Besorah

Besorah

*The Resurrection of Jerusalem and the
Healing of a Fractured Gospel*

MARK S. KINZER
and
RUSSELL L. RESNIK

CASCADE *Books* · Eugene, Oregon

BESORAH
The Resurrection of Jerusalem and the Healing of a Fractured Gospel

Copyright © 2021 Mark S. Kinzer and Russell L. Resnik. All rights reserved. Except for brief quotations in critical publications or reviews, no part of this book may be reproduced in any manner without prior written permission from the publisher. Write: Permissions, Wipf and Stock Publishers, 199 W. 8th Ave., Suite 3, Eugene, OR 97401.

Cascade Books
An Imprint of Wipf and Stock Publishers
199 W. 8th Ave., Suite 3
Eugene, OR 97401

www.wipfandstock.com

PAPERBACK ISBN: 978-1-7252-6400-7
HARDCOVER ISBN: 978-1-7252-6401-4
EBOOK ISBN: 978-1-7252-6402-1

Cataloguing-in-Publication data:

Names: Kinzer, Mark S., author. | Resnik, Russell L., author.

Title: Besorah : The resurrection of Jerusalem and the healing of a fractured gospel / by Mark S. Kinzer and Russell L. Resnik.

Description: Eugene, OR: Cascade Books, 2021 | Includes bibliographical references.

Identifiers: ISBN 978-1-7252-6400-7 (paperback) | ISBN 978-1-7252-6401-4 (hardcover) | ISBN 978-1-7252-6402-1 (ebook)

Subjects: LCSH: Bible. Luke—Criticism, interpretation, etc. | Bible. Acts—Criticism, interpretation, etc. | Israel (Christian theology)—Biblical teaching. | Jerusalem. | Eschatology. | Jews—Restoration. | Temple of Jerusalem (Jerusalem)—In the Bible. | Messianic Judaism. | Zionism.

Classification: BR158 K56 2021 (print) | BR158 (ebook)   06/03/21

Unless otherwise indicated, all Scripture quotations are from The ESV® Bible (The Holy Bible, English Standard Version®), copyright © 2001, by Crossway, a publishing ministry of Good News Publishers. Used by permission. All rights reserved.

Scripture quotations marked CJB are from the *Complete Jewish Bible*, copyright © 1998 and 2016 by David H. Stern. Used by permission. All rights reserved worldwide.

Scripture quotations marked NIV are from the Holy Bible, New International Version®, NIV® copyright ©1973, 1978, 1984, 2011 by Biblica, Inc.® Used by permission. All rights reserved worldwide.

Scripture quotations marked NRSV are from the New Revised Standard Version Bible copyright © 1989 National Council of the Churches of Christ in the United States of America. Used by permission. All rights reserved worldwide.

Scripture quotations marked TLV are from the Tree of Life Translation of the Bible. Copyright © 2015 by The Messianic Jewish Family Bible Society.

Dedicated to Roz, whose name is always good news to my ears.

—Mark Kinzer

Dedicated to Jane, my partner in life and in the riches of the besorah from the beginning.

—Russ Resnik

Contents

Acknowledgements | ix
Preface One | Mark S. Kinzer | xi
Preface Two | Russ Resnik | xv

Introduction: Jesus, Israel, and the Prophetic Gospel | 1

Part One: The Besorah of Messiah and Jerusalem, Crucified and Risen

Chapter One: The Besorah of Messiah | 11

Chapter Two: The Crucified Messiah and Jerusalem | 22

Chapter Three: The Resurrected Messiah and Jerusalem | 36

Part Two: The Besorah, the Temple, and the Covenant People

Chapter Four: The Holy Temple in Scripture | 55

Chapter Five: Luke's Portrayal of the Temple | 73

Chapter Six: The Jewish People and the Restoration to Come | 87

Chapter Seven: The Jewish People and the Torah in the Besorah of Luke | 100

Chapter Eight: The Jewish People and the Torah in the Book of Acts | 115

Contents

Part Three: The Besorah, Present and Future

Chapter Nine: The Return to Zion in Light of the Besorah | 133

Chapter Ten: Messianic Judaism and Restoration of the Besorah | 148

Epilogue | Russ Resnik | 163

Bibliography | 167

Scripture Index | 171

Acknowledgements

Many thanks to the friends and colleagues who read and provided invaluable feedback on the manuscript—Ed Loescher, Ari Waldman, and Troy Wallace. My wife, Jane, added her fresh insights and great ideas, as she does in most of my writing projects.

Our sons and daughters and their husbands and wives, and our grandchildren as well, provide steady encouragement and inspiration, along with our extended family and our friends in Albuquerque and in the Messianic Jewish community worldwide. In particular, our old and dear friends, Andrew (Eitan) and Connie Shishkoff have been with us throughout our whole experience of the besorah, and Eitan helped launch my writing career long ago as we prayed together on a camping trip in southern Utah.

I also join Mark Kinzer in thanking Robin Parry of Cascade Books, who edited both *Jerusalem Crucified* and the current volume, and who has never ceased to be a source of encouragement for living out the message both books convey.

—Russ Resnik

Thanks to all of those who have read *Jerusalem Crucified, Jerusalem Risen*, and who have shared with me their responses to the book. Thanks also to all who told me that they began reading *Jerusalem Crucified*, but could not finish because of its difficulty. They helped me see the need for the current volume, and for Russ's skillful touch.

—Mark Kinzer

Preface One

Mark S. Kinzer

At seventeen years of age, I decided to be a writer. To prepare myself for my future calling, I compiled vocabulary lists and drilled myself in their content.

Soon after graduating from college I was hired to do research and writing for a publisher run by an interdenominational community. Eventually that role involved my authoring several short teaching books aimed at a general audience. The new job helped me learn the practical skills required of a writer. But it also turned out to be an unexpected ordeal.

The words that came naturally to me were the ones that had appeared on my teenage vocabulary lists. In addition, my poor eyesight made it difficult for me to describe natural scenes in vivid detail. I was better at working with abstract ideas and recognizing the connections between things than at depicting concrete realities. I loved stories, but was more adept in analyzing than in telling them. Consequently, I sweated over those short teaching books, bringing them to birth only after a protracted and painful delivery. The final product was adequate—but, in my judgment, not as well-crafted as similar pieces by more gifted communicators.

In retrospect, I see that I benefited from the discipline of writing in a style that ran against my grain. My editors forced me to simplify my thinking and language, and they taught me to convey my ideas in a clearer and more straightforward manner. But my mental grain naturally tilted in a more scholarly direction.

Thus, a decade later when I began doctoral studies, I felt liberated. I wrote my dissertation in less than a year. After receiving my PhD in 1995, I took up the task of exploring the uncharted territory of Messianic Jewish theology. A series of articles and books followed. The writing process was not difficult. However, as my friends noted in my hearing, reading

Preface One: Mark S. Kinzer

the pieces was another story. Many unacquainted with theological texts would open a volume, and give up after a few pages. Others plowed ahead, and later said that they were glad that they had done so. But I had not made the job easy for them.

My most recent book, *Jerusalem Crucified, Jerusalem Risen*, was published in 2018. It deals with contemporary issues relevant to Christians, Jews, and the general reading public: the role played by the land of Israel and the Jewish people in the New Testament; the sources and limits of Christian Zionism; and the rupture between the Jewish and Christian traditions, viewed as an internal fracturing of the gospel itself. The book addressed these issues from a distinctive Messianic Jewish perspective, and set the issue of Messianic Judaism itself in a new perspective. As such, it was especially relevant for Messianic Jews and Jewish Christians. Moreover, in my own (admittedly biased) opinion, the volume approached all of these matters in a fresh and compelling manner. Nevertheless, it was written in my usual style, and so was destined to find only a modest number of readers.

One may now appreciate my ecstatic response to Rabbi Russ Resnik in the summer of 2019 when he proposed writing a book that repackaged the content of *Jerusalem Crucified* for a general reading audience. Russ is one of the most respected voices in the worldwide Messianic Jewish community. He has also proved himself a talented communicator adept at interpreting scripture for a general audience. He thus has a gift that I lack.

Russ understood all the nuances of *Jerusalem Crucified*, and loved the book. But he saw that its method and style would intimidate many who might otherwise be drawn to its message. Therefore, he offered to combine his talents with mine to create a new book capable of reaching a larger body of readers. In this way, *Besorah* was conceived and born.

The writing process was simple. With the material in *Jerusalem Crucified* as his starting point, Russ wrote chapters, and sent them to me for comment. I would suggest a few changes, and we would discuss them and quickly come to agreement. All went smoothly. I could not have asked for a more congenial co-author.

And he is truly a co-author. The main biblical and theological ideas, and some of the specific language, are drawn from *Jerusalem Crucified*, but the personal voice is entirely that of Rabbi Russ. He brings to the project a narrative flair and an informal style that I could never master—either in my youth, or now in my advancing age. I am grateful that he was willing

Preface One: Mark S. Kinzer

to partner with me to produce a work that might go beyond what either of us could do on our own.

Do not misunderstand me: this is not "Mark Kinzer for dummies." Russ writes intelligent books for intelligent readers. It will challenge your mind and your heart. But the challenge will not come from technical theological jargon or complicated refutations of contrary scholarly opinions. The challenge will come from the depth and richness of the biblical message itself, which Rabbi Russ opens up with transparent clarity. Read, enjoy, and embrace the challenge!

Ann Arbor, Michigan
September 2020/Elul 5780

Preface Two

Russ Resnik

I FIRST ENCOUNTERED YESHUA the Messiah as a young Jewish hippie. The story of that encounter leads right into the theme of this book: the report about Messiah Yeshua announced to our Jewish people millennia ago, and how that announcement remains good news to the Jewish people in the twenty-first century.

It was the early 70s and I was living with my wife-to-be, Jane, on a high mesa at about 8,000 feet elevation in a mountainous corner of northern New Mexico, on a ranchito that belonged to one of the locals named Facundo Martinez. Our Jewish-hippie friends Connie and Andrew joined us a while after we moved up there. In exchange for rent, Andrew and I did Facundo's irrigating during the growing season, waking up at whatever hour his share of the water distribution was scheduled to begin—sometimes in the middle of the night. We diverted the water out of the *acequia madre*, the main irrigation canal, into the smaller canals and ditches that covered his 80 acres of pasture and hayfields. In exchange we could garden an acre of the land for our own corn and potatoes and vegetables and live in the cabin, which lacked electricity, phone service, running water, and plumbing, but possessed a spectacular view of the red cliffs of Mesa Montosa in the foreground and the distant, snow-crested San Juan peaks of Southern Colorado far beyond.

One day in the early fall, Jane returned from a trip to our former commune with some winter supplies. She'd gotten a ride down to the commune with a friend and had brought our two little boys with her. When our two sons got sick on the commune, the resident hippies weren't much help, and Jane was stranded. Finally a friend offered to take her to a spot on Highway 44 in the town of Bernalillo, where we often caught rides back to our part of the state. As they neared the spot, Jane asked God—whoever he might be—to just get her home. She looked up and there was a made-over Greyhound bus idling by the side of the road, inscribed with the words, JESUS: ONE WAY. The Jesus people inside were from New Jersey, where they had felt directed by the Spirit to go to the mountains of New Mexico for a year to study the Bible. They'd laid hands on their bus before they left, praying that anyone who came into it would accept Jesus before he or she got off. So they gladly helped Jane get on board, along with the little boys and hundreds of pounds of winter supplies. After the bus got going, the transmission became stuck in second gear. The Jesus people laid hands on it and prayed for it to shift—and it did! So when they began to bombard Jane with Bible verses and urged her to "invite Jesus into your heart," she felt that she should listen; after all, this bus ride was an answer to prayer. And so it was that Jane, always the pioneer among us, became a believer in Jesus on that ride home.

Connie soon accepted Yeshua too, and she and Jane invited two young men from the bus to our cabin for dinner. After the meal, Andrew and I sat with them while they pointed out Bible verses to us by the light of a kerosene lamp. They told us that if we would accept Jesus in our hearts, and confess the words "Jesus is Lord," God would save us and place his Spirit within us. By the time we met these guys, my hippie dream of returning to nature and creating a community of peace and love was beginning to unravel. I remember standing one day at the edge of our mesa, looking out at the orange and ivory mesas and the majestic far-off peaks, and feeling like I was standing on the edge of an abyss. Our idealistic quest, the return to a simpler, uncorrupted way of life, to true peace amid the mountains and mesas—in a moment I saw it all as just a distraction from the truth that life was meaningless and headed nowhere. But now I was in for the greatest surprise of my life. As these young men started talking about faith in Jesus, I found myself believing it. Like any good Jewish hippie, I looked down upon Christianity (along with Judaism, I must add), but in recent months, the Bible, and Jesus above all, had begun to draw me.

Now, to my great surprise, the Spirit of God opened my eyes to see Jesus, who had been altogether foreign to me for most of my life, as Messiah, as the reality I had been seeking all along. My road in life had brought me to the edge of the mesa to stare out at the void. Now God stepped in, and suddenly I was turned in an entirely new direction. That night, by the light of the kerosene lamp, I believed. Jesus was and is the Messiah, and he came into my heart.

Preface Two: Russ Resnik

This encounter with Jesus was undeniable, but I still couldn't get myself to say "Jesus is Lord" as my new friends were hoping. In the polite Southern California Jewish home of my childhood, the name of Jesus was simply not spoken. Our Catholic next-door neighbors had an eerie picture of Jesus on their wall, staring out with longing eyes with his heart exposed in his chest. In an older part of town I had seen a neon sign that flashed the mysterious words "Jesus Saves." You could pick up redneck preachers invoking Jesus on the local radio. I remembered all this, along with Crusades and Inquisitions, forced conversions and expulsions. I wanted Jesus, but my long-neglected upbringing held me back. It had not protected me from all kinds of exotic religious practices in the recent past, but now it kept me from saying the words that I already believed in my heart. Finally, after three days, I was able to say aloud that Jesus was my lord.

But then came another surprise: my dormant Jewish identity suddenly revived. I wasn't sure what to do with it, but I knew deep down that it was important that I was Jewish. Somehow it was a major part of the plan God was drawing me into.

We spent that first winter reading the Bible, learning to pray, and slowly grasping the basics of following Jesus—we hadn't learned to say "Yeshua" yet. Somewhere along the way, we decided that we should spend time with other people who believed in Jesus. We knew about what the locals called the "Hallelujah" church, named Templo Cristiano, in the nearby village of Gallina, and started attending on Sunday nights.

I've come a long way from Templo Cristiano in the decades since, but this little Spanish-speaking mountain church was critical in my formation as a Jewish follower of Yeshua. Its initial impact was very simple: Templo Cristiano slapped down the welcome mat for this band of gringo hippies. We were still at a vulnerable stage of our Messiah-journey, still checking things out despite the intensity of our recent encounter, still asking, was it all for real?

That welcome mat was especially important for us as Jewish Yeshua-believers. We had grown up with the idea that Jesus was not for us. The Jewish community is diverse and open-minded, but one thing that just about all Jews agree on is that Jesus is not for us, and neither are the Christians. When I was five or six years old, attending a parade in my home town on the 4th of July, I was standing on the curb with my mother's best friend, Shirley Greenberg. A float came by, sponsored by a local church, and on it they were acting out a scene from the story of the

Good Samaritan. I even remember a live donkey on the float, but perhaps that's my imagination. Over the scene a banner read, "The Good Samaritan—Story of Christian Love." Shirley turned to me and said, "Christian love!? When did the Christians ever love us?"

Now, years later, I experienced the answer to that question at Templo Cristiano. We came through the doors, late, still looking pretty grubby even after we'd tried to clean up in our primitive conditions, with a few even grubbier kids in tow. When we showed up, the pastor, Brother Limas, stopped the service, switched from Spanish to English, and welcomed us warmly, "Come in! Our brothers and sisters from the Mesa! Welcome!" The little old ladies took our kids on their laps so we could pay attention to the service, and the whole church made us part of the family.

That welcome grounded us in the kingdom of God, convinced us it was all for real, and provided a vision of true community that stayed with us as we became involved in the Messianic Jewish congregational movement a few years later. It helped us see that the congregation could be the place that welcomed Jewish people to Messiah and into the kingdom of God.

Templo Cristiano had another influence on us, which leads right to this book that you're reading. It was a Pentecostal church, and those were the early days of the Charismatic movement and all its controversies. Brother Limas taught that the infilling and gifts of the Holy Spirit were for today, that the Book of Acts provides not just a history of the early Yeshua community, but a model for followers of Yeshua ever since. I've had my differences with the Charismatic and Pentecostal movements over the years, but I continue to believe that this is the right way to view Acts, and that the Holy Spirit remains active today, inspiring dramatic interventions and spiritual gifts such as healing, prophetic utterances, and speaking in tongues.

Brother Limas didn't cover this back then, but in addition to the Holy Spirit dimension, another part of the story in Acts is for today—a thriving Jewish movement for Yeshua that remains connected with Jewish life and tradition. When Paul made his last visit to Jerusalem, he reported to James and the other elders about all that God was doing among the gentiles. "And when they heard, they began glorifying God. They said, 'You see, brother, how many myriads there are among the Jewish people who have believed—and they are all zealous for the Torah'" (Acts 21:20 TLV). These Jewish believers in Yeshua remained among the Jewish community in Jerusalem, the Jewish capital; they worshiped in the temple (Acts 2:46; 5:42), and they were committed to Torah, the way of life that had shaped the Jewish people for centuries. If the Book of Acts is for today, as I learned so well at Templo Cristiano, this picture of a Yeshua movement of loyal Jews in the heart of the Jewish community is for today as well.

Loyalty to Yeshua coupled with loyalty to Jewish life and tradition (and the Jewish people) is evident not only in Acts, but also in the account of the life of Yeshua by the same author, Luke. *Besorah: The Resurrection of Jerusalem and the Healing of a Fractured Gospel* demonstrates that this indigenous Jewish movement for Messiah isn't just a fascinating historical note, but is at the heart of God's plan for Israel, and for the nations of the earth. It's an essential part of the good news that Luke and Acts present to us.

I'm using the term "good news" as a synonym for what's commonly called "gospel," as well as the term "besorah," which we develop in this book. Just as I had to struggle over the words "Jesus is Lord," I struggled over the word "gospel"—and it was also a distinctively Jewish struggle. It wasn't just that the gospel was foreign to us. After all, as Jewish hippies we'd embraced all kinds of religious words from Sanskrit, which was even more foreign. But "gospel" somehow seemed to be against the Jews. We tried to soften that sense by using the term "good news," which captured the meaning of the original Greek term *euangelion*. We also insisted that we were still Jewish—some would say "more Jewish than ever"—after accepting the good news. But I began to realize that a problem remained: this good news, originally announced to the Jewish people, seemed to contain the message that Jewish life and tradition were no longer valid. It didn't contain anything that would help explain *how* we were "more Jewish than ever." Even worse, it seemed to be telling us that all of our Jewish family and loved ones were spiritually altogether lost, that the customs we'd grown up with were obsolete, and that Judaism, which had sustained the Jewish people for centuries, was a false religion.

There was another problem with the good news that I had received, although that problem only became evident after years of walking with Yeshua and growing in my knowledge of scripture. The good news as I understood it from the guys on the Jesus bus was about Jesus all right, but it focused mostly on us accepting Jesus and what we'd get for doing that. We invited him into our hearts and we got a free, irrevocable ticket to heaven. Somewhere along the way, at Templo Cristiano or among other Christian friends later on, I heard people calling Jesus their "personal Lord and Savior." I couldn't find that phrase in the Bible, and after a while it began to sound like "personal trainer" or "personal coach." Except that Jesus the personal Lord and Savior didn't seem that interested in our spiritual condition after we signed up with him. I eventually came to see this form of the good news as distorted by modern Western individualism and self-absorption, and even promoting that form of spiritual malady. It assured us that we were born again, headed for heaven, in a personal relationship with him, and treated our behavior and actions in the world as side issues.

Community life, so central to the story in Acts, was among these supposedly side issues, and connection with Jewish life and the Jewish people wasn't even on the map. Being "more Jewish than ever" was a side-note to the good news we had received, and whatever it meant didn't seem to require spending much time among Jewish people, virtually all of whom lacked the ticket to heaven and were headed in the opposite direction. This number included our beloved parents and grandparents, including the *bubbe* who loved us unconditionally, fed us delightful food made with her own hands, blessed us, and sent us on our way. It included the six million murdered at the hands of the Nazis. The good news seemed to have little hope for the Jewish people as a whole and seemed to beckon Jews to leave their community and its miseries to find real life in God.

We left the mountains a couple of years after our encounter with Yeshua. Andrew and Connie moved to Santa Fe to be mentored and to work with an outreach to the hippies of Northern New Mexico called Shalom Ministries. Jane and I moved to Albuquerque to serve on the staff of DARE—Drug Addicts Recovery Enterprises—a Bible-based residential treatment program for drug addicts and ex-offenders. During our years at DARE, we met Eliezer Urbach, an older Jew who had fled Hitler's Europe, served in the Israeli war of independence, accepted Yeshua in the mid-50s, and eventually ended up in Denver, where he became a mentor and father-figure to many young Messianic Jews. Eliezer started visiting Albuquerque every month and soon took me under his wing. One day he invoked an old Yiddish saying, "Russell, with one *tuchas* you can't dance at two weddings. You'll have to decide—will your children take part in the Christmas pageant, or the Chanukah play?"

The choice seemed obvious enough to me, now with four children, but *how* to do it was not so clear. By 1980 I had become an elder of a charismatic, pro-Israel church with a sizeable Jewish contingent. Jane and I led a Friday-night home fellowship of about two dozen, mostly Jews and intermarried couples. Some of our friends in other parts of the country were leaving the church world altogether and joining Messianic Jewish congregations, and even Eliezer, who initially opposed the whole idea, dropped his reservations and became instrumental in founding a Messianic congregation in Denver. These were the people I trusted most in the world; shouldn't I go with them on this issue?

In the summer of 1983, things came to a head. One of our commune friends, Ed, had become involved in a Messianic synagogue in Philadelphia. Tired of arguing with us about Messianic Judaism, he offered to fly Jane and me to a big Messianic conference in Pennsylvania where we could see things for ourselves. There we were reunited with Andrew and Connie, who had moved east to join Beth Messiah congregation in Maryland. We were thrilled to hear so many Jewish voices praising the Lord with New York accents. We felt ourselves being drawn into the vision, and one night at the conference received our most powerful calling from God since we had accepted the Messiah. We were to give ourselves to the Messianic movement.

We returned to Albuquerque with a vision to transform our home group into a Messianic congregation. But first Eliezer sent me to another conference, hosted by a new group called the Union of Messianic Jewish Congregations (UMJC). There I encountered the same broad vision, but with more focus on establishing congregations, building community, and connecting leaders. Our home-group-in-transition joined the Union as an associate member, and by the next year, with help and encouragement from the UMJC, we qualified for full membership. Since then the vision has matured, from the early realization that it was OK to be Jewish even though we were saved and born again, to a conviction that as Jewish Yeshua-followers we were called to live Jewish lives and remain connected to Jewish tradition and community.

In 2002, the Union released a statement defining Messianic Judaism in line with this conviction:

> The UMJC envisions Messianic Judaism as a movement of Jewish congregations and groups committed to Yeshua the Messiah that embrace the covenantal responsibility of Jewish life and identity rooted in Torah, expressed in tradition, and renewed and applied in the context of the New Covenant. Messianic Jewish groups may also include those from non-Jewish backgrounds who have a confirmed call to participate fully in the life and destiny of the Jewish people. We are committed to embodying this definition in our constituent congregations and in our shared institutions.
>
> (*This is the version updated by UMJC delegates in 2005.*)

This definition implies that the *euangelion*, the good news of Yeshua's atoning death and life-giving resurrection, was still good news for the Jewish people. It confronts all of us, Jews and gentiles, with our need to get right with God, but it doesn't call Jews out of being Jewish. After all, the good news is at its heart a concept from the Hebrew Bible, rooted especially in the prophecies of the second half of Isaiah (chapters 40–66). In Isaiah, the word "besorah" refers to the announcement that God has arrived, or is about to arrive, to deliver and restore his people, *and to establish his glorious reign over all the earth*. The besorah declares that the time has come, that this kingdom has drawn near, and that we are to make ourselves ready by turning back to the ways of the kingdom. Yeshua appeared on the human scene declaring this very message:

> The time has come,
> God's Kingdom is near!
> Turn to God from your sins
> and believe in the besorah! (Mark 1:15 CJB, modified)

For a Jew, turning to God from your sins includes, in the words of the UMJC definition, returning to "the covenantal responsibility of Jewish life and identity" founded in scripture. The revolutionary insight of Messianic Judaism is that combining loyalty to Yeshua and deep participation in Jewish life and identity isn't just permissible, isn't just an attractive option, but is *essential* to God's purposes, not only for the Jewish people but also for all humanity.

This insight leads to another benefit of the term "besorah" in comparison with other terms like "gospel" or "good news." Not only is the besorah clearly good news for the Jewish people, but it also is up-to-date and relevant good news for all people. It is a communal announcement, a call to turn from our own ways and become participants in a kingdom that belongs to God and encompasses all who have been made right with God through the work of Messiah Yeshua—people from every background, race, ethnicity, and creed. The besorah lifts us out of our twenty-first-century hyper-individualism and self-absorption, which is linked to the pandemic of anxiety, depression, and addictive behaviors of this age. In contrast, the good news that's often presented in the modern American church world is highly individualistic, the story of "me and Jesus" and the good things I get by believing in him. This part of the story is real, but it's far too narrow. It can encourage us to focus on our own experience with God and our escape

Preface Two: Russ Resnik

from this world to the glories of heaven so that we miss the communal, world-redeeming, kingdom dimension of the besorah.

One of the authors of the definition of Messianic Judaism was Mark Kinzer, who led a UMJC-affiliated congregation in Ann Arbor, Michigan, at the time. The definition allows for a wide range of thought and practice, but Kinzer's writings, most notably his 2005 book *Postmissionary Messianic Judaism*,[1] were a major influence. His more recent book *Jerusalem Crucified, Jerusalem Risen*[2] provides a deeply biblical foundation for the Messianic Jewish community, and for Christian understanding of God's purposes for the Jewish people. And, as I implied above, understanding God's purposes for Israel leads to understanding his purposes for all of humankind, including you and me.

The book you are reading draws heavily upon *Jerusalem Crucified, Jerusalem Risen* to tell the same story in a more popular and accessible format. It is a privilege for me to be working with Mark to make that book accessible to a wider audience.

I'll conclude this preface with another thing I learned decades ago at Templo Cristiano and have held to ever since: *Yeshua is coming again!*

Most people who take the Bible seriously believe in the return of the Messiah in some way or another, but Templo Cristiano was a real second-coming church. In those days people expected Jesus to be back within five years, or ten on the outside. I remember a young man, Johnny, who testified at one of the services back then. He had been out in a field, plowing with his tractor, when he stopped the engine to take a break. Everything was quiet, even silent. There was not a soul in sight, and Johnny alone in the field had a moment of panic, thinking the rapture had happened and he had been left behind! His story had a good ending, though, because it led him to recommit his life to the Lord.

Forty-five years later, I'm still inspired by this level of expectancy, and I still believe in the return of Messiah myself. But I see part of the picture more clearly than I did back then. Yeshua is coming back to fulfill all that God promised in the scriptures, including his promises to restore the Jewish people. God has tied his reputation to the destiny of the Jewish people, and this age cannot come to a close without a great move of God's Spirit among

---

1. Mark S. Kinzer, *Postmissionary Messianic Judaism: Redefining Christian Engagement with the Jewish People* (Grand Rapids: Brazos, 2005).

2. Mark S. Kinzer, *Jerusalem Crucified, Jerusalem Risen: The Resurrected Messiah, the Jewish People, and the Land of Promise* (Eugene, OR: Cascade, 2018).

us. Speaking of the regathering to the land of Israel, which is currently underway, the Lord tells the prophet Ezekiel, "Therefore say to the house of Israel, Thus says the Lord God: It is not for your sake, O house of Israel, that I am about to act, but for the sake of my holy name . . ." (Ezek 36:22). The Lord then reveals that he will bring the House of Israel back to the land of Israel. There in the land of Israel, the regathered Jewish population will be cleansed of their misdeeds, filled with the Spirit of God, and empowered to walk in obedience to the statutes and ordinances of the Lord (Ezek 36:23–27)—all to the glory of God and the enhancement of his name.

> And I will give you a new heart, and a new spirit I will put within you. And I will remove the heart of stone from your flesh and give you a heart of flesh. And I will put my Spirit within you, and cause you to walk in my statutes and be careful to obey my rules. (Ezek 36:26–27)

The gift of the Spirit that we believed in and received in the Jesus-people days doesn't push aside God's promises to Israel or Israel's calling to be a light to the nations. It prepares the Jewish remnant regathered in Jerusalem to welcome Yeshua back to his own people and city, as Yeshua himself said to Jerusalem, "You will not see me again until you say, 'Blessed is he who comes in the name of the Lord'" (Matt 23:39). This profound welcome and reconciliation between the Jewish people and the Jewish Messiah isn't just an accessory to the good news of Messiah, the besorah, but is its very heartbeat, as we will see in the chapters to come.

Introduction

Jesus, Israel, and the Prophetic Gospel

> Now I would remind you, brothers, of the gospel I preached to you ... that Christ died for our sins in accordance with the Scriptures, that he was buried, that he was raised on the third day in accordance with the Scriptures, and that he appeared to Cephas, then to the twelve. (1 Cor 15:1, 3–5)

> ... the gospel of God, which he promised beforehand through his prophets in the holy Scriptures, concerning his Son, who was descended from David according to the flesh and was declared to be the Son of God in power according to the Spirit of holiness by his resurrection from the dead, Jesus Christ our Lord. (Rom 1:1–4)

A Jewish and Prophetic Gospel Restored

THE GOSPEL OR GOOD news that Paul and his fellow apostles proclaimed transformed the ancient world. It reshaped the lives of individuals as well as the life of the societies in which they lived.[1] Some found its message neither believable nor beneficial, but those who embraced the message celebrated it as "the power of God for salvation" (Rom 1:16).

This message spoke of a particular Jewish man, who was heralded as the "Christ"—the royal Messiah "descended from David" whom the Jewish people had long awaited. The message had been "promised beforehand ... in the holy scriptures"—the sacred writings composed, preserved, and

---

1. The word "gospel" is not capitalized in general usage, but only when used as part of a title, such as the Gospel of Luke. The same rule applies to "besorah," which is capitalized only as part of a title, for example, Luke's Besorah.

studied by generations of Jews. All of the original witnesses to Messiah's resurrection were Jews, as were the first people who received their message, and the movement they launched had its worldwide center in Jerusalem, the capital city of the Jewish people.

Nevertheless, within a century the community born from this message had become largely non-Jewish. More significantly, the way its gentile members interpreted the message resembled nothing that a Jew would call "good news." These gentiles saw the Jewish people as an enemy, and rejoiced at the destruction of the city of Jerusalem at the hand of Rome in 70 CE. They understood that event as the end of the Jewish people's priestly role among the nations. Some expected a future restoration of Jerusalem, while others rejected that idea as a crass material hope. Regardless, few of these gentile heirs of the gospel thought that Jews would have any distinctive identity or role in the age to come. The few individual Jews who managed to overcome these obstacles and seek baptism were discouraged or even forbidden from observing Jewish practices or participating in the Jewish community. The "good news" as now proclaimed by the Christian community could hardly be recognized as "the power of God for salvation" for the Jewish people, or as in any sense "good" from a Jewish perspective.

Few Christians of the twenty-first century would condone the anti-Jewish rhetoric that developed in the first few centuries after the fall of Jerusalem. Most Christians today respect their Jewish neighbors and the Jewish tradition. Many take seriously Paul's assertion that "the gifts and the calling of God are irrevocable" (Rom 11:29) and believe that the Jews remain special to God. But this belief in the enduring character of God's choice of the Jewish people has little direct connection to the "gospel" these Christians affirm and proclaim. This gospel differs little in its Jewish implications from the one announced in the second century. The death and resurrection of Jesus still have no positive bearing on the historical life or destiny of the Jewish people as a priestly nation, or so this gospel seems to declare.

In this book we argue that it was not always so, and that it should no longer be so. We present an understanding of the good news in which the death and resurrection of Jesus are inseparable from the historical journey and destiny of the Jewish people, and we refer to this good news by the term *besorah*, the Hebrew equivalent of *euangelion* or gospel.

The besorah declared by the apostles is *prophetic* in character. It points to a finished act of redemption by Israel's Messiah, and also to the present and future outworking of that act in the life of Messiah's Israel.

Moreover, it declares that Messiah and his own Jewish people together retain a special bond with a place—the land of Israel and the city of Jerusalem. The death and resurrection of the Messiah are as tied to the destiny of that place as they are to the destiny of that people. We aim in this book to recapture this foundational aspect of the good news. It is seen most clearly in Luke and Acts, but it was largely lost during the second century and never fully recovered. Our recovery effort will help us see the universal impact of Messiah's life, death, and resurrection in light of their particular prophetic meaning for the Jewish people.

Luke, Acts, and the Besorah

In our quest to recover the Jewish character of the besorah as good news for Israel, we focus on the Gospel (or Besorah) of Luke and the Acts of the Apostles—two significant texts within the New Testament. But the New Testament, Israel's disputed scripture, can't be isolated from Israel's undisputed scripture, the *Tanakh*.[2] We see this connection, for example, in Paul's use of the phrase "in accordance with the scriptures"—that is, the Tanakh—in his summary account of the gospel in 1 Corinthians 15, cited above.

We will show that Acts (read in light of the Gospel of Luke) presents a besorah that is directed especially to the Jewish people, and that relates to the fulfillment of Jewish history. This future fulfillment involves the return of the exiled Jewish nation to its land and its capital city. The Jewish people remain in covenant with God and in relationship with the risen Messiah even in exile, and the Torah remains the guiding document of that covenant. Moreover, Acts pictures a messianic community that has Torah-faithful Jews at its heart, a community that others from the nations enter in order to be linked in fellowship with the Jewish people.[3] As such, the community of Yeshua-followers in Acts represents a prophetic foretaste of the future promised in the besorah, in which Israel and the nations are joined together through the resurrected Messiah.

---

2. A traditional Jewish acronym referring to the Torah, the Prophets (i.e., *Nevi'im*), and the Writings (i.e., *Ketuvim*). "Torah" refers primarily to the Five Books of Moses, Genesis through Deuteronomy, and more broadly to the body of laws and customs derived from the Five Books, or in other contexts to the whole body of scripture. The books of the Tanakh in different order comprise the Christian Old Testament.

3. The word "messianic" is not capitalized in general usage, but is capitalized when referring to the contemporary movement of Messianic Judaism, or contemporary Messianic Jews.

Introduction

It is evident from the prologues of Luke and Acts, both addressed to the same Theophilus (Acts 1:1; Luke 1:3), that these two volumes derive from the same author. For most of the last century, however, scholars have gone beyond this hint of common authorship to discuss the literary unity of the two books. These scholars have studied Luke and Acts not as separate works composed by the same person, but as two parts of a single unified narrative which they call "Luke-Acts." This unified narrative provides the biblical foundation for the book that you are now reading. But even though scholars recognize the literary unity of these two volumes, they tend to treat Luke and Acts separately in other discussions. The Besorah of Luke (like Mark) lives in the shadows of Matthew and John, and Acts is treated as a historical sourcebook for the early church and the writings of Paul. As a result neither Luke nor Acts has played a major role in theological study. We see this as a mistake that we seek to correct, especially when it comes to interpreting the meaning of the besorah in relation to the Jewish people.

Considered together, Acts and Luke "dominate the landscape of the New Testament," making up "almost one-fourth of its total verses."[4] But their unique significance within the New Testament derives as much from their content as from their quantity. Acts provides a vision of the life and teaching of the early Jesus-community as a fitting sequel to Luke's account of the life and teaching of Jesus. In this way, these books help knit the diverse strands of the New Testament writings into a unified whole.

Furthermore, the author of Acts identifies with the figure of Paul, who is of course another major source of New Testament scripture. Paul's story takes up all of Acts chapters 13 through 28, and Luke often uses the first-person plural when telling this story (see Acts 16:10–17; 20:5–15; 21:1–18; 27:1—28:16). Luke presents himself as a member of Paul's company, and so as sharing Paul's perspective. Paul reveals the Jewish character of this perspective when he speaks about himself in Acts, consistently identifying himself as a loyal member of the Jewish people and faithful to the Jewish tradition (see, for example, Acts 23:6; 24:14–21; 25:8; 26:5–7; 28:17). As we'll see, this approach reflects the approach of the whole messianic Jewish community, especially in Jerusalem. Therefore, we suggest that Luke views Paul's perspective as a model, which he reflects in his own treatment of scripture.

Given the central issue addressed in this book—the relationship between the besorah and the ongoing life of the Jewish people—the reasons

---

4. Juel, *Luke-Acts*, 1.

Introduction

for choosing Luke-Acts as our primary text should be clear. We may now proceed to introduce the chapters of this volume and the logic of their arrangement.

Chapter Preview

Part One: The Besorah of Messiah and Jerusalem, Crucified and Risen

In Part One we define our keyword *besorah* and show how it announces the coming judgment and restoration of Jerusalem and the Jewish people, as well as the death and resurrection of Messiah. This linkage reveals a prophetic dimension to the besorah, which will be emphasized throughout this book.

Chapter One: The Besorah of Messiah

We open with Yeshua's visit to his home synagogue in Nazareth (Luke 4:16ff), where he announces his mission "to proclaim good news to the poor," as foretold in Isaiah 61. The term "gospel" was introduced in Mark, the earliest account of Yeshua's life and ministry, where it is also linked to Isaiah 40–66. This chapter explores what "gospel" means in Mark and Luke, and how it relates to the Hebrew term "besorah." The irony is that besorah is normally an announcement of triumph, as in Isaiah, but this besorah includes apparent defeat, that is, the crucifixion. Only with the crucifixion is the ultimate triumph of resurrection made possible. The besorah of the death and resurrection of Messiah includes what God will do for Israel through this death and resurrection.

Chapter Two: The Crucified Messiah and Jerusalem

In Luke, the besorah of Messiah includes crucifixion and resurrection—both of Jesus and of Jerusalem, which stands for the Jewish people as a whole. We open with a brief view of Luke's birth and infancy narrative (which will be revisited in chapter 7) to see how Luke introduces the besorah as a message for and about all Israel. This expanded besorah informs four key passages in Luke, which show how Jesus defines his crucifixion as linked to the judgment to come upon Jerusalem, thus hinting at the hope of resurrection for the holy city.

Introduction

Chapter Three: The Resurrected Messiah and Jerusalem

In Acts, the emphasis shifts from Messiah's crucifixion to his resurrection, which points toward the eventual resurrection of Jerusalem. Peter's early sermons on Shavuot (Pentecost) and Paul's later sermons—all directed toward Jews—emphasize the resurrection both as validating Jesus' messianic claims, and as the source of hope for Jerusalem's restoration. This emphasis is reinforced by the geographical structure of Luke-Acts and the conclusion of Acts in Rome, both of which serve to heighten the expectation of Jerusalem's restoration in the end.

Part Two: The Besorah, the Temple, and the Covenant People

These chapters explore the outworking of the besorah as presented in Part One regarding the people and land of Israel, represented by Jerusalem. We begin with a discussion of the temple, which is the heart of Jerusalem and a key to its significance, as well as its future. Then we discuss Luke's emphasis on the calling of the Jewish people, which entails the continuing role of the Torah as Israel's covenant document and guide to its communal life.

Chapter Four: The Holy Temple in Scripture

The temple is the heart of Jerusalem and a key to the city's lasting significance. To provide background for the place of the temple in Luke-Acts, this chapter briefly traces its portrayal in the Tanakh, showing how the temple (and the earlier tabernacle) was always portrayed as a symbol pointing to realities beyond itself. This portrayal is the key to properly understanding the place of the temple in the New Testament, including in Paul's writings, Hebrews, Revelation, and John.

Chapter Five: Luke's Portrayal of the Temple

In line with the rest of the Bible, Acts highlights the continuing significance of the temple, and thereby Jerusalem. But Stephen's speech in Acts 7 is often interpreted as denying any role of the temple after Messiah's resurrection. We will see how Stephen supports rather than denies the continuing significance of the temple and of the Jewish people as well. His speech is consistent with the rest of Acts in emphasizing the promised return of

INTRODUCTION

God's presence to Zion, the place made holy for generations past, present, and future.

Chapter Six: The Jewish People and the Restoration to Come

After the resurrection of Messiah, Israel remains a covenant people and heir of the promised redemption. Because of this, the besorah goes out to the Jewish people in a mission distinct from the mission to the gentiles. This chapter covers Peter's sermon to the Jews of Jerusalem in Acts 3, and Paul's sermons in the diaspora connected with his thrice-repeated pivot to the gentiles. We conclude with Paul's final words in Acts 28, to counter interpretations of these events based on supersessionism or replacement theology.

Chapter Seven: The Jewish People and the Torah in the Besorah of Luke

The continuing role of the Jewish people means a continuing role for the Torah, which has confirmed and guided Israel's covenant relationship with God through the centuries. Beginning with his infancy narrative in chapters 1 and 2, Luke portrays a Jewish remnant faithful to Torah and seeking the fulfilment of God's promises for Israel contained in Torah and the Prophets. He goes on to present Jesus as a Torah-faithful Jew in both his teaching and his practice, a Jewish teacher who summons all who hear him to repentance in response to the Torah.

Chapter Eight: The Jewish People and the Torah in the Book of Acts

Luke portrays Jesus' followers, like Jesus himself, as faithful to Torah from the beginning of Jesus' ministry through the entire narrative of Acts, showing that Torah-faithfulness in Israel is an integral part of the besorah. This chapter covers two passages often employed wrongly to argue against the validity of the Torah and the continued calling of the Jewish people after the resurrection, Acts 10 (Peter's dream) and Acts 15 (the Jerusalem council).

Part Three: The Besorah, Present and Future

The besorah is prophetic, meaning that its message and perspective include past, present, and future. We will conclude with a look at recent events in Jewish history, and the anticipated future of Israel, in light of the besorah, including two realities currently in process—the Jewish return to Zion and the emergence of contemporary Messianic Judaism.

Chapter Nine: The Return to Zion in Light of the Besorah

The besorah as presented in Luke-Acts, which speaks both of Jesus and Israel, has become fractured, reflecting the fractured community of God's people in history. But two events of our times point toward a prophetic restoration of the fractured besorah. This chapter considers the first of these events, the Jewish return to Zion, and its meaning in light of the besorah.

Chapter Ten: Messianic Judaism and Restoration of the Besorah

Like the Jewish return to the land of Israel, Messianic Judaism properly understood is a foretaste of the restoration to which the besorah points. It is also a key to the healing of the fractured besorah, a healing that will benefit Jerusalem—that is, the Jewish people—the entire body of Jesus-followers, and all the nations of humankind.

Terminology

An observant reader will notice some inconsistency in our use of "Yeshua" and "Jesus," and "Messiah" and "Christ," as well as other names. We use "Yeshua" within specifically Jewish contexts, and "Jesus" everywhere else. Our practice is determined by the cultural feel and context as we present our case, rather than from defined rules of usage. Likewise, we avoid terms like "church" and "Christian," not out of any disrespect, but because these terms have different meanings and implications within different cultural settings. They often carry connotations that imply the fractured understanding of the people of God that we are seeking to correct. Sometimes it is necessary to make familiar terms unfamiliar in order to challenge unconscious assumptions regarding their meaning.

Throughout our book, first-person anecdotes derive from the experience of co-author Russ Resnik.

With that, we are ready to begin our journey through what up to now has been largely unexplored territory: the prophetic besorah of Israel's crucified and risen Messiah that is truly good news for Jerusalem and the world.

Part One

The Besorah of Messiah and Jerusalem, Crucified and Risen

Chapter One

The Besorah of Messiah

THE VILLAGE OF NATZERET was a scattering of stone huts spread over a hillside, far enough from the bustling shore of the Kinneret to be mostly forgotten by the other Jews of Galilee. The houses and the paths between them looked quiet enough, but on this Friday morning a steady buzz droned behind the walls and in the few shady spots outside. The villagers were talking about one of their own, the son of Yosef and Miriam, who had left town just a few months before. Stories about him were already making the rounds through all of Galilee: He had gone down to the Jordan to be immersed by Yochanan and the crowds there heard a voice from heaven when he emerged from the waters. He had returned to the lively fishing towns of the Kinneret and healed scores of sick folks. He'd even driven out demons on several occasions. He taught in different synagogues every Shabbat and folk all around the Galilee couldn't stop talking about what they'd heard.

Natzeret was out on the fringes of this excitement, but the villagers were talking about all these things among themselves. They were also wondering what had gotten into this young man who had grown up among them. But they wouldn't have to wait long to find out, one of them said, because rumors had it that he was on his way to Natzeret, coming home, and he'd be there before Shabbat arrived at their doors.

Rumors don't always come to pass—indeed they rarely do—but the next morning, when the men of Natzeret gathered in the largest house in the village to study and pray together, Yeshua ben Yosef showed up. The room had been cleared of its meager furnishings to make space for the little congregation, and it was crowded that morning when Yeshua stepped in to join them, as he had done so many times before over the years. After the reading from the Torah scroll—the villagers were proud to possess their own *sefer Torah*—the man leading the service invited Yeshua up to read from the scroll of the Prophets, since he had just come home from a long absence. Yeshua rose, smiled and nodded to some of the others, and opened the scroll.

It was all a familiar enough ritual, with familiar enough players, but something felt different that morning as Yeshua unrolled the scroll, gazed down at the words for a brief moment, and then in clear and rounded tones chanted the words:

> The Spirit of Adonai is upon me,
>   because he has anointed me
>   to proclaim good news to the poor.
> He has sent me to proclaim liberty to the captives
>   and recovering of sight to the blind,
>   to set at liberty those who are oppressed,
> to proclaim the year of Adonai's favor.

Yeshua left off there, in the middle of the verse, rolled up the scroll, gave it back to the attendant, and sat down. He could feel the eyes of all the men bearing down on him—neighbors and friends, older men whom he had learned to respect as a youth, and young men who as boys had played with him in the hills around Natzeret. They all were silent and he let their silence settle in. Then he said the words: "Today this scripture has been fulfilled in your hearing." He could hear the murmuring this saying stirred up, some praising him but others asking what Yosef's son could mean by that statement. Yeshua looked at the men around him, "Doubtless you will quote the proverb to me, 'Physician, heal yourself.' What we heard that you did in Capernaum, do here in your hometown as well. But I'm telling you, no prophet is honored in his hometown."

The men gasped: "Yeshua is comparing himself to the prophets? He's doing favors for the fishmongers of Capernaum that he won't do for us?" Yeshua could feel the tension mounting, but he went on to talk about the great prophets of old, Eliyahu and Elishah, and how God sent them to help gentiles despite all the needs among their own people.

These hard-working and under-appreciated men could only understand Yeshua's words as insults. Five or six of them jumped up from their rough benches, grabbed Yeshua by the shoulders, and pushed him outside. The whole assembly followed, shouting and shoving him toward a rocky crag about a hundred yards off, where they were accustomed to throw their meager trash. But somehow Yeshua simply turned around, stepped away from the crowd, and walked away.

"Proclaim good news to the poor"

We don't know whether Isaiah 61 was part of a communal reading cycle in those days, or simply a passage that Yeshua chose for himself. But either way the message on that Sabbath morning was unmistakably clear. Yeshua was saying that the Spirit of Adonai, the LORD, was upon *him*—which meant that he was a prophet himself.[1] And if that wasn't clear enough, he applied the next line to himself as well, "God has anointed *me*," reading the Hebrew word from which we get Messiah, the anointed one. If Yeshua wasn't yet claiming to be Messiah, he was hinting at it—and clearly claiming to be a prophet, one of the anointed ones of the Tanakh, the Hebrew scriptures, who had now appeared to proclaim "good news to the poor."

"Proclaim good news to the poor"—this phrase is the tagline for the entire second half of Isaiah's prophecy (chapters 40 through 66), and for Jesus' mission as Luke narrates it. *Proclaim-good-news* is all one long word in Greek: *euangelisasthai*. As exotic as that word looks, Luke will pick it up again a little later to translate Jesus' own words, not just his reading of Isaiah. After Jesus leaves Nazareth, he returns to Capernaum and continues to heal the sick and demonized, so that reports about him spread out over the whole region. Proclaiming good news isn't just a verbal exercise; it's also an on-the-ground demonstration of the realities it announces. In the midst of these amazing events, a friendly crowd (and yes, Jesus encountered some friendly Jewish crowds) approaches Jesus and begs him not to leave their area. But he replies, "I must *proclaim-good-news* of the kingdom of God to the other towns as well; for I was sent for this purpose."

Proclaim-good-news bookends the description of Jesus' opening activity in Galilee after returning from Judaea. The section begins with Jesus revealing himself as the Spirit-anointed one proclaiming good news (Luke 4:16–30), and it closes with Jesus in action, proclaiming good news (Luke 4:43). But what exactly is the good news? What is the message "of the kingdom of God" that Jesus proclaims "to the poor" (4:18)? The phrase "good news" is often translated as "gospel" or "glad tidings" and is termed "the Message" in Eugene Peterson's popular translation, but these options don't really answer our question. What exactly is this good news?

In the two passages in Luke, the word is a verb. The Greek original sounds like evangelize/evangelizing, and that's a plausible translation,

---

1. See the linkage between the Spirit coming upon someone and prophecy in Numbers 11:29; 1 Samuel 10:6; 19:20–4; and Joel 2:28.

but it triggers images of modern evangelists and evangelism, and misses the sense of the ancient Hebrew original. The noun form of good news doesn't appear in Luke's extended narrative until Acts 15:7 (and just one other time, in Acts 20:24). But Luke was almost certainly familiar with the writings of Mark, the earliest account of the life of Jesus, and Mark uses the word in noun form. We can turn there briefly to get a sense of what the word meant in its first-century Jewish context. The noun "good news" appears at the very opening of Mark's account: *The beginning of the good news of Jesus the Messiah, the Son of God.*

Return from Exile

Mark is a master builder and he lays his foundation in this opening verse. He sets weighty words like massive stones in a solid row, stones upon which the entire structure of his account will rest: "The beginning of the good news of Jesus the Messiah, the Son of God." And as soon as this foundation is laid, Mark characteristically plunges into the action:

> As it is written in the prophets,[2]
>
> "Behold, I send my messenger before your face,
>   who will prepare your way,
> the voice of one crying in the wilderness:
>   'Prepare the way of the Lord,
>   make his paths straight,'"
>
> John appeared, baptizing in the wilderness and proclaiming a baptism of repentance for the forgiveness of sins. (Mark 1:2–4)

The "beginning of the good news" for Mark is the voice of one crying in the wilderness. This voice, which belongs to a man named John, isn't itself the good news, but it rises up at the beginning to prepare the way for the good news. Mark frames his wilderness scene in words from Isaiah 40. For Jewish readers—or better, hearers—of the word in those days and long since, a single line can evoke the whole passage. One vibrant image can paint the whole picture in the mind of the hearer. So "the voice of one crying in the wilderness" describes John and also paints the backdrop for the whole drama being enacted before us. Mark in his concise approach just cites one verse from Isaiah 40. Luke, when he describes the same scene,

---

2. The ESV lists this reading in the margin. In the body of the text it reads "As it is written in Isaiah the prophet." The first two lines, however, are actually from Malachi 3:1.

cites three verses of Isaiah (Luke 3:4–6). But both accounts are meant to bring the whole passage to mind:

> A voice of one crying in the wilderness:
> "Prepare the way of the Lord,
>   make his paths straight."
> Every valley shall be lifted up,
>   and every mountain and hill be made low;
> the uneven ground shall become level,
>   and the rough places a plain.
> And the glory of the Lord shall be revealed,
>   and all flesh shall see it together,
>   for the mouth of the Lord has spoken. . . .
>
> Go on up to a high mountain,
>   O herald of good news to Zion;
> lift up your voice with strength,
>   O herald of good news to Jerusalem;
>   lift it up, fear not;
> say to the cities of Judah,
>   "Behold your God!" (Isa 40:4–5, 9, ESV marginal reading)

"Herald of good news" in this passage is a single word in Hebrew, *mevaseret*. One of the suburbs of modern Jerusalem is named Mevaseret Zion, the phrase translated above as "herald of good news to Zion." I have close friends in Mevaseret Zion, and I've been there many times. From various vantage points in the city, you can look out at the hilly streets and byways of Jerusalem. You can see Highway 1, the busy thoroughfare from Tel Aviv that leads into the Jewish capital. This sort of scene is the background for Isaiah's imagery. *Mevaseret* or *mevaser*, herald-of-good-news, is originally a military term for a messenger, and his message is a related term, *besorah*, a report from the battlefield. The terms play a part in the accounts of the deaths of Saul (2 Sam 4:10) and Absalom (2 Sam 18:19–27), where they don't necessarily mean *good* news. Isaiah, however, definitely has good news in mind as he pictures the herald watching out over the highway leading into Jerusalem (Zion is a synonym for Jerusalem in this passage), eager to announce the approach of someone. Since the entire block of Isaiah's prophecy beginning in chapter 40 is about Israel's return from captivity in Babylon, we understand that Isaiah's herald is watching the highway that comes from Babylon back to the land of Israel, back to Jerusalem.

What is most striking in this passage, however, is that the herald isn't watching only for the return of the *Israelites*, but also—and above all—for the return of *their God*. God's presence has gone into exile with Israel and his presence will return, leading them back to the land of their inheritance. Then the herald will cry out the good news to Jerusalem, "Behold your God!"

Isaiah focuses on the end of exile; the prophet Ezekiel pictures the beginning of the same exile, as God's presence departs from Jerusalem. "And the glory of the LORD went up from the midst of the city and stood on the mountain that is on the east side of the city" (Ezek 11:23). This mountain is the Mount of Olives, and one midrash captures the comments on this verse by the ancient sage Rabbi Jonathan:

> Three and a half years the *Shechinah* [God's presence] abode upon the Mount of Olives hoping that Israel would repent, but they did not; while a *Bath Kol* [voice from heaven] issued announcing, "*Return, O backsliding children* (Jer 3:14), *Return unto Me, and I will return unto you* (Mal 3:7)." (Lamentations Rabbah, proem)

The midrash speaks of Israel's need to repent, and then describes that repentance in the words of the prophets as a *return* to God. The Hebrew term for repentance, *teshuvah*, means "return" or "turning." As Rabbi Jonathan notes, Israel did not return to God in Ezekiel's time, and the Shechinah departed from the Mount of Olives. (The Mount of Olives will play a vital role in Luke and Acts, as we'll see later.)

Before Ezekiel saw the glory of God leave the city, however, he saw it leave God's house or sanctuary (Ezek 10:18–19), and he heard God's reassuring words about Israel his people: "Though I removed them far off among the nations, and though I scattered them among the countries, yet I have been a sanctuary to them for a while in the countries where they have gone" (Ezek 11:16). God himself will be a sanctuary for his people wherever they are scattered in exile, and so God himself is with them in exile. Later Ezekiel, like Isaiah, pictures God's return:

> And behold, the glory of the God of Israel was coming from the east. And the sound of his coming was like the sound of many waters, and the earth shone with his glory. . . . And I fell on my face. As the glory of the LORD entered the temple by the gate facing east, the Spirit lifted me up and brought me into the inner court; and behold, the glory of the LORD filled the temple. (Ezek 43:2, 3b–5)

In Isaiah, the herald is watching the highway so that he can announce God's promised return, but first he calls on the people to prepare the way, using images of highway building: "make his paths straight," and "the uneven ground shall become level, and the rough places a plain." Centuries later, when Mark quotes Isaiah, he applies these phrases as metaphors for repentance, for returning to God. After citing Isaiah's call to prepare the way of the Lord, Mark writes, "John appeared, baptizing in the wilderness and proclaiming a baptism of *repentance* for the forgiveness of sins" (Mark 1:4, emphasis added).

The "good news" in Mark is that the God of Israel is returning to his people *and* that the people need to return to God. This aspect of the good news is front and center the next time Mark employs the term:

> Now after John was arrested, Jesus came to Galilee, proclaiming the good news of God, and saying, "The time is fulfilled, and the kingdom of God has come near; repent, and believe in the good news." (Mark 1:14–15 NRSV)

This passage seems a bit odd at first glance. Part of the "good news" is the call to "believe in the good news"! We can understand this phrasing better by remembering that in the context of the Tanakh and the Jewish world of Jesus' day, "believe" means more than intellectual agreement or abstract faith. The word implies trust in the message, faithfulness toward it, which goes hand-in-hand with repentance to produce a whole-hearted, behavioral response to this message about the kingdom of God. Mark has already called this message "the good news of Jesus the Messiah," implying that it is in and through Jesus that the kingdom of God has drawn near.

Just as in Isaiah, to proclaim the good news means announcing the return of the king and calling those who hear to prepare the way for him. This is good news for Israel, the Jewish people. It's the fulfillment of all that the prophets have promised and all the people have come to hope for. Mark reveals that God is restoring his kingdom in and through his Son, Jesus the Messiah, and that John has begun the process of preparation by calling the people to respond fully to this announcement and return to their God.

Besorah Defined

This good news, then, rests squarely on the prophecies of Isaiah—Isaiah 61 as Jesus announced to the home-town assembly in Nazareth, and Isaiah 40 as

Part One: The Besorah of Messiah and Jerusalem

Mark, followed by Luke, reveal in their accounts of Jesus' immersion in the Jordan. To underline this allusion to Isaiah we will employ the Hebrew term for "good news," reflecting the language of the prophet: *besorah*.

The besorah is the announcement that the divine King is returning to his people Israel to fulfill all that the prophets have promised. In light of this gracious intervention, the besorah also announces that the time has come for his people to bring their lives back into alignment with the King and his ways.

This besorah is prophetic, revealing the deeper meaning of past and present events, and looking far ahead into the future. It is deeply rooted not only in Isaiah, but also in the Torah and all the prophets, and now its "time is fulfilled."[3] Now Jesus enters Israel's story as the One who will activate and accomplish the besorah in his own life. All humankind will benefit from the besorah of Jesus the Messiah, but its fulfilment is linked in an essential way with Israel, the Jewish people, and with the land of Israel, their inheritance. Luke will explore that linkage in the most thorough fashion, both in the Besorah that bears his name and in the Book of Acts.

Before we return to Isaiah 61 to conclude this chapter, we'll listen as Isaiah employs similar terminology in another key prophecy:

> How beautiful upon the mountains
>   are the feet of the *mevaser*, the herald-of-*besorah*,
> who announces peace, the herald-of-*besorah* of good,
>   who announces salvation,
>   who says to Zion, "Your God reigns!"
> Your watchmen lift up their voice,
>   their voice together for joy;
> for eye to eye they see
>   the return of the Lord to Zion. (Isa 52:7–8[4])

Here again the "*return* of the Lord to Zion" implies that he has been *absent*—in exile with Israel, as we saw earlier. The watchmen here, as in Isaiah 40, are looking out over the road to Jerusalem, the highway back from exile, and now they lift their voices in joy at the Lord's return.

---

3. The word "Torah" will appear many times throughout this book, and it's difficult to translate with one English term. In some cases, like this sentence, it refers to the Five Books of Moses, or the Pentateuch. It can also be used to refer to scripture in general, as well as to Jewish commentary on scripture. In other contexts it is understood, and translated, as "Law," but this term can be misleading because the word Torah itself means "teaching" or "instruction," and includes narrative as well as legal content.

4. Authors' translation.

God's return from exile is even clearer in the conclusion to this section, as the prophet tells the Jewish refugees:

> For you shall not go out in haste,
>   and you shall not go in flight,
> for the Lord will go before you,
>   and the God of Israel will be your rear guard. (Isa 52:12)

Isaiah 52 is part of a traditional *haftarah* reading. The haftarah, or haftarot in the plural, are traditional passages from the writings of the Prophets that are read each week in the synagogue. This particular haftarah begins at Isaiah 51:12 and ends here at Isaiah 52:12. The reading for the following week begins at Isaiah 54:1. Isaiah's famous prophecy of the suffering servant in 52:13—53:12 is skipped entirely, and it doesn't appear anywhere else in the cycle of haftarot. Does Jewish tradition deliberately overlook the prophecy of the servant who "has borne our griefs and carried our sorrows" (Isa 53:4), perhaps as a snub to the claims of Yeshua's followers? We cannot know all the motives of those who crafted the haftarah cycle, but Isaiah 53 does not actually suit the occasion in which its surrounding chapters are read. Isaiah 51:12—52:12 and Isaiah 54 are two of a series of haftarah readings leading up to Rosh Hashanah, the Jewish New Year. The series begins with Isaiah 40:1, "Comfort, comfort my people" and the theme of comfort or consolation provides a transition from *Tisha B'Av*, the day marking the destruction of the temple, to Rosh Hashanah seven weeks later. This haftarah reflects the theme: "the Lord has comforted his people" (Isa 52:9). Isaiah 53 doesn't speak explicitly about the theme of comfort at all.

In the light of Messiah's life, death, and resurrection, however, we can see a connection between Isaiah 53 and the comforting message of the Lord's return to Zion. Isaiah 52:1–12 sounds a joyous note of restoration, but we might ask *how* this restoration will be achieved. Isaiah 52:13 opens the next section with the answer:

> Behold, my servant shall act wisely;
>   he shall be high and lifted up,
>   and shall be exalted.

This exalted servant is the key to Israel's restoration, but as Isaiah tells his story, the tone of exaltation quickly shifts to suffering, rejection, and death. Only toward the end do we hear the hint of restoration and resurrection to come:

> Yet it was the will of the LORD to crush him;
>> he has put him to grief;
> when his soul makes an offering for guilt,
>> he shall see his offspring; he shall prolong his days;
> the will of the LORD shall prosper in his hand.
> Out of the anguish of his soul he shall see and be satisfied.
> (Isa 53:10–11a)

It's up to Mark and Luke to show the fulfilment of this hint in the life, death, and resurrection of Jesus of Nazareth, who is revealed to be the "servant of the LORD."

The Coming Jubilee

With this background in mind, we're ready to return to dusty Natzeret, and to listen again to the words Yeshua read from the scroll of Isaiah on that shocking Shabbat morning long ago.

> The Spirit of the LORD is upon me,
>> because he has anointed me
>> to proclaim-besorah to the poor.
> He has sent me to declare liberty to the captives,
>> recovery of sight to the blind,
>> and the end of bondage to the oppressed,
> to proclaim the year of the LORD's favor. (Luke 4:18–19[5])

This passage is Isaiah's final use of basar/besorah terminology, which he combines here with terminology about the year of Jubilee. "Liberty" is *dror* in Hebrew, a specialized term to describe the release and restoration of Jubilee "when each of you shall return to his property and each of you shall return to his clan" (Lev 25:10). Those who had to sell their holdings because of poverty are restored to their property in the year of Jubilee. Even those whose poverty was so desperate that they had to sell themselves into bondage are set free and can return to their families. Isaiah's "year of the LORD's favor" also suggests Jubilee, as do the specific blessings that Yeshua reads off: liberty, recovery, the end of bondage. Finally, the Greek word in this passage for "liberty" and "end of bondage" is *aphesis*. This word is drawn from the ancient Greek translation of Isaiah 61 known as the Septuagint, and also appears numerous times in the Septuagint version of Leviticus 25, describing the Jubilee.

---

5. Authors' translation based on the Hebrew of Isaiah 61.

Isaiah employs the Jubilee language of Leviticus to give us a foretaste of the Jubilee to come, when the Anointed One, the one upon whom the Spirit rests, will bring an end to the oppression and loss of this age. In that end-times Jubilee, the people of Israel will be restored to their land, which they inhabited as mere tenants under the Roman occupation of Yeshua's day. It's no wonder that Yeshua's neighbors in Natzeret were amazed, stunned, even shocked, when he said, "Today this scripture has been fulfilled in your hearing." Was he implying that the Jubilee to come had already begun? And that he was the one to bring it to fulfilment? It's no wonder that the neighbors could so readily turn against Yeshua when he had hinted at such an audacious claim.

And so we've come full circle. When Jesus announced his assignment to proclaim-good-news to the poor, he was invoking the besorah foreseen by Isaiah—and revealing that he was the one to bring it to pass. As we continue through Luke's account in his Gospel and Acts, we will learn that Jesus must endure death and resurrection to accomplish this task. Luke will reveal how the besorah concerning the death and resurrection of Jesus is simultaneously the besorah of God's coming reign in Jerusalem. This two-pronged impact is inherent in the term "besorah" that we use throughout this book. Besorah is a main character in the whole story that we retell, second only to Jesus himself in the drama that will unfold.

The irony is that "besorah" is normally an announcement of triumph, as in Isaiah, yet this besorah includes apparent defeat—the agonizing death by crucifixion. But only with crucifixion can the ultimate triumph of resurrection be achieved. And indeed, Jesus has already undergone crucifixion and risen again to inaugurate the resurrection to come, and this is good news not only about what God *has* done, but also about what God *is* doing and *will* do. The besorah is a prophetic declaration of God's past, present, and future saving deeds in the life of the people of Israel through Israel's resurrected Messiah, Jesus of Nazareth.

Chapter Two

The Crucified Messiah and Jerusalem

> To Jerusalem, Your city,
> may You return in compassion,
> and may You dwell in it as You promised.
> May You rebuild it rapidly in our days
> as an everlasting structure,
> and install within it soon the throne of David.
> Blessed are You, Lord, who builds Jerusalem.

A GENERATION AFTER JESUS of Nazareth was crucified at the hands of Rome, the Jewish people and their beloved Jerusalem suffered a similar fate. Roman legions crushed a major Jewish uprising, burned Jerusalem, and destroyed the holy temple. The Jewish people have prayed and longed for the restoration of Jerusalem ever since. The prayer above is one of a series of blessings called the Amidah, or "Standing" prayer. According to Jewish tradition, it became part of the formal liturgy in the days of Gamaliel II, leader of the Jewish community in the generation after the fall of the temple.[1] The flames of Jerusalem's destruction had barely been quenched when prayers for her restoration began to arise—and they have continued to ascend to God's throne through all the long centuries since.

In the course of these same centuries, the death of one Jewish figure on a hill outside the walls of Jerusalem, just forty years before the temple fell, has seemed to those reciting these prayers irrelevant or averse to the fulfillment of their hopes. In this book, however, we are claiming that the besorah of the death and resurrection of Jesus the Messiah is also, and inextricably, a prophetic vision of the death and resurrection of Jerusalem, the very restoration longed for in the prayers of the Amidah.

---

1. *Koren Siddur*, 108–9, 122.

But how can this be? How can Jesus' saving act in offering himself to God, and God's saving response in raising him from the dead, have a redemptive impact on the people of Israel and their land?

These questions focus on the linkage between Jesus and his people. And they also *assume* a linkage between that people and its land, because the redemption we're speaking of centers on Jerusalem, a real city in the heart of the ancestral Jewish homeland. Beginning with the call of Abraham in Genesis 12 and continuing throughout the biblical narrative, the land of Israel is an essential sign of God's blessing upon the people of Israel. The status of the Jews as God's covenant people has never depended on their inhabiting the land, but Jewish religious identity has always included a passionate hope of return to the land. As Jewish prayer amply demonstrates, Judaism looks forward to the regathering of the people to the land promised to Abraham, Isaac, and Jacob. "Bring us back in peace from the four quarters of the earth and lead us upright to our land."[2]

We are proposing the radical idea, based on the writings of Luke, that Jesus died and rose again as the messianic representative of the Jewish people, *and* that his death and resurrection have ordered the course of Jewish history ever since, including the promised restoration to the land. When Jesus suffers and dies he participates in advance in the intensified exile of the Jewish people that will begin a generation later when the Romans destroy Jerusalem. Because of Jesus' suffering, this destruction becomes not only punishment but also a source of purification and renewal for the Jewish people. In the same way, Jesus' resurrection serves as the pledge and empowerment of Jerusalem's ultimate redemption, of the future return from exile and restoration to the covenant land of Israel.

Jerusalem and the Early Church

In line with the Torah and Prophets, Luke views the holy city as the fulcrum of God's action in human history. He also sees it as bound inseparably to the crucified and risen Messiah. Since the capital city represents the land as a whole, when Jesus identifies himself with Jerusalem, as he does in the passages we'll review in this chapter, he identifies himself with the land as well. At the same time, he identifies with the Jewish people to whom that land was promised. But, sadly, Luke and Acts haven't traditionally been read in

---

2. *Koren Siddur*, 96.

this way. A quick review of Christian attitudes towards Jerusalem in the early centuries will help us understand why.

In the decades after the fall of Jerusalem in 70 CE, at least some Jewish followers of Jesus shared the grief of their fellow Jews over that event. Consider Hegesippus, a second-century Jewish believer in Jesus. He wrote about James the Just, brother of the Messiah and leader of the Torah-observant branch of the early Yeshua-movement. Hegesippus portrays James as a Nazirite maintaining a strict code of ritual purity (Num 6:1–21), who, like the high priest on the Day of Atonement, devoted himself to prayer in the Jerusalem temple, "asking forgiveness for the people." Hegesippus recounts the martyrdom of James, in which he follows his brother's example by praying for the forgiveness of those who are putting him to death. And Hegesippus concludes his narrative by noting that the Roman siege of Jerusalem begins not long after the death of James. For Hegesippus, the intercessory prayers of this righteous man, who loved his people and his city, had preserved them from evil, and when he died the city lost its protection and fell under God's judgment. Historians today might argue over the details in the story of James the Just as told by Hegesippus, but it demonstrates that there were disciples of Jesus in the second century who, like the ideal figure in the story—and its author himself—loved Jerusalem and its Jewish inhabitants, and grieved over its destruction by the Romans.[3]

Other Jesus-followers of the second century, who were not Jewish, reveal a far different attitude toward Jerusalem. Like the James of Hegesippus, writers such as Justin Martyr and Irenaeus loved and longed for the city; but, unlike James, they loved a Jerusalem that was not a Jewish city rooted in Jewish memory and symbolizing the Jewish people as a whole. Instead, they looked to an *eschatological* Jerusalem. (The terms *eschatology* and *eschatological* refer to the age to come, the glorious future envisioned by both the New Testament and rabbinic tradition.) The Jerusalem they hoped for would be the center of a restored and glorified messianic kingdom inhabited and ruled only by members of the church. Jewish Jerusalem had been judged and brought to a decisive end; but the Son of God would return, and a glorious "Christian" Jerusalem would rise from its ashes.

The contrast between this attitude toward Jerusalem and the attitude of most Jews comes to vivid expression in the opposing reactions during

---

3. The writings of Hegesippus appear in *Ecclesiastical History*, by the fourth century historian and bishop Eusebius. The citations in this paragraph are from *Ecclesiastical History* 2.23.

the second and third centuries to the Temple Mount itself. Two generations after the fall of the temple, the Jews mounted another revolt against Rome and suffered another disastrous defeat in 135 CE. Afterwards, the Romans rebuilt Jerusalem and renamed it Aelia Capitolina. Jews were forbidden to live in the city, but they were permitted to gather on the Mount of Olives opposite the Temple Mount to mourn for the desolated temple and Jewish city, and to pray for their restoration. As a result, a new type of pilgrimage emerged among Jews, very unlike the joyful festival pilgrimages of the Torah (Exod 23:14–17; Deut 16:1–17). This was a pilgrimage of lamentation and longing for the glory of the messianic age to come.

While Jewish worshipers were creating this new type of pilgrimage, something similar developed in the church, but with a radically different perspective. Unlike their Jewish counterparts, Christians came not to mourn but to exult. They considered the destruction of the temple and the Jewish city— and the exile of its Jewish inhabitants—to be an act of divine vindication of Jesus. For these gentile believers, the sight of the temple ruins demonstrated that "Christianity" had triumphed over Judaism. The scattered stones of the Temple Mount bore witness that the Jews had been rejected by God, and that the church now constituted God's beloved people.

This view of Jerusalem changed dramatically with the conversion of the Roman emperor, Constantine, early in the fourth century. Always alert to the power of symbols, the emperor sanctioned an excavation at the Jerusalem site that generations of local Jesus-believers had identified as the place of Messiah's execution and burial. Apparently this local tradition was reliable, for in 327 the excavations uncovered a tomb that was assumed to be the place at which the Son of God was raised from the dead.[4] This discovery sent shock waves through the worldwide church, and ultimately produced a dramatic change in attitude toward the earthly Jerusalem. Fourth-century Christians focused not on the Jerusalem of eschatological expectation, as did Justin and Irenaeus; nor did they care about the Jerusalem of Jewish memory, as did Hegesippus; the city that captured their imagination in this era was *the Jerusalem of Jesus.*

Constantine built a church at the site of the tomb, which eventually became the earthly center of the church's spiritual universe and the primary destination for pilgrims from throughout the world. Churches were also

---

4. Recent archaeological excavations support the reliability of this tradition. See https://www.nationalgeographic.com/news/2017/11/jesus-tomb-archaeology-jerusalem-christianity-rome/, accessed 9/1/19.

constructed at other sites associated with events in the life of Jesus, such as the Last Supper and the Ascension. Jerusalem was now a "Christian" holy city, a city of shrines, whose earthly stones had the power to connect members of the church to both the redemptive events of the past and the heavenly realities to which they pointed. In the following centuries, the stature of the Jerusalem church was elevated until it attained the sort of prestige that had earlier been enjoyed by the messianic Jewish community of Jerusalem under the leadership of James the Just.

It came as an enormous shock, therefore, when Persian armies trampled Jerusalem in 614, and Arab invaders took the city in 637. At this time, gentiles who had once mocked Jews for grieving over the fall of Jerusalem took up the language of lament themselves. "The Christians had sharply differentiated their experience in Jerusalem from that of the Jews. Now as they went into exile in their turn, they turned naturally to the gestures and psalms of their predecessors in the Holy City, and like the Jews they spoke of God and Zion in the same breath."[5] These gentiles had come to share a love for the earthly city comparable to the love that animated the Jewish people, and as a result they now experienced a similar pain in her loss. Yet, this shared pain did nothing to heal the relationship between the Jewish people and the church, but only intensified their mutual hostility. The bitter fruit of that animosity would ripen four and half centuries later, when Crusaders from the West recaptured the holy city in an attempt to restore its "Christian" glory, and killed many of its Jewish inhabitants in the process.

Church history testifies to the enduring power of Jerusalem as a sign of the saving work of God in the world that inspires passionate devotion. Gentile believers in Jesus came to see the earthly Jerusalem as central to their faith; but the Jerusalem they loved was the city of Jesus, the Jerusalem of an already accomplished redemption—not the Jerusalem of the Jewish people, the city of a redemption still to come. Just as Jesus had been torn from the people who were his own flesh and blood, so the city of Jewish hope had likewise become exclusively "Christian" property.

But, we might ask, how does this Christian attempt to own Jerusalem compare with Jesus' way of relating to the city?

---

5. Armstrong, *Jerusalem*, 214.

Four Crucial Scenes

Four scenes from Jesus' story in the Besorah of Luke point toward an answer to that question. These scenes treat the death of Jesus and the fall of Jerusalem in ways that make each event an interpretation of the other. As we move toward their climax, we'll see how Jesus not only mourns over Jerusalem's coming fall and maintains hope in her restoration, but also identifies himself with Jerusalem in the suffering and death—and by implication the resurrection—that await him.

1. "O Jerusalem, Jerusalem" (Luke 13:31–35)

Jesus is in Galilee, going "through towns and villages teaching and journeying toward Jerusalem" (Luke 13:22). During a break some Pharisees come up and warn him that Herod, the ruler of Galilee, is seeking to kill him, so he'd better move on. Jesus replies,

> Go and tell that fox, "Behold, I cast out demons and perform cures today and tomorrow, and the third day I finish my course. Nevertheless, I must go on my way today and tomorrow and the day following, for it cannot be that a prophet should perish away from Jerusalem." O Jerusalem, Jerusalem, the city that kills the prophets and stones those who are sent to it! How often would I have gathered your children together as a hen gathers her brood under her wings, and you were not willing! Behold, your house is forsaken. And I tell you, you will not see me until you say, "Blessed is he who comes in the name of the Lord!"

When Luke notes that it's Pharisees who warn Jesus of Herod's murderous intentions, he is distinguishing them from the Jerusalem authorities of the following verses, who will carry out Herod's wish. This distinction reflects Luke's moderate portrayal of the Pharisees in both his Gospel and Acts. It also reflects his portrayal of the chief priests as the primary actors behind the arrest and conviction of Jesus and the persecution of his followers in Jerusalem.

The other three scenes that we'll visit in this chapter appear only in Luke, and so does the first part of this passage, verses 31–33. This section concludes with words that highlight the special role Jerusalem must play in the drama of redemption: "It cannot be that a prophet should perish away from Jerusalem."

Part One: The Besorah of Messiah and Jerusalem

The next two verses (34–35) appear also in Matthew 23:37–39, but in a different context. In Matthew, Jesus says these words not *on the way* to Jerusalem, as in Luke, but *after* his triumphal entry into the city when the crowds had called out, "Blessed is he who comes in the name of the Lord!" (Matt 21:9). In Matthew's version, therefore, the promise "you will not see me" contains an added word—"again" (Matt 23:39). This minor detail suggests that the triumphal entry was a prophetic enactment of Yeshua's future return, when Jerusalem will see him "again" and cry out "Blessed is he who comes in the name of the Lord!" And there's another difference in the two accounts. In Matthew 23:37, Yeshua says to Jerusalem, "you were not willing" after having a number of disputes with Jerusalem authorities (Matt 21:10—22:46). In Luke's version, however, Jesus says "you will not see me" *before* he has even arrived in Jerusalem, and *before* he has tested Jerusalem's "willingness" to respond.

How then do we interpret Jesus' sorrow over Jerusalem's rebuff, apparently before it even happens? How can Jesus claim that the city "will not see" him, shortly before he shows up and is seen there? Luke here seems to be presenting Jesus as a prophet speaking God's own words on his behalf. As commentator Robert Tannehill argues, the words "how often have I desired to gather you" (Luke 13:34) refer to "the long history of God's dealing with Jerusalem," and the words "you will not see me" likewise refer not to Jesus, but to *God*: "Verse 35 is speaking of the departure of Jerusalem's divine protector, who will not return to Jerusalem until it is willing to welcome its Messiah, 'the one who comes in the name of the Lord.'"[6] This interpretation is unusual, but it makes sense of what might otherwise be a puzzling text. It also reflects the idea of God in exile, which sets the stage for the Lord's return to Zion, the theme of the besorah in Isaiah, which we covered in chapter 1.

In summary, then, Luke 13:31–35 focuses attention on the city of Jerusalem and its temple authorities as those who persecute the prophets and who will put to death the Messiah. The Pharisees are distinct from this persecuting body and in some measure opposed to it, as are the Galileans who accompany Jesus on his journey to the capital. The longing for Jerusalem's welcoming response belongs not only to Jesus but even more to God, whose love for the city and whose grief at its wickedness is not a recent development but has extended through multiple generations. The predominant tone of Jesus' words, as in all four of the scenes we are now

---

6. Tannehill, *Luke*, 225.

considering, is one of lament. Nevertheless, a more positive note emerges in the end: "You will not see me *until you say*, 'Blessed is he who comes in the name of the Lord!'" (Luke 13:35). There is reason to hope that the divine presence, whose departure renders the city vulnerable to its enemies ("Behold, your house is forsaken"), will return again, to comfort and glorify Jerusalem. And this passage makes the condition for such a future return unmistakably clear: The city—apparently still in its character as the capital of the Jewish people—must offer the same welcome to the Messiah that he will receive from his Galilean disciples later in Luke's account, when he enters the city a few days before Passover. Jesus will not fulfill his ministry apart from the city with which he identifies so fully. Jerusalem's welcome of Jesus is essential to the besorah.

2. Jesus Weeps for Jerusalem (Luke 19:41–44)

When Jesus told those around him that he had to go to Jerusalem, he described the city's spiritual hardness and warned of its fate. But now, as he actually approaches the holy city and gazes upon it, Jesus weeps, saying,

> Would that you, even you, had known on this day the things that make for peace! But now they are hidden from your eyes. For the days will come upon you, when your enemies will set up a barricade around you and surround you and hem you in on every side and tear you down to the ground, you and your children within you. And they will not leave one stone upon another in you, because you did not know the time of your visitation.

Ironically these words of lament come amid Jesus' so-called "triumphal entry." He has already descended the Mount of Olives on the back of a donkey and now he's at the base of the hill, looking up at the city walls and the magnificent temple. Luke has made it clear that it's "the multitude of his disciples" who greet him with shouts of joy and praise as he rides by (19:37), with no mention of the city as a whole. Even amidst this cheering little crowd, some Pharisees raise their voices and call on Jesus to rebuke his disciples for their words—"Blessed is the King who comes in the name of the Lord"—but Jesus refuses (19:38–39). The disciples are responding properly to Jesus' entry, but the city as a whole does not respond . . . and now Jesus weeps over it. He weeps because in one glance he beholds two prophetic pictures, one superimposed on the other: the first is his own suffering and death, which will reveal that Jerusalem has not "known the things that make for peace" or the time of her "visitation"; the second is Jerusalem's coming destruction at the hands of the Romans, who "will tear you down to the ground, you and your children within you" (19:44).

It's striking to see how these phrases of lament echo the joyous Song of Zechariah in Luke 1:68–79. Zechariah, father of John the immerser, is filled with the Spirit at his son's circumcision and utters a song. It's a celebration of the saving power of "the Lord God of Israel" (1:68), who acts in accordance with his oath to Abraham (1:73), his merciful covenant with all the patriarchs (1:72), and the words spoken "by the mouth of his holy prophets from of old" (1:70). In all this, the *tone* of the song is the opposite of the tone of Luke 19:41–44. Even more, the *content* of Jesus' prophetic words as he approaches the city appears to be the direct opposite of Zechariah's song. In the births of John and Jesus, God has "*visited* and redeemed his people" (1:68), "to give *knowledge* of salvation to his people" (1:77). But now, in contrast, Jerusalem "did not *know* the time of [its] *visitation*" (19:44). The specific words of Jesus' lament in Luke 19 actually echo in ironic contrast the words of Zechariah's song in Luke 1.

Zechariah sings that God has come to "give light to those who sit in darkness" and "to guide our feet into the way of *peace*" (1:79); Jesus mourns that "the things that make for *peace*" are "hidden from your eyes" (19:42), implying that those he's speaking to still "sit in darkness." Zechariah proclaims that God's work through John and Jesus will result in Israel's being saved and rescued from its *enemies* (1:71; 73), but now Jesus foresees the coming siege and destruction of Jerusalem by Israel's *enemies* (19:43–44).

We have here far more than a *non-fulfillment* of what was promised; the echoing words draw attention to the blatant *contradiction* between what Zechariah anticipated and what is actually taking place. Furthermore, this contradiction can't be evaded (as Bible interpreters have sometimes tried to do) by distinguishing the "Israel" of Zechariah's Song from the "Jerusalem" that Jesus approaches. Luke treats the redemption of *Israel* (1:68) as equivalent to the redemption of *Jerusalem* (2:38). If Jerusalem is judged rather than redeemed, then Israel is judged rather than redeemed—but Zechariah's whole song speaks of Israel being redeemed.

This contradiction between the joyful expectation of Jerusalem's redemption in Luke's infancy narrative and the actual events that occur in Jerusalem in both 30 and 70 CE might suggest that Luke's story concerning Israel should be read as a tragedy. It begins in great promise but ends in catastrophe. And a tragic element is undeniable, but it's highly unlikely that

Luke thinks the promises to Israel in his infancy narrative have been—or can be—thwarted in the end. To see God's dealings with Israel as ultimately tragic would mean that God's dealings with Jesus also result in failure. Jesus mourns over the coming suffering of Jerusalem just as many in Jerusalem will mourn over *his* suffering (23:27–31). But the suffering of Jesus and the grief it causes are swallowed up in the joy of his resurrection (Luke 24:41, 52). Since Zechariah, moved by the Holy Spirit (Luke 1:67), sings of Israel's redemption shouldn't we also expect Jerusalem's suffering and grief to be swallowed up in the joy of redemption?

If redemption is Luke's vision of Israel's future, as Jesus' words in Luke 13:35 suggest, then the allusion in Luke 19:41–44 to the Song of Zechariah is neither ironic nor contradictory. Instead it is a way of signaling that the sad events taking place in Jerusalem are not the end of Jerusalem's story. In fact, the judgment of Jerusalem—and Jesus' bearing of that judgment on the cross—will be instrumental in achieving her ultimate redemption. When Jesus addresses Jerusalem here, he sees the coming judgment on the city as clearly as he sees his own coming crucifixion. And since he identifies so clearly with Jerusalem, his coming resurrection is also an enactment of the city's restoration.

3. The End of the Times of the Gentiles
(Luke 21:20–24)

After Jesus descends the Mount of Olives he goes up into the holy city and enters the temple courts. There he encounters merchants selling animals for sacrifice right in the midst of this holy place, and drives them out. To the gatekeepers of the temple, and the chief priests, this Nazarene is a troublemaker and a nuisance. They seek a way to get rid of him, perhaps permanently, but Jesus keeps returning to the temple to teach and proclaim his besorah. As the religious authorities vie with each other to trip him up, Jesus doesn't back down.

In the temple courts, tensions are mounting, but during a moment of calm, Jesus hears some of his followers admiring the temple and its magnificent chiseled stones. He warns them that the temple's days are numbered. "As for these things that you see, the days will come when there will not be left here one stone upon another that will not be thrown down" (Luke 21:6). Jesus' followers are shocked. The temple torn down!

But they've learned to pay attention to the words of the Master and so they ask him when this disaster will happen.

Jesus' answer to that question appears in Mark and Matthew, as well as Luke, but with a different emphasis. In Mark 13 and Matthew 24 Jesus' discourse combines references to the destruction of Jerusalem by Rome and the great distress at the end of the age in a way that superimposes one event on the other. In contrast, Luke's version of the discourse makes a clear distinction between what will happen in Jerusalem in 70 CE and what will happen at the end of the age.

> But when you see Jerusalem surrounded by armies, then know that its desolation has come near. Then let those who are in Judea flee to the mountains, and let those who are inside the city depart, and let not those who are out in the country enter it, for these are days of vengeance, to fulfill all that is written. Alas for women who are pregnant and for those who are nursing infants in those days! For there will be great distress upon the earth and wrath against this people. They will fall by the edge of the sword and be led captive among all nations, and Jerusalem will be trampled underfoot by the Gentiles, until the times of the Gentiles are fulfilled.

Mark's account speaks of the "abomination of desolation" standing in the temple (Mark 13:14); Luke uses the same Greek word for the "desolation" that will come not just upon the temple, but upon the whole city (21:20). The sign of that desolation is the armies surrounding Jerusalem rather than the idolatrous altar implied in Mark's account. Mark goes on to speak of "such tribulation as has not been from the beginning of the creation that God created until now, and never will be" (Mark 13:19), implying the time of final judgment. Luke's version speaks of a more limited judgment, "wrath against *this people*," that is, the Jewish people who inhabit Jerusalem. Most significantly, in Luke 21 the world in its unredeemed form—and the Jewish people—remain in existence after this event, for not all of the inhabitants of Jerusalem are slain but some will "be taken away as captives among all nations," and "Jerusalem will be trampled underfoot by the Gentiles, until the times of the Gentiles are fulfilled." This concluding statement implies that an extended period of time will elapse between the destruction of Jerusalem and the end of the age—which will occur only *after* "the times of the Gentiles are fulfilled."

Jesus paints a grim picture here, but it's a picture that aligns with what he said in the two earlier events on the way to Jerusalem. Jesus foresees judgment *and* a future redemption for Jewish Jerusalem. Perhaps the period in which the gentiles "trample" Jerusalem will end when the Jewish people corporately welcome Jesus as the promised Messiah with the words, "Blessed is he who comes in the name of the Lord." If so, such "trampling" must be compatible with a continued Jewish presence in the city, since Luke 13:35 speaks of a welcome extended to Jesus by the Jews *of Jerusalem*. On the other hand, the transition from the "times of the Gentiles" to the fullness of the messianic age might be an extended process rather than a singular event—a process that culminates in the corporate Jewish welcoming of the Messiah, but begins well before that greeting. This second interpretation will become especially relevant when we consider the extraordinary events in Jewish history that mark the twentieth century. This detail aside, it's clear that the city is to undergo judgment/death and eventual restoration, just as Yeshua is about to undergo death on the cross and resurrection on the third day.

4. The Daughters of Jerusalem Weep (Luke 23:27–31)

The conflict in Jerusalem reaches its breaking point with the approach of Passover. One of Jesus' closest followers betrays him to the chief priests and temple officers, who have him arrested at night, rush him through a sham trial, and hand him over to the power of Rome. The Roman governor, Pilate, agrees to have Jesus executed by the hideous Roman method—crucifixion. As imperial soldiers lead Jesus away, they seize a Jewish bystander, Simon of Cyrene, to carry his cross.

> And there followed him a great multitude of the people and of women who were mourning and lamenting for him. But turning to them Jesus said, "Daughters of Jerusalem, do not weep for me, but weep for yourselves and for your children. For behold, the days are coming when they will say, 'Blessed are the barren and the wombs that never bore and the breasts that never nursed!' Then they will begin to say to the mountains, 'Fall on us,' and to the hills, 'Cover us.' For if they do these things when the wood is green, what will happen when it is dry?"

These verses, which appear only in Luke, add a number of crucial features to the story:

1. The women who mourn and wail over Jesus' fate show that the city is divided in her response to Jesus, just as she will later be divided in her response to the twelve (Acts 5:33–39), to Stephen (Acts 8:2), and to Paul (Acts 23:6–10). Not everyone in Jerusalem approves of

the actions of their leaders. Nevertheless, in the end those who are sympathetic to Jesus and his disciples are unable to carry the day.

2. These women respond to what is happening to Jesus in the same way that he had responded to Jerusalem's fate as he anticipated his arrival in the city (Luke 13), and later as he actually approached its gates (Luke 19). This besorah has already sounded the note of grief, and these women are but echoing a note that we've heard before.

3. This echo helps prepare us for Jesus' words when he points the wailing women to what they should really be grieving over. The passages that are echoed—Luke 13 and 19—also help us understand the tone of Jesus' words to the women. He doesn't speak harshly or vindictively, but instead beckons the women to join him in his own grief for Jerusalem, grief that is coming to a head as he reaches his place of execution.

4. Jesus' words about the blessing upon barren women in that coming day allude to a verse from our previous passage (Luke 21:20–24): "Woe to those who are pregnant and to those who are nursing infants in those days!" (21:23). "Woe" and "Blessed" are parallel but contrasting terms. Those who are "blessed" here in our fourth passage are those who are not subject to the "woe" of our third passage. Thus, Luke's narrative here in chapter 23 echoes all three of the earlier grieving-for-Jerusalem texts (13:31–35; 19:41–44; 21:20–24) as it sets the stage for their dramatic enactment. This echo confirms the bond connecting all four texts, and the message that they all convey: Jesus' profound identification with Jerusalem in her suffering.

5. A final point concerns the closing words of this passage: "For if they do this when the wood is green, what will happen when it is dry?" (23:31). Jesus is innocent of violent insurrection, yet he suffers the punishment reserved by the Romans for just such offenders. He is the green wood, which will be burned up in the "baptism of fire" that he must undergo (Luke 3:16; 12:49–50). If one innocent of offense suffers in this way, what will be the fate of the rebellious city as a whole and its leaders—the dry wood—when the torch is tossed in their pile? In this way, Jesus takes his place as the innocent representative of his people, who bears in advance the judgment that they merit and will eventually receive.

Bible commentator and theologian N. T. Wright describes Jesus' words here as a "riddle" revealing the meaning of his crucifixion:

> It suggests, in its dark riddling way, that Jesus understood his death as being organically linked with the fate of the nation. He was dying as the rejected king, who had offered the way of peace which the city had rejected; as the representative king, taking Israel's suffering upon himself. . . . Having announced the divine judgment upon Temple and nation alike, a judgment which would take the form of awful devastation at the hands of the pagan forces, Jesus was now going ahead of the nation, to undergo the punishment which, above all, symbolized the judgment of Rome on her rebel subjects. If they did this to the one revolutionary who was not advocating rebellion against Rome, what would they do to those who were, and those who followed them?[7]

Jesus here signals that his death is "organically linked with the fate of the nation." Rather than attempting to dissuade the daughters of Jerusalem from grieving at his death, Jesus urges them to recognize how his death—his "baptism of fire"—anticipates the national conflagration to come. He thus invites them—and us—to grieve *with* him rather than merely *for* him. And so we return to the prayer for the restoration of Jerusalem with which this chapter opened: "To Jerusalem, Your city, may You return in compassion, and may You dwell in it as You promised." It's a traditional Jewish prayer, recited multiple times daily by observant Jews . . . and it reflects a longing expressed by the Jewish Messiah, Yeshua of Natzeret.

Conclusion

We've seen how Jesus identifies with Jerusalem to the fullest extent, bearing in his own body the judgment to come upon the holy city. Now we turn to Luke's second volume, the Book of Acts, to see how he identifies through his resurrection with the coming redemption of Jerusalem. The besorah that comes into focus through both volumes includes crucifixion and resurrection—both of Jesus and of Jerusalem, which stands for the Jewish people as a whole. This fully orbed besorah opens our eyes to God's purposes, not only in the first century, but throughout history and in the day in which we live.

---

7. Wright, *Jesus and the Victory of God*, 570.

Chapter Three

The Resurrected Messiah and Jerusalem

All day long on the journey from Jerusalem down to Jericho, Miriam had been thinking about the happy days of Passover that she'd just spent in the holy city with her husband, Yosef, and their twelve-year-old son, Yeshua. Miriam was traveling with other women on the long descent to Jericho, the city of palms. It was the month of Aviv, springtime, and the weather was mild. The soil was still moist from the winter rains, and on shaded hillsides along the road Miriam could catch glimpses of the last of the wildflowers, bursting forth in yellow, orange, and red against the pale green grass.

The sun was at their backs as the caravan skirted Jericho and then turned north to head up the valley of the Jordan and back to Galilee. After an hour or two the pilgrims stopped and began to prepare for the night. Smaller children had been left at home with friends or family members, but some of the women had infants to nurse and settle down for sleep. Miriam decided to walk on ahead a half mile or so to where the men and older boys were setting up their encampment. She wanted to make sure that all was well with Yosef and Yeshua and wish them a good night. When Miriam spotted Yosef at a distance, Yeshua was nowhere to be seen, but she thought he could be anywhere among this traveling crowd, visiting relatives or spending time with other boys.

Yosef saw Miriam approaching and raised his hand to greet her, but he wondered why Yeshua wasn't with her. The two parents soon realized that neither of them knew where Yeshua was, and started racing through the encampments, asking relatives and friends from Natzeret if they'd seen their boy. After a couple of hours it was too dark to search any longer. In anguish they realized their only option was to turn around and start the long ascent back to Jerusalem as soon as they had enough sunlight to travel again.

Finally, three anxious days after Yosef and Miriam realized Yeshua was missing, they found him in the temple courts. They had arrived early in the morning and had seen a cluster of men gathered around some Torah scholars, their voices raised in the lively conversational study of holy texts that students loved. And there, in the middle of it, was Yeshua sitting at the scholars' feet—listening, asking questions, and answering questions they posed. Some of the men had the look of serious Jerusalem Torah scholars and others looked like pilgrims, who had probably stayed in the holy city a few extra days hoping to learn something new. And all these men were looking at Yeshua in amazement as they heard the questions and answers coming from this twelve-year-old's lips. Yosef and Miriam were amazed too, but then, during a break in the discussion, Miriam remembered her worry and fear over the past three days and pulled Yeshua aside. "Son, why have you treated us like this? Look, your father and I were worried sick searching for you." And now it was Yeshua who looked surprised. "Why were you looking for me?" he said. "Didn't you know that I must be in my Father's house?" (Luke 2:48b–49).

Jerusalem, the City of Jesus

It's a charming tale, and as Luke recounts it, he makes a profound point: Jerusalem belongs to Jesus. "My Father's house" can refer to the temple or to the city as a whole. Both belong to Jesus' own Father and Jesus is the rightful heir. Luke describes Jesus in 2:43 with the Greek word *pais* or "boy," the same word he uses for David as God's son (Luke 1:69; Acts 4:25) and for Jesus as David's heir (Acts 3:13, 26; 4:27, 30). Jerusalem was the city of David and his dynasty, and therefore it is also the city of Yeshua ben David, the son of David. There may even be a play on words with "Father" in 2:49—the city of Jerusalem and its temple belong ultimately to God (Jesus' divine Father), and God has bestowed it as an inheritance upon David (Jesus' earthly father or ancestor). In both senses Jesus can rightly call the temple "my Father's house."

Jerusalem is the city of Jesus. In our last chapter we saw how Jesus tied the destruction of his beloved Jerusalem to his own death, indicating that he would bear in his own body the judgment to come upon the holy city. This linkage raises a question that is rarely asked: does Luke picture the same sort of connection between Jesus' resurrection and the future redemption of Jerusalem? As we turn to Acts, we'll discover good reasons for answering that question with a "yes"—beginning with Luke's pattern of associating the resurrection of Jesus with God's promises to David and his dynasty, which includes Jesus himself. Jerusalem is the city of David, and the promises to David are therefore promises concerning Jerusalem as well. Let's see how Luke highlights this connection in the two most important speeches that he records in Acts, Peter's initial public proclamation of the besorah on Shavuot (Pentecost), and Paul's speech in the synagogue of Pisidian Antioch on his first apostolic journey.

Two Key Speeches

Jesus and his parents traveled to Jerusalem for Passover, one of the three annual festivals on which Jews made a pilgrimage to Jerusalem and its temple, in obedience to the Lord's instructions: "Three times in the year you shall keep a feast to me.... Three times in the year shall all your males appear before the LORD God" (Exod 23:14, 17). The other two pilgrimage holidays were Shavuot (the Feast of Weeks or Pentecost) and Sukkot (the Feast of Tabernacles).

During the first Shavuot after Jesus' resurrection, Jesus' followers were gathered in Jerusalem, praying together. Suddenly, amidst a great noise like a rushing wind, the Holy Spirit came upon them with such power that they began to prophesy and praise God in languages they'd never learned. The streets all around them were filled with worshipers from throughout Israel and all the surrounding lands, and their joyful proclamations started to draw a big crowd. Peter took the opportunity to step out and tell his fellow Jews what was going on.

Peter's Sermon on Shavuot

This is the first of our two key speeches. In it, Peter quotes Psalm 16, including verse 10: "For you will not abandon my soul to Hades, or let your Holy One see corruption" (Acts 2:27). Peter explains that these words couldn't apply to David, their author, but had to refer to someone else. "Brothers," he says to his fellow Jews,

> I may say to you confidently of our ancestor David that he both died and was buried, and his tomb is with us to this day. Since he was a prophet, he knew that God had sworn with an oath to him

that he would put one of his descendants on his throne. Foreseeing
this, David spoke of the resurrection of the Messiah, saying,

> "He was not abandoned to Hades,
> nor did his flesh experience corruption."
>
> This Jesus God raised up, and of that all of us are witnesses.
> (Acts 2:29–32 NRSV)

David had spoken words that were fulfilled in the resurrection of his descendant Jesus: "You will not abandon my soul to Hades, or let your Holy One see corruption." Instead of seeing Hades and corruption, Jesus was raised up from the dead—and Peter and his friends can provide eye-witness testimony of that. Peter continues, citing another of David's writings, Psalm 110:

> Being therefore exalted at the right hand of God, and having received from the Father the promise of the Holy Spirit, he has poured out this that you both see and hear. For David did not ascend into the heavens, but he himself says,
>
> "The Lord said to my Lord,
> 'Sit at my right hand,
> until I make your enemies your footstool.'"
>
> Therefore let the entire house of Israel know with certainty that God has made him both Lord and Messiah, this Jesus whom you crucified. (Acts 2:33–36 NRSV)

Peter explains to this crowd of Jewish worshipers what's going on right before their eyes: the crucified and risen Messiah has been exalted to God's right hand in the heavens, and from there he has poured out the Holy Spirit upon his disciples, as they can see and hear. In this way, Jesus has revealed himself to them as the promised son of David, who did not see corruption, but who ascended to heaven and was enthroned as Lord and Messiah.

Paul's Sermon in Pisidian Antioch

A few years later, Sha'ul of Tarsus, also known as Paul, gives the second of our two key speeches.

Paul is sent out with Barnabas from the city of Antioch in Syria to spread the besorah among the gentiles. Paul and Barnabas come to another Antioch, in the region of Pisidia, and, as is their custom, attend the local synagogue on the Sabbath. The synagogue rulers recognize the two men as visitors and invite them to bring "a word of encouragement for the people." Paul takes this invitation and runs with it, giving a word that defines his entire mission, and displays the same logic as Peter's speech on Shavuot.

Paul opens with a recap of Israel's history up to the founding of David's dynasty, and underlines Jesus' lineage as David's descendant and heir (Acts 13:22–23). He then cites Psalm 2 as a prophecy of the resurrection—"You are my Son, / today I have begotten you"—followed by the same verse from Psalm 16 that Peter quoted earlier: "You will not let your Holy One see corruption" (Acts 13:33–35). Between these two verses from Psalms, Paul adds an illuminating text from Isaiah 55:3: "And as for the fact that [God] raised him from the dead, no more to return to corruption, he has spoken in this way, 'I will give you the holy and sure blessings of David'" (Acts 13:34). In this way, Paul claims that the resurrection of Jesus stands at the heart of the "holy and sure blessings of David."

The resurrection, therefore, isn't only the raising of one holy Galilean prophet in whom God was uniquely present. And it isn't only a sign of Jesus' victory over death, or of God's vindication of his rejected Messiah. It is also, for Paul as for Peter, the glorification of Israel's Davidic king, Yeshua of Natzeret, whose eternal reign cannot be divorced from the city chosen to be the place of his throne. If the Son of David has been raised from the dead, and if the city of David is destined likewise to be raised from the dead, as the prophets declare, we have reason to see the resurrection of the Son as a firm pledge, an advance sign, and even the catalyst of the resurrection of the city.

Paul's Later Speeches

Paul's final speeches in Acts reinforce this conclusion. In them he presents the resurrection of Jesus as the source of hope for Israel's national resurrection. Let's take a look.

When Paul appears before the Sanhedrin in Acts 23, he identifies himself as a Pharisee, a member of a party for whom Israel's future resurrection is a fundamental tenet of faith. He goes on to claim, "It is with respect to the hope and the resurrection of the dead that I am on trial" (Acts 23:6). The word "dead" here is plural ("resurrection of *those who are dead*"). Paul in this way is referring to the hope for Israel's future resurrection, a hope that he shares with his fellow Pharisees. This claim was a shrewd political maneuver, setting the Pharisees in his audience against the Sadducees who were present as well, but it was also an entirely accurate statement. Paul was on trial for his proclamation of the risen Messiah of Israel, whose resurrection funded a firm and joyful hope in Israel's destiny as a people.

Paul restates this claim when he appears before Felix, the Roman governor (Acts 24:15, 21), but the fullest expression of Paul's message of national hope and resurrection comes later when he appears before King Agrippa:

> According to the strictest party of our religion I have lived as a Pharisee. And now I stand here on trial because of my hope in the promise made by God to our fathers, to which our twelve tribes hope to attain, as they earnestly worship night and day. And for this hope I am accused by Jews, O king! Why is it thought incredible by any of you that God raises the dead [plural]? . . . To this day I have had the help that comes from God, and so I stand here testifying both to small and great, saying nothing but what the prophets and Moses said would come to pass: that the Christ must suffer and that, by being the first to rise from the dead, he would proclaim light both to our people and to the Gentiles. (Acts 26:5–8, 22–23)

Jesus is only "*the first* to rise from the dead," and Paul implies that his resurrection will be instrumental in bringing about the resurrection of all Israel, the "promise . . . to which our twelve tribes hope to attain." In this speech, Paul doesn't link Jesus' resurrection to the restoration of Jerusalem, but more generally to Israel's national hope of restoration.

Paul makes his final speech in Acts to the Jewish leaders of Rome. He reiterates his claim that his message concerns the destiny of all Israel: "For this reason, therefore, I have asked to see you and speak with you, since it is because of the hope of Israel that I am wearing this chain" (Acts 28:20). The "hope of Israel" here isn't Jesus himself, but the resurrection, the renewal of Israel in the messianic age that Jesus will accomplish. In the years following Paul's declaration, however, Zion was not glorified but instead burned to the ground, and these words pointed to a future redemption of the city that would be a true resurrection from the dead.

The portrayal of Jesus' resurrection in all these speeches aligns perfectly with Luke's portrayal of Jesus' death. Both events are set within a prophetic context in which they are inseparably bound to Israel's ultimate destiny, a destiny most clearly revealed in the story of Jerusalem exiled and restored.

Jerusalem and the Geographical Structure of Luke and Acts

For Luke, as for the prophets, Jerusalem represents both the *people* of Israel and the *land* of Israel, fusing in one vivid image the shared life of the Jewish people and the site promised as their inheritance. Luke emphasizes the unique role of Jerusalem by structuring the narrative within his two volumes geographically, with Jerusalem as its center. No other books in the New Testament adhere to such a defined geographical pattern. As we examine the geographical structure of Luke and Acts, therefore, we'll gain fresh insight into the unique message concerning Jerusalem that the two volumes convey.

The Geographical Structure of the Besorah of Luke

Among the four Gospels, only Luke begins in Jerusalem—and not only in Jerusalem, but in the temple itself, with Zechariah, future father of John the immerser, offering incense in the holy place. Both Matthew and Luke describe Jesus' birth near Jerusalem in Bethlehem, but only Luke depicts the presentation of the infant Jesus in the Jerusalem temple, accompanied by the prophetic blessings of Simeon and Anna. Only Luke provides readers with a story of Jesus as a youth, a story that recounts his visit to Jerusalem for Passover. Thus, Luke's two-chapter introduction centers on the city of Jerusalem and its temple.

Then, from the beginning of chapter 3 to the final paragraphs of chapter 9, Luke shifts his focus to Galilee, following for the most part the order of events recorded in the Gospel of Mark. After that, he opens a new section of his narrative, which includes material that appears only in his account, beginning with, "When the days drew near for him to be taken up, he set his face to go to Jerusalem" (Luke 9:51). The next nine chapters of Luke's "Special Section" form an extended travel narrative tracing Jesus' final journey to Jerusalem (Luke 9:51—18:14). The material itself is only loosely geographical in character, but Luke has chosen to organize all the material around the journey to Jerusalem, with occasional reminders of the geographical context (for example, Luke 13:22 and 17:11). In this way, the central section of Luke's narrative, which occurs outside Jerusalem, treats the holy city as its point of orientation.

As in all four Gospels, the events of Luke's passion narrative occur in Jerusalem and its immediate environs. But only Luke restricts the resurrection appearances to that area, and only Luke includes Jesus' command to his disciples to remain in the city (Luke 24:49). Then Luke's Besorah ends as it began—in the Jerusalem temple, with a community of Jews worshiping the God of Israel (Luke 24:53).

Among the four Gospels, then, only Luke *begins in* Jerusalem, *ends in* Jerusalem, and orients its central narrative around a *journey to* Jerusalem. Taken together with Luke's special treatment of the destruction and redemption of Jerusalem considered above, this emphatic geographical structure underlines Luke's unique concern for the holy city and her enduring significance. Luke's overall portrayal of the life, death, and resurrection of the Messiah aligns with the other Gospels, but we should not overlook the unique elements that he adds, which integrate the redemption of Jerusalem into the very structure of his Besorah of Jesus the Messiah.

The Geographical Structure of Acts

In the opening scene of Acts (following a brief preface), the risen Messiah has been with his followers for forty days, "speaking about the kingdom of God." He instructs them not to leave Jerusalem, but to wait there for the promised immersion in the Holy Spirit (Acts 1:3–4), and these instructions raise a question among the disciples.

> So when they had come together, they asked him, "Lord, will you at this time restore the kingdom to Israel?" He said to them, "It is not for you to know times or seasons that the Father has fixed by his own authority. But you will receive power when the Holy Spirit has come upon you, and you will be my witnesses in Jerusalem and in all Judea and Samaria, and to the end of the earth." (Acts 1:6–8)

These verses are crucial for a proper interpretation of the entire book of Acts. Readers often assume here that Jesus wants to correct the ethnocentric worldview of his disciples. They think Jesus wants his followers to look beyond Jerusalem and the Jewish people and develop a new universal worldview. In the text itself, however, the focus remains on Israel, and the question is specifically about "the time" of Israel's final restoration. Will it occur *now* (or *later*)? Jesus doesn't deny the restoration to come for Israel,

PART ONE: THE BESORAH OF MESSIAH AND JERUSALEM

but he tells his disciples the timing is in God's hands. Then he continues: "But you will receive power when the Holy Spirit has come upon you, and you will be my witnesses in Jerusalem and in all Judea and Samaria, and to the end of the earth." Generations of interpreters have noted that this verse supplies us with a rough geographical outline of Acts, a geographical structure, we'll add, that is *centered on Jerusalem*.

Like the Besorah of Luke, Acts begins in Jerusalem, within a community gathered around the temple (Acts 2:46; 3:1–10; 4:1–2; 5:12, 20–21, 42).[1] The story develops as the message and power of Jesus radiate outwards—first to the towns of Judea and Samaria (Acts 8:1, 4–25), then to Damascus (Acts 9:1–2, 10, 19). In Acts 10, Peter brings the message of Jesus to the gentile Cornelius and his household in the coastal city of Caesarea. Then in Acts 13 Paul begins his travels, wending his way through Asia Minor (modern-day Turkey), and eventually crossing over to Europe and establishing Jesus-believing communities in Greece. The story concludes with Paul in Rome, capital of the Empire.

But this popular narrative outline, like the condensed summary of Acts 1:8, leaves out a particular detail that has profound implications for the book's geographical structure: Jerusalem remains the center and focal point throughout. While radiating steadily outwards, *the story continually reverts back to Jerusalem.*

- Paul encounters Jesus on the road to Damascus, *and then returns to Jerusalem* (9:26–29).

- Peter proclaims Jesus to Cornelius in Caesarea, *and then returns to Jerusalem* (11:2).

- A congregation arises in Antioch, *and then sends aid to Jerusalem* in a time of famine (11:27–30).

---

1. Readers of Acts are sometimes puzzled by the disciples' continuing attachment to the temple, now that the final sacrifice of Yeshua has been accomplished. As will be evident throughout this book, the new realities brought into being through the death and resurrection of Messiah Yeshua do not negate or invalidate the institutions established in the Torah. The significance of the temple and of its sacrificial rites may be modified after the definitive sacrifice of Yeshua, but those Torah institutions remain central to the worship and devotion of the early Jewish followers of Yeshua. This view is often seen as in conflict with the teaching of the book of Hebrews. For a perspective on Hebrews that is consistent with our reading of Acts, see 67–68, and also Kinzer, *Jerusalem Crucified*, 85–94.

- Paul and Barnabas journey from Antioch to Asia Minor, *and then return to Jerusalem* for the central event in the book of Acts—the Jerusalem council (15:2).
- From Jerusalem Paul travels with Silas to Greece, *and then returns again to Jerusalem* (18:22).
- Paul takes his final journey as a free man, *and then returns to Jerusalem*, where he is arrested (21:17—23:11).

This feature of the geographical structure of Acts is often missed, but one commentator sees it clearly:

> Although Acts begins in Jerusalem and ends in Rome, it is inaccurate to conclude that Jerusalem falls out in favor of Rome.... Even when Paul is in Rome, his memory reverts to Jerusalem to reiterate his fate there (28:17). Hence, Acts does not delineate a movement away from Jerusalem, but a constant return to Jerusalem. In the geography of Acts emphasis repeatedly falls on Jerusalem from beginning to end.[2]

If indeed Acts 1:8 is a geographical outline of the book, then its language supports this conclusion, for it describes Rome as being located at "the *end* of the earth." Rome may be the capital of a gentile empire, holding political control over much of the earth, but for Luke it was neither the *center* nor the true capital of the world. That honor belonged to Jerusalem alone.

In both the greater story of the advance of the apostolic message and the more specific story of Paul, the heart beats in an alternating diastolic and systolic rhythm, with Jerusalem as the perpetual center *to which all must eventually return*. And Jerusalem restored is an inherent element of the besorah of the death and resurrection of Messiah, essential to its fulfillment.

The Puzzling Conclusion to Acts of the Apostles

But Acts does end in Rome rather than in Jerusalem. Moreover, it ends with Paul's rebuke of the Jewish leaders of Rome as those whose hearts had been dulled by a divine judgment. In many ways this is a puzzling conclusion to these two volumes, especially given the Jerusalem-centered theology that we're outlining. Let's look at it more closely.

---

2. Brawley, *Luke-Acts and the Jews*, 35–36.

Part One: The Besorah of Messiah and Jerusalem

The second half of Acts deals exclusively with the work of Paul, who will die in Rome as a martyr not long after the events described in Acts 28, and in all likelihood before Luke had completed his writing. Luke could have probably brought closure to his narrative of the early messianic community by recounting Paul's heroic death, yet he refrains from doing so. We propose that this lack of closure in Acts 28 constitutes an essential message of its own: the story Luke is telling is not concluded, but has in fact only just begun. Ending with the death of Paul could signal that the proclamation and manifestation of the kingdom of God and its transforming power had come to a suitable narrative climax. But Luke sends a different signal by concluding with Paul alive and well in Rome: "He lived there two whole years at his own expense, and welcomed all who came to him, proclaiming the kingdom of God and teaching about the Lord Jesus Christ with all boldness and without hindrance" (Acts 28:30–31). The work must continue; the kingdom to come must still be proclaimed, lived, and awaited.

This reading of the end of Acts finds its most powerful support in the beginning of Acts.

As we just saw, Acts opens with a question: "Lord, will you at this time restore the kingdom to Israel?" (Acts 1:6). The apostles ask this question on the Mount of Olives, overlooking Jerusalem, where the Messiah has just been raised from the dead. They clearly anticipate the imminent restoration of the Davidic kingdom in its ancestral capital, but they seem to have forgotten Jesus' earlier teaching regarding the destruction of Jerusalem: "Jerusalem will be trampled underfoot by the Gentiles, until the times of the Gentiles are fulfilled" (Luke 21:24). Jesus' response to the apostles echoes this earlier teaching: "It is not for you to know times or seasons that the Father has fixed by his own authority" (Acts 1:7).

The death and resurrection of the Messiah have begun the process that will lead to the overthrow of the final gentile empire, but much suffering still remains for the people of Israel and the city of Jerusalem. Since Jerusalem will soon be "trampled underfoot by the Gentiles," it is evident that the kingdom is now being restored to Israel in only a partial and imperfect fashion. Luke still awaits that day when "the times of the Gentiles are fulfilled," which will also introduce the "time" when God will "restore the kingdom to Israel." Therefore, he rightly leaves his narrative without closure, for the narrative of God's dealings with Jerusalem, Israel, and the nations has not yet been closed.

Luke wants his readers to grasp the rhythmic geographical flow of his narrative, which streams out from Jerusalem always to return again, like waves that beat on the rocks and then return to their ocean home. He leaves his narrative in mid-flow, in anticipation of its future consummation, which will occur at some point *after* the judgment of Jerusalem. Rome may be at the "end of the earth," but it is not the end of the story. The story must end where it began—in Jerusalem.

Mount of Olives: Ground Zero of Redemption

The first chapter of Acts records an astounding event, which confirms that the story must end where it began—in Jerusalem. Jesus answered the apostles' question about the restoration of the kingdom by telling them they couldn't know the timing of that restoration, but in the meantime they'd be empowered as his witnesses "to the end of the earth." And then, as they stood there watching, "he was lifted up, and a cloud took him out of their sight."

> And while they were gazing into heaven as he went, behold, two men stood by them in white robes, and said, "Men of Galilee, why do you stand looking into heaven? This Jesus, who was taken up from you into heaven, will come in the same way as you saw him go into heaven." (Acts 1:9b–12)

It's not hard to imagine the apostles staring upward with jaws dropped as Jesus rises up into the clear blue skies above Jerusalem. We might also imagine them wondering what the two men in white robes mean when they say that Jesus "will come in the same way as you saw him go." Luke hints at the answer by telling us that this all happened on the "mount called Olivet"—the Mount of Olives—which evokes the prophecy of Zechariah:

> For I will gather all the nations against Jerusalem to battle. . . . Then the LORD will go out and fight against those nations as when he fights on a day of battle. On that day his feet shall stand on the Mount of Olives that lies before Jerusalem on the east. . . . Then the LORD my God will come, and all the holy ones with him. (Zech 14:2–5)

What do the two mysterious men mean by the phrase, "in the same way"? Just as Jesus ascends now *from* the Mount of Olives, so he will descend in the end *to* the Mount of Olives, as Zechariah foretells. Just as the Mount of

Olives serves now as his point of departure from Jerusalem, so that same site will mark his point of entry to the city when he returns.

This dramatic scene also reminds us of Ezekiel's prophecy of the departure and return of the divine glory, which we cited in chapter 1. When the glory departs from the holy temple it first stops and rests on "the mountain east of the city" (Ezek 11:23)—that is, the Mount of Olives. Later, when the glory returns to the temple, it comes "from the east" (Ezek 43:2)—that is, from the Judean exile in Mesopotamia. The prophet views the returning glory from the vantage point of the Temple Mount, which looks eastward toward the Mount of Olives and beyond. Thus, Ezekiel sees the glory return "in the same way" as he saw it depart.

Jerusalem will suffer many things, as the prophecies of Zechariah, Ezekiel, and Jesus all foretell. But in the end the city will be consoled when the LORD comes to defend her, his feet standing on the Mount of Olives. "On that day," when the LORD comes and "all the holy ones with him," he will be welcomed by Jerusalem in a fitting manner. "On that day" the leaders and the people of the city—not just the "multitude of his disciples"—will go out together to meet him, proclaiming with joy, "Blessed is he who comes in the name of the Lord" (Luke 13:35; 19:37–38).

The narrative of Jesus' ascension from the Mount of Olives provides us with *the strongest and clearest evidence for the Jerusalem-centered eschatology of Luke and Acts.*

The Three Pilgrimage Festivals and Their Message

Zechariah 14 unlocks the meaning of the Mount of Olives, and it suggests another key to the narrative of Luke-Acts and its hope for "the redemption of Jerusalem." This key is the approach taken in the narrative to the pilgrimage festivals of Israel, the "three times in the year [when] all your males [shall] appear before the LORD God" (Exod 23:17).

We opened this chapter with the story of Yeshua and his family journeying to Jerusalem in obedience to this commandment to celebrate the early-spring festival of Passover (Luke 2:41). The central narrative of Luke is then structured around Jesus' journey to Jerusalem, again to celebrate Passover (Luke 22:1, 7–8, 11, 13, 15). Acts has a similar orientation to the late-spring pilgrimage festival, Shavuot, the day on which the Spirit is poured out on the followers of Jesus (Acts 2). Later Acts describes Paul's final journey to Jerusalem in a way that makes it resemble Jesus' pilgrimage before his death. But whereas Jesus went to Jerusalem to celebrate Passover, Paul goes for Shavuot (Acts 20:16). The narrative of Acts is thus focused on Shavuot in the same way as the narrative of Luke is focused on Passover.

The two accounts, then, cover the first two pilgrimage festivals of Israel—but what about the third, the autumn feast of Booths, or Sukkot? The festival year is incomplete without this crucial feast, which anticipates the final harvest and Israel's redeemed life (along with the nations) in the world to come.

In Jewish tradition, likely going as far back as the first century, a key reading for Sukkot is Zechariah 14: "And the LORD will be king over all the earth. . . . Then everyone who survives of all the nations that have come against Jerusalem shall go up year after year to worship the King, the LORD of hosts, and to keep the Feast of Booths" (Zech 14:9, 16). If the Besorah of Luke is related to Passover, and the Acts of the Apostles to Shavuot, then the as-yet-unwritten conclusion to this trilogy will be related to Sukkot. In the eschatological celebration that will fulfill the meaning of this festival, the nations will join Israel in Jerusalem to glorify the One who is the "king over all the earth." Thus will be realized the "kingdom of God" which, according to the final verse of Acts, Paul proclaimed in Rome "with all boldness and without hindrance" (Acts 28:31). *Only in a future day will the story find its ultimate closure.*

If we read the conclusion of Acts in relation to the beginning of the book, we'll see how clearly it points to the future redemption of Jerusalem. The geographical structure of Luke and Acts conveys the same hopeful message with an essential addition: The resurrection of Jesus is the pledge and power that ensures Jerusalem's future redemption. Only when that redemption comes to pass will the "kingdom of God" reach its appointed goal.

Joy in the Midst of Exile

Luke's vision of Israel's exile and restoration, however, is complex. On the one hand, the resurrection of Jesus constitutes the first-fruits and source of Israel's ultimate restoration. On the other hand, Luke also portrays the coming destruction of Jerusalem as a new stage in Israel's enduring exile, which will not end until "the times of the Gentiles are fulfilled." Jesus' suffering and death anticipate the intensified exile soon to come upon his people at the hands of the Romans. Moreover, Luke portrays Jerusalem as both the enduring capital

PART ONE: THE BESORAH OF MESSIAH AND JERUSALEM

of the Jewish people, and as the capital and international center of the community of Jesus' disciples—and indeed of the world itself. The coming agony and humiliation of the city at the hands of the Romans inspired in his work a profound sense of grief rather than exultation.

No better witness to this complex vision of exile and restoration exists than Jesus' remarks about feasting and fasting. Messiah is still in Galilee and is enjoying a feast thrown by Levi the tax-collector, whom he has just called to follow him. Some Pharisees are watching the festivities and they challenge Jesus: "The disciples of John fast often and offer prayers, and so do the disciples of the Pharisees, but yours eat and drink." Jesus replies, "Can you make wedding guests fast while the bridegroom is with them? The days will come when the bridegroom is taken away from them, and then they will fast in those days" (Luke 5:33–35).

N. T. Wright comments:

> Fasting in this period was not, for Jews, simply an ascetic discipline, part of the general practice of piety. It had to do with Israel's present condition: she was still in exile. More specifically, it had to do with commemorating the destruction of the Temple. Zechariah's promise that the fasts would turn into feasts [Zech 8:18–19] could come true only when YHWH restored the fortunes of his people. That, of course, was precisely what Jesus' cryptic comments implied.[3]

Wright helpfully characterizes the practice of fasting as a corporate Jewish response to exile. He also rightly sees Jesus' feasting rather than fasting as a sign that Jesus is the one who will bring the exile to an end. But Wright goes beyond these helpful insights as he continues:

> This is . . . a claim about eschatology. The time is fulfilled; the exile is over; the bridegroom is at hand. Jesus' acted symbol, feasting rather than fasting, brings into public visibility his controversial claim, that in his work Israel's hope was being realized; more specifically, that in his work *the Temple was being rebuilt*.[4]

But this interpretation only holds up if we ignore Jesus' final words: "The days will come when the bridegroom will be taken away from them, and *then they will fast in those days*" (Luke 5:35). In other words, Jesus implies that his earthly presence served as a sign of the coming restoration, but

---

3. Wright, *Jesus and the Victory of God*, 433.
4. Wright, *Jesus and the Victory of God*, 434. Emphasis original.

was not the final restoration itself. Fasting was not appropriate in his physical presence, but it would again be appropriate *after his ascension*. The resurrection and ascension of Jesus may secure the ultimate end of exile, but before that end comes, the bridegroom will be taken away for a time, and fasting will resume. During this period—between Messiah's resurrection/ascension and his return—the condition of exile in some sense endures.

The restoration has begun, and now, through faith in Jesus, the gift of the Spirit, and participation in the apostolic community, one could receive an authentic foretaste of the final redemption. Nevertheless, the coming destruction of Jerusalem will constitute a new stage in the exile rather than its conclusion.

This new stage of exile, however, also contains positive elements, even for Jews outside the apostolic community. Here are three:

1. The doors of the apostolic community remain open to all, and there the powers of the messianic age are already available.

2. Messiah's resurrection and ascension—and his continued presence in the world by his Spirit—stand as a sure pledge, even amid the continuing exile, of Jerusalem's ultimate restoration.

3. Jesus took upon himself Jerusalem's suffering when he died upon the cross. This established a dynamic link between his redemptive work and the suffering endured by the Jewish people. Jesus' radical identification with the Jewish people in his suffering and death—and in his resurrection and ascension—solidifies a bond that is thereafter unbreakable.

Conclusion

When Miriam and Yosef found the young Yeshua in the holy temple, he called it—and by implication the holy city as well—"my Father's house." Jerusalem belongs to the son as his inheritance, and he identified with it through his sacrificial death, bearing in his own body the judgment to come upon the holy city. The Book of Acts looks beyond the crucifixion to link the resurrection of Jesus with the coming redemption of Jerusalem.

Jerusalem is the city of David and the city of David's greater son, the city of the holy temple, the city that Jesus loved, and the city in which he died and rose again from the dead. Acts opens after Jesus' resurrection,

PART ONE: THE BESORAH OF MESSIAH AND JERUSALEM

with the community of his disciples taking root in Jerusalem, which is paradoxically in servitude—a kind of exile—under the power of Rome. The early messianic community is a prophetic sign of the meaning of that exile and a pledge of the restoration to come. Later, with Paul, the messianic community takes up temporary residence in Rome itself, at the *end* of the earth—but without losing her expectation of returning home to Zion, the true capital of the world.

Luke presents Jerusalem as the center of the land of Israel, the center of the Jewish people, the center of the messianic community, and the center of the entire world. His Besorah depicts the suffering and death of Jesus as a prophetic participation in the suffering and destruction of Jerusalem to come, implying that his resurrection is the pledge and catalyst of Jerusalem's future restoration. Luke's vision covers not only the city itself, but also that which the city represents—the whole land of Israel and the Jewish people. According to Luke, the death and resurrection of the Messiah are bound inextricably to both the land and the people of Israel. In the final analysis, therefore, Jesus' saving work either includes them in its scope, or fails in its purpose.

This claim implies an understanding of the gospel that expands upon the one most Christians have held through the centuries, including our own. It affirms the saving work of Jesus through his death and resurrection, but goes beyond the individualistic and spiritualized understanding of that work so prevalent today. The gospel as Luke presents it demonstrates the inextricable linkage between the death and resurrection of Jesus and the destiny of the Jewish people, which in turn unlocks the destiny of all nations. To reflect this expanded understanding, we've been using the word "besorah" instead of "gospel." In our next section, we'll look more deeply at the ramifications of this besorah for the people and land of Israel, beginning with the temple, which lies at the heart of Israel's story and is an irreplaceable key to its future.

Part Two

The Besorah, the Temple, and the Covenant People

Chapter Four

The Holy Temple in Scripture

Yeshua's pilgrimage as a twelve-year-old boy was just one of many visits to the temple he made throughout his life. John records two of these visits early in his Besorah, first for Passover (2:14–15), and later for an unnamed "feast of the Jews" (5:1, 14). Between these two visits, Yeshua returned to Galilee by way of Samaria, and the temple remained in clear focus even in that non-Jewish region.

It's about noon and Yeshua and his band take a break at a spot known as Jacob's well. After Yeshua's followers go off to find food, a Samaritan woman arrives at the well and Yeshua asks her for a drink of water. She's surprised and asks this Jewish stranger why he's even talking with her, a Samaritan woman. In reply Yeshua offers her "living water," something far better than the water he's asking her to share. Then he goes on to mention details of her life that he'd normally have no way of knowing. The woman is taken aback. She realizes that Yeshua must be a prophet—a Jewish prophet—so she raises an old controversy with him: "Our fathers worshiped on this mountain, but you say that in Jerusalem is the place where people ought to worship." Yeshua responds simply, "You worship what you do not know; we worship what we know, for salvation is from the Jews" (John 4:10–22).

Yeshua tells the Samaritan woman that the site of true worship is Jerusalem, and salvation for the whole world will come from that place and "from the Jews"—the people who have long been devoted to it. The Jerusalem temple is a sign of a future salvation that will far transcend it. This answer might not have won fans in Samaria, but it reflected an idea already at play in Jewish thought of the time. Yeshua takes a huge stride beyond the Jewish consensus, however, when he adds that this future salvation is already unfolding through the Spirit:

Part Two: The Besorah, the Temple, and the Covenant People

> Woman, believe me, the hour is coming when neither on this mountain nor in Jerusalem will you worship the Father.... But the hour is coming, and is now here, when the true worshipers will worship the Father in spirit and truth, for the Father is seeking such people to worship him. (John 4:21, 23)

After Jerusalem and its temple were destroyed by Roman troops in 70 CE, Christians began to interpret these words in stark terms: the temple was part of an earthly, outdated system that has now been replaced by true, spiritual worship of the Father. This sort of interpretation of John 4 is still popular today, but does it reflect the whole biblical picture of the temple? Is it consistent with the besorah presented in Luke and Acts?

That besorah, as we've seen, links Jesus' suffering and death to the suffering that was to come upon Jerusalem in 70 CE and beyond. Moreover, for Luke, Jesus' resurrection foreshadows the future restoration of Jerusalem. So if Jesus' resurrection serves as a pledge that the city will be restored in the end, can we say the same about the future of her temple? Will it also be restored in the end?

This is where problems arise. Numerous New Testament texts seem to challenge the hope for a restored temple in the age to come. The New Testament sometimes portrays Jesus himself as the true temple, and his followers as part of that temple through union with him. Some texts imply or even say outright that there will no longer be a temple building after Jesus returns (for example, Hebrews 9:6–10 and Revelation 21:22). These texts assume that the temple belongs to the present age, when access to the Holy One is available but restricted. In the future age, however, such access will be open to all, and a temple no longer necessary. This appears to be what Jesus is telling the Samaritan woman.

Moreover, if the temple represents Jerusalem, as Luke seems to assume, then the transformation of the temple from a building to a living reality might imply a similar, "spiritual" transformation in the character of the city. And this is exactly what many Christian commentators have concluded. From there they claim that such a transformation of temple and city suggests a similar transformation of Israel's land and people, in which the particular calling of the Jewish people yields to a new, universal faith. This perspective is widespread in Christian thought—and it runs counter to our whole thesis regarding the besorah and its message about the resurrected Messiah, the Jewish people, the city of Jerusalem, and the land of promise.

In this chapter we respond to this perspective by seeing how the temple is understood in the Bible outside of Luke's writings, exploring its history and significance in relation to the land, the city, and the people. In the next chapter we'll return to Luke and Acts to make the same exploration within those texts. A proper understanding of the temple and its role in the Bible is essential to a proper understanding of the besorah itself.

The Temple in the Hebrew Scriptures

In the history of Israel up to the cataclysmic year of 70 CE, the city of Jerusalem, the land of Israel, and the people of Israel were all relatively stable in meaning, with boundaries that most Israelites could agree upon.

- **Jerusalem** was a city in the mountainous spine of the land of Canaan, straddling the border that separated the northern from the southern tribes of Israel. The location of the city walls shifted over time and, like all cities, Jerusalem expanded and contracted. Yet, Jerusalem always remained Jerusalem. We speak of the First and Second Temples, divided in time by the Babylonian exile, but we do not speak of the First and the Second Jerusalems. The city ravaged by Nebuchadnezzar was the same city that was later restored under Cyrus, to be vanquished again by Rome.

- **The land of Israel** had Jerusalem at its heart and, like Jerusalem, remained the land of Israel despite the fluctuations of history. The maximal boundaries of the land promised to the patriarchs and matriarchs were somewhat fluid, but everyone recognized that Judea, Samaria, and Galilee formed the core of that inheritance.

- **The people of Israel** had a more complex definition, but within the Bible itself, the core characteristics of the people are clear enough. Those who were descended from Abraham, Isaac, and Jacob, worshiped the God of Israel, and participated in the life of the covenant community were members of the people.[1] This unambiguous corporate reality was identifiable and relatively stable through time.

---

1. *Halakhah*, Jewish law, considers the child of a Jewish mother to be Jewish, regardless of the father's identity. The wider Jewish community will often consider the child of a Jewish father and non-Jewish mother to be Jewish as well. Our point here is that the core reality was unambiguous and agreed-upon by all, and that dispute arose only over borderline cases (such as a person with only one Jewish parent), which were far less common in the ancient world than in the world today.

Part Two: The Besorah, the Temple, and the Covenant People

In contrast, the temple pointed to realities beyond itself, as we'll see in the next section, and changed dramatically throughout its history. To understand the unique nature of the temple, we need to review its history from the tabernacle at Sinai to Solomon's temple in Jerusalem.

The ark of the covenant resided in the holy of holies of the tabernacle constructed at Sinai (Exod 40:18–21). After Israel entered the land, the ark (and its tabernacle) came to rest at Shiloh (Josh 18:1; 1 Sam 3:3), a sanctuary overseen by the priestly family of Eli.[2] Threatened by the Philistines, the army of Israel took the ark with them into battle, and it was captured by enemy forces. But the Philistines soon regretted taking this booty, which brought them only trouble, and returned it to Israel. It ended up in the town of Kiriath Yearim, where it remained for twenty years (1 Sam 4:1–7:2).

At the same time, the descendants of Eli operated a sanctuary at Nob without the ark, but with other sacred items such as the bread of the presence (1 Sam 21:1–9). After the priests of Nob were slaughtered by Saul (1 Sam 22:6–23), what became of this sanctuary? According to the Chronicler, the tabernacle and the altar of burnt offering were situated at Gibeon during David's reign, even after he brought the ark to Jerusalem (1 Chr 16:37-40; 21:29; 2 Chr 1:3-6). Thus, for a time, the items that were essential parts of the temple worship—the ark, the altar, the bread of the presence, the tabernacle—were divided between at least two distinct sites.

Finally King David brought the ark to his newly established capital city and desired to build a house for it, but the prophet Nathan told him it was not he but his son who was to accomplish that task (2 Sam 7:1–13). Nevertheless, God revealed to David precisely *where* in Jerusalem the "house of the Lord" was to be located—on the threshing floor of Ornan the Jebusite (1 Chr 21:15—22:1). On that site King Solomon erected the temple, bringing together the sacred items that for many years had been divided.

This history reveals the three fundamental elements that came together to make the Jerusalem temple a site unique in holiness: (1) the ark, (2) the tabernacle and its furnishings, and (3) the location itself. This location had already played a major role in Israel's long drama:

> Then Solomon began to build the house of the Lord in Jerusalem on *Mount Moriah*, where the Lord had appeared to David his father, at the place that David had appointed, on the threshing floor of Ornan the Jebusite. (2 Chr 3:1, emphasis added)

---

2. Judges 20:26–28 states that the ark was at Bethel in an earlier period, namely, during the priestly tenure of Phinehas, grandson of Aaron.

Mount Moriah is the very site where Abraham had long before bound Isaac as a sacrifice in obedience to the Lord's command (Gen 22:2). Now, in the days of David and Solomon, Abraham's wholehearted devotion to the Lord becomes the model for Israel's true worship at the temple, fulfilling Abraham's saying that the Lord will be "seen" at the place where he had offered up Isaac (Gen 22:14). Genesis 22, then, establishes Moriah as a holy site centuries before Moses is commanded to build the tabernacle, and even more centuries before the Lord directs David and Solomon to build the temple there. Evidently this is the place foretold in Torah, "the place that the Lord your God will choose out of all your tribes to put his name and make his habitation there" (Deut 12:5).

When Solomon finally completes the temple, the holiness of the Temple Mount, even apart from the ark and the tabernacle furnishings, is evident in his prayer of dedication. He asks God to hear the prayers directed toward that place, even when the people of Israel are taken into exile—when, presumably, the temple service is no longer conducted (1 Kgs 8:46–53). The Book of Daniel testifies to precisely this practice of praying toward Jerusalem even when the ark has disappeared, the temple is destroyed, and the people have been taken into exile (Dan 6:10).

Thus, the Temple Mount was holy before Israel crossed the Jordan with the ark and the tabernacle, and it remains holy after the ark and the tabernacle furnishings are destroyed and Israel is taken back across the Jordan into captivity.

After the Babylonians destroyed Jerusalem in 586 BCE, the ark of the covenant disappeared from history and played no further role in the worship practices of the Jewish people. The Holy of Holies of the Second Temple, dedicated in 515 BCE, was an empty room. Sacrifices were again presented on the bronze altar; the fragrance of incense rose again from the golden altar; the menorah was again lit; and the bread of the presence rested again on the golden table; but the central article of the desert tabernacle and the First Temple, which represented the throne of the Lord, was nowhere to be found. For almost six centuries this ark-less temple served as Israel's most holy site. And then, in 70 CE, Jerusalem fell to the Roman legions, and the Second Temple underwent the same fate as the first.

Nearly two millennia have passed since that day. The ark and the temple have both vanished from history—yet the Jewish people remain, with their worship still directed toward the Temple Mount in Jerusalem. Anyone who has prayed at the ancient stones of the Kotel, the Western Wall, surrounded by Jewish worshipers from around the world wearing black hats and baseball caps, caftans and t-shirts, can see how the temple still lives as a symbol of Jewish faith and identity. The Western Wall is part of a massive retaining structure around the Temple Mount dating back to the time of Jesus. It's a place of unmistakable power and holiness, the site of ongoing Jewish prayer for centuries, and a reminder of the ancient temple, which lives on as an indestructible symbol within the Jewish imagination.

Even when the temple still stood, however, the Tanakh portrays it as a mixture joining the three separate elements of ark, tabernacle furnishings, and geographical site. As a mixture that was always in danger of fragmenting into its separate elements, the temple lacked the stable coherence of the city, land, and people it represented. Whether or not the three temple elements of ark, tabernacle, and place are ever reassembled, Jerusalem and the Jewish people retain their unparalleled significance.

The Temple as a Symbol Pointing to Realities beyond Itself

In the Hebrew Bible, Jerusalem, the land, and the covenant people are concrete realities and each one plays a significant role in the ongoing drama of God's dealings with the world. The temple, on the other hand, always pointed (and gave access) to realities beyond itself, including these four realities: the heavenly temple, the cosmic temple, the eschatological temple, and the human temple.

1. The heavenly temple

Isaiah was worshiping as a young man in the Jerusalem temple, when he suddenly found himself transported to its heavenly correlate. He saw the LORD "sitting upon a throne, high and lifted up," with the hem of his robe filling the temple (Isa 6:1). Jewish Bible scholar Jon Levenson describes the significance of this scene:

> In Isaiah's ecstatic experience, he sees and hears a session of the divine council.... The earthly Temple is thus the vehicle that conveys the prophet into the supernal Temple, the real Temple, the

Temple of YHWH and his retinue, and not merely the artifacts that suggest them.[3]

This same heavenly temple, according to later Jewish tradition, had been revealed to Moses on Sinai as the model for the earthly tabernacle he was to build—"Exactly as I show you concerning the pattern of the tabernacle and of all its furniture, so you shall make it" (Exod 25:9). Levenson considers this traditional interpretation of Exodus 25 to be a faithful reflection of the text itself:

> The Temple on Zion is the antitype.... The real Temple is the one to which it points, the one in "heaven," which cannot be distinguished sharply from its earthly manifestation. Thus, when Moses is to construct Israel's first sanctuary, the Tabernacle in the wilderness, he does so on the basis of a glimpse of the "blueprint" or "model" of the heavenly shrine which he was privileged to behold upon Mount Sinai (Exod 25:9, 40).[4]

The terminology of "earthly" and "heavenly" temple suggests that the (earthly) Jerusalem temple could not be severed from its heavenly archetype without losing something essential to its very nature.

2. The cosmic temple

The second reality that the Jerusalem temple pointed to was the cosmic temple, or the cosmos itself—the entire created order—*as* a holy temple. Levenson shows how the narrative of the construction of the tabernacle in Exodus 35–40 corresponds in several ways to the narrative of the creation of the world in Genesis 1:1–2:3, and the description of building Solomon's temple in 1 Kings follows the same pattern.[5] These texts support Levenson's thesis: "in the Hebrew Bible . . . the Temple is the epitome of the world, a concentrated form of its essence, a miniature of the cosmos. . . . [T]he Temple (or mountain or city) is a microcosm of which the world itself is the macrocosm."[6] God indwells his whole creation; worship in the temple reflects processes in this creation, and in turn has an impact on those very processes.

---

3. Levenson, *Sinai and Zion*, 123.
4. Levenson, *Sinai and Zion*, 140.
5. Levenson, *Sinai and Zion*, 142–44.
6. Levenson, *Sinai and Zion*, 138–39.

PART TWO: THE BESORAH, THE TEMPLE, AND THE COVENANT PEOPLE

3. The eschatological temple

The third reality to which the Jerusalem temple pointed was the temple of the age to come. The prophet Ezekiel describes a vision of this future temple (beginning in chapter 40), which he received thirteen years after the destruction of the First Temple. The temple he sees isn't the one later constructed by Zerubbabel, nor its even later expansion by Herod. Ezekiel sees a new temple, and he also sees a transformation of the landscape of Jerusalem and its surrounding region. He describes a stream of water "issuing from below the threshold of the temple toward the east" that becomes "a river that I could not pass through . . . deep enough to swim in" (47:1–5). Such a dramatic deepening of the water defies natural explanation, for there are no other streams flowing into the river to raise its water level. Moreover, the water itself has life-giving qualities beyond anything known in the present order of the world: "And wherever the river goes, every living creature that swarms will live" (Ezek 47:9; see also v. 12). Nourished by these life-giving waters, the land of Israel now resembles the Garden of Eden.

Other prophetic texts also anticipate an eschatological temple and a transformed natural order. According to Joel 3:18, "And in that day . . . a fountain shall come forth from the house of the LORD and water the Valley of Shittim." Likewise, Zechariah writes, "On that day living waters shall flow out from Jerusalem"—presumably issuing from "the house of the LORD." The order of nature will be transformed to eliminate the cold of winter and the darkness of night (Zech 14:6–8).

The connection between the Jerusalem temple and its heavenly and cosmic correlates is found in our earliest sources, but this connection with the eschatological temple emerges only in later sources, after the destruction of Solomon's temple. The temple had always pointed *upwards* (to the heavenly temple) and *outwards* (to the cosmic temple); now it also pointed *forwards* (to the eschatological temple-to-come).

4. The human temple

Finally, the Jerusalem temple also pointed beyond itself to a human temple—namely, the people of Israel. The LORD's aim for the tabernacle was not to dwell "in *it*" but "among *them*" (Exod 25:8). The tabernacle and temple were not ends in themselves but instruments of this greater purpose. Israel was not made for the temple, but the temple for Israel.

The implications of this reality only become clear at the time of the Babylonian exile. The prophet Ezekiel, taken into exile ten years before the destruction of Jerusalem, sees a vision of the holy city and its temple in their current state (Ezek 8–11). He sees the "glory," the divine presence, departing from the temple because of the people's sins (see 8:3–4, 6; 9:3; 10:1–22). Later he sees the glory return from the east, the direction of exile, from where the people of Judah will return as well (Ezek 43:2–7). The glory that had dwelt within the temple, rendering it holy, still dwells among the people, the human temple, in their exile, as well as in their return.

As we've seen, Isaiah shares a similar vision of "the return of the Lord to Zion." He proclaims to Israel:

> The voice of your watchmen—they lift up their voice;
> > together they sing for joy;
> for eye to eye they see
> > *the return of the Lord to Zion.* (Isa 52:8, emphasis added)

The Judeans leave Babylonia as the Israelites left Egypt centuries before, but this time their exodus is peaceful rather than in fear and haste. Isaiah continues:

> For you shall not go out in haste,
> > and you shall not go in flight,
> for the Lord will go before you,
> > and the God of Israel will be your rear guard. (Isa 52:12)

The return of the Lord to Zion is inseparable from the return of the Lord's people to Zion. This picture only makes sense if Isaiah sees something similar to what Ezekiel sees: the Lord returns *with* the exiles because the Lord had accompanied them *in* their exile.

These prophecies imply that the divine presence was bound to the *people* of Israel (and especially to the faithful among them) even more closely than to the building they had constructed as its residence. Just as the temple pointed away from itself to its heavenly, cosmic, and future correlates, so it likewise pointed to its human correlate—the people chosen to be "God's sanctuary" (Ps 114:2).

PART TWO: THE BESORAH, THE TEMPLE, AND THE COVENANT PEOPLE

The Temple in the Non-Lukan Writings of the New Testament

The tabernacle in the wilderness and the temple that came after it play a vital role throughout the Hebrew scriptures. But the role is complex and fluid, in contrast with the more concrete and stable role of the land and people of Israel and the city of Jerusalem. The temple pointed beyond itself to the heavenly temple, the cosmic temple, the eschatological temple, and the human temple, four realities that play out in the portrayal of the temple within the New Testament as well.

The Letters of Paul

Paul's writings are often pictured as a major departure from the teachings of what Christians call the "Old Testament"—especially when he's speaking about anything Jewish, like the temple. But the picture of the temple that we've just traced in the Tanakh casts an entirely different light on Paul.

When Paul wrote to the community he had formed in Corinth, for example, he spoke of it as an expression of the human temple to which the Jerusalem temple pointed (2 Cor 6:14—7:1; see also 1 Cor 6:19–20). In other writings he pictured his own life and the lives of his followers as priestly in character, and their service as analogous to temple sacrifice (Rom 12:1; 15:15–16, 27; Phil 2:17; 4:18). This extension of temple concepts beyond the boundaries of the Jerusalem institution didn't contradict the Hebrew Bible, but it was actually based upon it—and it was common within the Jewish world of Paul's time. It was meant to amplify rather than diminish the honor bestowed on the temple.

Paul displays his continuing esteem for the temple in several important texts. In Romans 9:4, for example, Paul includes the "glory" and the "worship" among the privileges given to Israel. These terms are connected to the temple, the place of *worship* where the *glory* of God dwells. In this verse, Paul presents the temple as an integral part of Israel's story—and of the special status bestowed on Israel—along with Israel's adoption (Exod 4:22), the covenants, the Law, and the promises. Paul leaves no doubt as to his favorable view of the temple and its regimen of worship.

This favorable view is also evident in 1 Corinthians 9:13, where Paul cites the example of the Jerusalem priests to argue that apostles have the right to receive material provision for their labor. "Do you not know that those who are employed in the temple service get their food from the temple, and those who serve at the altar share in what is sacrificed on the altar?" In Paul's view, the office of apostle involves a type of priestly service. To defend the priestly privileges of the apostles, he assumes the enduring value of the temple and its worship. And he speaks of temple worship in the present tense even after the resurrection of Messiah. Paul's "priesthood" doesn't nullify the Aaronic priesthood, but extends it in a new direction, while implicitly validating it.

In the next chapter of 1 Corinthians, Paul builds on this favorable view of the temple to argue against participating in pagan sacrificial banquets.

> [16] The cup of blessing that we bless, is it not a sharing in the blood of Messiah? The bread that we break, is it not a sharing in the body of Messiah? [17] Because there is one bread, we who are many are one body, for we all partake of the one bread. [18] Consider the people of Israel; are not those who eat the sacrifices partners in the altar? [19] What do I imply then? That food sacrificed to idols is anything, or that an idol is anything? [20] No, I imply that what pagans sacrifice, they sacrifice to demons and not to God. I do not want you to be partners with demons. [21] You cannot drink the cup of the Lord and the cup of demons. You cannot partake of the table of the Lord and the table of demons. (1 Cor 10:16–21 NRSV)

Paul is comparing three ritual actions here: (1) sharing in the Lord's Supper; (2) eating meat sacrificed at the temple in Jerusalem; and (3) participating in a sacrificial meal at a pagan temple. In verse 18, Paul uses the example of eating the Jerusalem temple sacrifice (ritual 2) to explain what he means by "sharing in the body of the Messiah" (ritual 1; the Lord's Supper) in verse 16. Then, in verse 21, he presents the Lord's Supper (understood as a sacrificial banquet) as a reason to avoid pagan sacrificial banquets (ritual 3): "You cannot partake of the table of the Lord and the table of demons."

This argument requires a positive view of the Jerusalem temple and its sacrificial service. To be "partners" in the altar is to be partners of the God who is represented by that altar. As in 1 Corinthians 9, Paul speaks of this partnership in the present rather than the past tense: those who eat the temple sacrifices—"the people of Israel"—*are* (rather than *were*) partners in the altar. Paul's conviction that Jews participated with God when they worshiped at the Jerusalem temple provides the foundation for his assertion that disciples of Jesus likewise participate in the Messiah through the Lord's Supper—and so should *not* participate with the demons of pagan sacrifice.

All these texts make it clear that Paul affirms the continuing significance of the Jerusalem temple. But a passage in Ephesians, 2:11–22, seems to suggest that the church is superior to the temple. Temple imagery pervades this whole passage and its conclusion: "In him [Jesus] the whole building is joined together and grows into a holy temple in the Lord; in whom you also are built together into a dwelling-place of God in the Spirit" (Eph 2:21–22).[7]

The central verse of Ephesians 2:11–22 tells how the Messiah has united Jews and gentiles in himself, and "has broken down the dividing wall, nullifying in his flesh the hostility between us" (2:14). Given the dominant role of temple imagery in the unit as a whole, this verse likely alludes to the barrier in the temple courts that prevented gentiles from drawing near to the sanctuary proper. In this way Ephesians asserts that the sacrifice of Messiah has effected a change in the status of gentiles who are united to him. They are now able to draw near to God in a way that was prohibited in the Jerusalem temple. This change of status challenges Jewish conventions of the time, but doesn't actually violate the Torah, which imposes no such barriers to gentile participation. Moreover, the prophetic message of Isaiah (for example, 56:6–8; 66:18–23) would lead one to expect just such a change in gentile status in the age to come.

According to Ephesians, the sacrifice of Messiah brings blessing not only to gentiles (who had been "far off") but also to Jews (who were already "near"): "So he came and announced-good-news of peace to you who were far off and peace to those who were near; for through him we both have access in one Spirit to the Father" (2:17–18). This promise of a more intimate "access" to God for Jews as well as for gentiles suggests that the temple barrier (which did not exclude Jews) wasn't the only obstacle that had been removed by the Messiah's sacrifice. Ephesians may here be hinting at what the letter to the Hebrews emphatically asserts—that the way is now open "to enter the holy places by the blood of Jesus" (Heb 10:19; see 6:19–20). The proximity to God, formerly granted only to the high priest, and to him only one day per year, is now the constant privilege of all who are united to the Messiah.

This ongoing proximity to God makes the community of Messiah's people a temple in which God resides. This is the sort of human temple that the Jerusalem temple had already been pointing toward. This temple in some ways goes beyond the Jerusalem temple, but doesn't dishonor or

---

7. All citations from Ephesians 2:11–22 are from Dr. Kinzer's own translation. For an extended exposition of Ephesians 1–3, see Kinzer, *Searching Her Own Mystery*, 65–82.

diminish it. Nor does focus on the human temple invalidate the enduring bond between the resurrected Messiah and the Jewish people, the city of Jerusalem, and the land of Israel.

Hebrews

Scholars of the last century often featured the Letter to the Hebrews as the poster-child for an early "Christianity" that left Judaism and the Jewish people behind—and by implication for a gospel that leaves out the Jewish people as a distinct nation. Here's a characterization of Hebrews, by a Jewish scholar and a Christian scholar, which typifies this view:

> The Temple in Jerusalem has in Hebrews been replaced by a conception of the divine throne in heaven and the faithful congregation on earth. . . . The author understands Israel, literally, as a thing of the past, the husk of the first, now antiquated covenant. . . . The true high priest has entered once and for all (9:12) within the innermost recess of sanctity, so that no further sacrificial action is necessary or appropriate.[8]

Like Paul, the author of Hebrews focuses on one of the realities that the Jerusalem temple points to in the Tanakh. As we've seen, Paul focuses exclusively on the *human* temple, but Hebrews concentrates on the *heavenly* temple. The passage above, then, seems to be reading Paul into Hebrews when it says, "The Temple in Jerusalem has in Hebrews been replaced by . . . the faithful congregation on earth." This idea of the human temple doesn't actually appear at all in Hebrews. Instead, Hebrews emphasizes the heavenly temple, which exists at the same time as the earthly temple, but in a different realm. Like other Jewish texts of the time, Hebrews asserts the superiority of this heavenly temple over its earthly antitype:

> But when Messiah came as a high priest of the good things that have come, then through the greater and perfect tent (not made with hands, that is, not of this creation), he entered once for all into the Holy Place. . . .
>
> For Messiah did not enter a sanctuary made by human hands, a mere copy [*antitype* in the Greek original] of the true one, but he entered into heaven itself, now to appear in the presence of God on our behalf. (Heb 9:11–12a, 24 NRSV)

---

8. Chilton and Neusner, *Judaism in the New Testament*, 182–83, 180.

Jesus cannot serve as a priest in the earthly temple, according to the Torah, because he is descended from David rather than Aaron. But he does qualify for a heavenly priesthood by the "power of an indestructible life" (Heb 7:16), which he now possesses through his resurrection and ascension. By virtue of his resurrection power, Jesus enters into the heavenly sanctuary and there exercises his priestly calling. His priesthood is heavenly, not earthly.

In a recent volume, scholar David Moffitt interprets this reality in a way that challenges past readings of Hebrews, like the one we cited above.

> The author emphasizes Jesus' ascension and heavenly session in part because *he acknowledges the authority of the Law, at least on earth*. Jesus can serve as high priest only if he is in heaven.... *The authority of the Law remains valid on earth*, and on earth a lawfully appointed order of priests already exists. Therefore, Jesus, being from the tribe of Judah (7:14), cannot serve in that priesthood.[9]

For Jesus to be an earthly priest and for his sacrifice to be an earthly sacrifice, these earthly Torah institutions would need to be *replaced*. But since Jesus' priesthood and sacrifice are both heavenly, they may *coexist* with the earthly institutions that prefigure them. Hebrews doesn't deal with the destruction of Jerusalem in 70 CE, although that event is often read back into it. Rather, until "the one who is coming" actually comes (Heb 10:37), the order of the earthly sanctuary remains in effect. It's not replaced by a superior earthly reality, that is, by "the faithful congregation on earth," as the two scholars claim in the reference above.

Hebrews doesn't delegitimize the temple and its order of worship in this age, nor does it negate the significance of the city of Jerusalem, the land of Israel, or the Jewish people. The traditional scholarly view that Hebrews sees Israel as "a thing of the past, the husk of the first, now antiquated covenant"[10] should be discarded.

Revelation

Like Hebrews, the Revelation of John focuses on the heavenly temple—but, unlike Hebrews, Revelation doesn't comment on the limitations of the earthly temple. Instead, it provides a description of the heavenly sanctuary

---

9. Moffitt, *Atonement and the Logic of Resurrection*, 220; 199. Emphasis added.
10. Chilton and Neusner, *Judaism in the New Testament*, 183.

that reflects a detailed correspondence to the earthly sanctuary ordained in the Torah and embodied in the Jerusalem temple.

Revelation shares with Hebrews the conviction that Jesus consummates his sacrifice in heaven rather than on earth. This is the meaning of the extraordinary scene in which the Lamb appears in heaven "standing as though it had been slain," takes the scroll from the one seated on the throne, and receives the worship of the four living creatures, the twenty-four elders, myriads of angels, and all creation (5:6–14). The Lamb is the Davidic Messiah (first described as the "Lion of the tribe of Judah," 5:5) who conquers through the sacrificial shedding of his blood. His sacrifice takes full effect only after he presents his resurrected martyred body before the throne in the heavenly temple.

Throughout most of the book of Revelation, this is the only temple in view. This changes, however, in the final chapters, when the heavenly Jerusalem descends to earth. At that climactic moment a voice issues from the throne, saying, "See, the tent [*skēnē*] of God is among human beings, and he will dwell (or pitch-his-tent [*skēnōsei*]) among them" (21:3).[11] This event fulfills the purpose the LORD first announced at Sinai: "And let them make me a sanctuary, *that I may dwell in their midst*" (Exod 25:8, emphasis added).

It appears that Israel's deepest hopes are now to be realized, but as John proceeds to describe this new Jerusalem, we are surprised to learn that the city contains no temple. We shouldn't interpret this fact as being anti-temple, however. Revelation doesn't take that sort of position elsewhere in dealing with the temple or with Jewish symbols in general. So how are we to interpret the absence of a temple here? The answer comes from the dimensions of the city, which John recounts just before he states that he "saw no temple in the city" (21:22): "its length and width and height are equal" (21:16). This cubical shape presents the city as a massive "holy of holies," which was likewise a perfect cube. If the city is now the holy of holies, then the new creation, centered in this new Jerusalem, has become a universal cosmic temple. The city has no temple because it *is* the temple, or its most essential part, the holy of holies, where God's glory now dwells among his people.

What we have here is a unique coalescing of two of the four temple motifs we see in the Tanakh—the expansive holiness of the *eschatological* temple blended with the universality of the *cosmic* temple—to form a powerful vision of a world-to-come filled with the presence of God.

11. Authors' translation.

Like Hebrews, Revelation sees the sanctuary ordained in the Torah, the Jerusalem temple, as appropriate for the present age, in which access to the divine presence is available but restricted. But the reality that this sanctuary pointed to—the reality of God dwelling on earth in intimate communion with human beings—is fully attained only in the age to come. Nevertheless, nothing in either book undermines the validity of temple worship in the present age, and nothing in either book challenges the enduring significance of the city of Jerusalem, the land of Israel, or the Jewish people.

The Gospel of John

Now we're ready to return to the account of Jesus' encounter with the Samaritan woman. John's Besorah reveals a unique theology that honors the temple while asserting that its purpose has been realized in a greater way through one person who in effect becomes the temple, Jesus the Messiah. Unlike Hebrews and Revelation, John shows little interest in the heavenly temple or in the temple of the age to come as a future hope. And he never depicts the messianic community as a temple. For John, the Jerusalem temple points to one supreme reality that is both earthly *and* heavenly: the flesh-and-blood person of Jesus, the embodied Logos (John 1:14), now risen from the dead.

Still, despite this profound innovation, John doesn't criticize the Jerusalem temple. Instead, he sees it as ordained by God and holy. In John, as in Luke, Jesus refers to the building as "my Father's house" (John 2:16). When he drives money-changers out of the temple, his disciples recall the verse, "Zeal for your house will consume me" (Ps 69:10, cited in John 2:17). Jesus is outraged at how the affairs of the temple are being conducted, but this outrage derives from his high regard for its holiness. Jesus also expresses his regard for the temple by teaching and proclaiming the kingdom there during various festivals—Passover (2:14–15), an unnamed holiday (5:1), Tabernacles (7:14, 28; 8:20, 59), and Hanukkah (10:23). Through his frequent presence Jesus displays an exceptional devotion to the Jerusalem temple that demonstrates his "zeal" for his Father's house. It's between two early visits to the beloved temple that Jesus passes through Samaria and meets the Samaritan woman. He tells her, "Woman, believe me, the hour is coming when neither on this mountain nor in Jerusalem will you worship the Father. . . . But the hour is coming, and is now here, when the true worshipers will worship the Father in spirit and truth, for the Father is seeking such people to worship him" (John 4:21, 23). Jesus isn't advocating some abstract, disembodied form of "spiritual" worship that replaces the traditional earthy practices of the Jerusalem temple. He doesn't deny the enduring value of worshiping God on Mount Zion. He isn't interested in *constricting* the realm of worship at all, but in *expanding* it. The resurrected Jesus will be accessible in every place through the gift of his Spirit, enabling his followers—wherever they may find themselves—to taste in this age the richness of the temple of the age to come.

Still, despite these expressions of respect for the Jerusalem temple, John's central message isn't about that edifice or the tent of meeting that preceded it, but about the person of Jesus to whom both structures pointed. This message is evident early in John's Gospel—"And the Word became flesh and pitched-his-tent [*eskēnōsen*] among us" (1:14).[12] The verb here is the same one we saw in Revelation 21:3, and both verses allude to the tent of meeting in the wilderness. The Word of God, which God placed first in the tent of meeting and later in the Jerusalem temple, now resides permanently in the consecrated flesh of Jesus the Messiah.

John reiterates this theme in his next chapter when he tells of Jesus' zeal for the temple. Jesus is asked to provide a sign to justify his act of driving out the money-changers, and he responds, "Destroy this temple, and in three days I will raise it up" (2:19). His questioners assume he's referring to the temple where they're standing, but actually Jesus is "speaking about the temple of his body" (2:21), which will be destroyed and raised up again. In this way John, like Luke, establishes a connection between the death of Jesus and the destruction of Jerusalem in 70—a connection reflecting the words of Jesus himself. John, like Luke, also connects Jesus' resurrection with Israel's future restoration, but his focus is on the preliminary restoration that has already occurred through the death and resurrection of Messiah. According to John, *the risen Jesus is himself the temple of the age to come*, accessible now to all who put their faith in him.

John's theology of the temple is unique in the New Testament, and in the world of first-century Judaism. But this theology is based on the Tanakh and its portrayal of the temple as pointing to the reality of the divine presence in the midst of the people of Israel (i.e., the human temple). As the king of Israel and the individual embodiment of his people, the resurrected Messiah fulfills in himself the purpose of the temple. He also

---

12. Authors' translation.

sustains God's enduring earthly promises to the land, the city, and his own family, the children of Israel.

Conclusion

We've surveyed the history and significance of the temple in the Hebrew scriptures and in several crucial strands of New Testament tradition. The Tanakh clearly portrays the temple as the heart of Jerusalem and the key to its significance in this age, as well as in the age to come. But readers of the New Testament often miss any similar portrayal there. Instead, they see the temple as part of an earthly, outdated system that has now been replaced by true, spiritual worship through Jesus Christ.

Moreover, if the temple represents Jerusalem as a whole, then its transformation from a building into a spiritual reality might imply a similar, "spiritual" transformation in the character of the city. And this is exactly what many Christian commentators have concluded. From there, they claim that such a transformation of temple and city suggests a similar transformation of Israel's land and people, in which the particular calling of the Jewish people yields to a new, universal faith. This sort of reading furthers the rift between the Jewish Messiah and the Jewish people, adding to the fracturing of the besorah.

Such interpretations, however, must downplay or set aside much of the Hebrew scriptures, which of course are part of the Word of God. They also, as we've seen, often overlook the particular wording of various New Testament passages, or read into them presuppositions about the temple and the Jewish people. After our brief survey of New Testament writings from a temple-positive perspective, we're ready to look more deeply into Luke-Acts to answer the question we posed early in this chapter: if Jesus' resurrection serves as a pledge that the city will be restored in the end, can we say the same about the destiny of her temple? The answer to this question reveals the ongoing place of Israel within the besorah.

Chapter Five

Luke's Portrayal of the Temple

Yeshua stood on the crest of the Mount of Olives and gazed across the Kidron Valley toward the holy city, where the temple rose up, its massive stones glowing white and golden in the morning sunlight. The valley and surrounding hillsides were green from the recent spring rains. Yeshua could see the road leading to the gates of Jerusalem already filling up with pilgrims, although Passover was still a few days away. He thought about another procession that would be coming from the opposite direction, from the Roman capital of Caesarea on the Great Sea, escorting the prefect, Pilate, in a display of power and pomp to the Praetorium on the western side of the Temple Mount.

A couple of hours earlier, when Yeshua and his entourage were still walking up the eastern slope of the Mount, he had sent two young followers ahead to a nearby village with an errand. "When you enter the village you'll find a donkey colt tied to a post. It's a colt that no one has yet ridden; untie it and bring it to me." The two young men had glanced at each other with a puzzled look. The master's instructions were simple enough, but they raised lots of questions: How would they be able to tell whether the colt had ever been ridden? Who did it belong to, and why was it standing there tied up? And most importantly, wouldn't they be mistaken for thieves? But before they could ask these questions—or decide not to ask—the master answered: "If anyone asks you, 'Why are you untying that colt?' tell him, 'The Lord has need of it.'" Apparently things would just work out, as they so often did in their travels with Yeshua.

And now, as Yeshua turned his gaze away from the holy temple to glance back toward the village, he could see his two followers headed his way, leading a donkey colt. When they brought it to Yeshua, other followers gathered around. Some of them quickly pulled off their traveling cloaks and put them on the donkey as a seat for their teacher. When the donkey's back had enough padding, they started spreading their cloaks on the road that led down the mount and then up toward the holy city. Yeshua mounted the donkey and prodded it forward, its first steps cushioned by the cloaks on the road. Yeshua's followers surrounded him and began to cry out, "*Baruch ha-melech ha-ba!* Blessed is the king who comes in the name of the Lord! Peace in heaven and glory in the highest!"

Some Pharisees among the crowd of pilgrims heard these shouts and challenged Yeshua to rebuke his followers, but he refused. He let his followers cry out in joy and praise, but when he looked up at the city walls he wept and spoke to the city itself: "The days will come upon you, when your enemies will tear you down to the ground, you and your children within you. And they will not leave one stone upon another in you, because you did not know the time of your visitation."

When Yeshua arrived in the city, he entered the temple courts and was confronted with another sorrowful sight. The holy place—the longed-for goal of pilgrims from all over the known world—looked like an ordinary market, filled with the tables of money-changers and stalls of animals being sold as sacrifices.

The Temple's Starring Role

The holy temple remains on center stage as the drama of redemption unfolds throughout the Hebrew scriptures and into the New Testament. But, as we've discussed, its role is complex and in some biblical texts it's transformed beyond easy recognition. Commentators often claim that this transformation suggests that a similar transformation takes place in the role of the holy city, the land of Israel, and its people. In their view, the special calling of the Jewish people yields to a new universal faith, and the gospel shifts the focus of God's purposes away from the land and people of Israel. We saw in the last chapter how such interpretations miss important balancing texts within the scriptures. Now we return to Luke's writings, where we'll see how the Jerusalem temple remains front and center, not only in the climactic scene of Jesus' entry into Jerusalem that we've just revisited (Luke 19:28–46), but throughout Luke's two volumes. The temple continues to support the ongoing role of the land and people of Israel.

Luke's Portrayal of the Temple

As we've seen, the Besorah of Luke opens in the temple, and its first dialogue occurs within the holy place itself (Luke 1:8–22).[1] The book closes in the same location: "And they worshiped him and returned to Jerusalem with great joy, and were continually in the temple blessing God" (Luke 24:52–53). Acts opens on the same Mount of Olives that Jesus descended on his way to the temple, and in its following scenes Jesus' followers keep returning to the temple courts (Acts 1:6–12; 2:46; 3:1; 5:12, 42).

Shaul, later referred to as Paul, takes the stage in Acts 8 and dominates the action from chapter 13 to the conclusion of the book. He embarks on three journeys as Messiah's emissary. Each journey extends further west but, as we have already seen, each one concludes with a return to Jerusalem. Paul's third and final visit to Jerusalem plays an especially significant role in the narrative of Acts, and the temple figures prominently in it. Paul has planned his itinerary so that he arrives in Jerusalem in time for the feast of Shavuot (Acts 20:16). In this way Paul's journey recalls Jesus' final ascent to Jerusalem for the feast of Passover. This parallel is reinforced by the grave warnings of what will befall Paul upon his arrival, echoing the grave warnings Jesus gave his followers on their way to Jerusalem, concerning what would befall him (Acts 21:4, 10–14; Luke 18:31–33).

After Paul enters the city and meets with James, leader of the Jerusalem assembly, he seeks to demonstrate his loyalty to the Torah and the Jewish people by engaging in a public rite in the temple. In the process, he is falsely accused of bringing a gentile into the sacred space restricted to Jews, and is arrested (Acts 21:17–28). Paul's accusers portray him as an apostate, a religious traitor: "This is the man who is teaching everyone everywhere against the people and the law and this place [the temple]" (Acts 21:28; similar charges were brought earlier against Stephen in Acts 6:11–14, as we'll see shortly).

In the scenes that follow, Paul defends himself against both the specific charge related to his conduct in the temple, and the general accusation of apostasy: "Neither against the law of the Jews, nor against the temple, nor against Caesar have I committed any offense" (Acts 25:8; see also 24:11–13). Paul is not only innocent of the charges, he's actually deeply devoted to the temple. He tells a Jewish crowd in Jerusalem about a vision he had while praying in the temple. Just as God appeared to Isaiah

---

1. Depending on the context, when we refer to the temple, we include the sanctuary, which can only be entered by the priests, and its surrounding courts, which were open to all worshipers.

when the prophet worshiped in the temple (Isaiah 6), so Jesus appeared to Paul (Acts 22:17). Apparently, for Luke, the temple is especially suited to a revelation of the risen Lord.

Throughout the scriptures, the tabernacle/temple points to realities beyond itself. Likewise, in Luke's writings, the temple plays a role that points to the abiding place of the land and people of Israel at the heart of the besorah. Luke's portrayal of the temple and its intimate association with Jerusalem, as well as the geographical structure of his two volumes, point toward Israel's future restoration as the center of God's plan of redemption for all humankind.

Temple Worship and the Messianic Community

Worship at the temple included the *tamid* offering, presented twice each day—once in the morning, and once in the late afternoon (Exod 29:38–42; Num 28:1–8). Jews who weren't priests or Levites could participate in the temple worship by praying at the time of the sacrifice, either in the temple courts, or towards the temple structure if they couldn't be present. When the Besorah of Luke opens in the temple, with Zechariah offering incense, it's part of the tamid liturgy—accompanied by the prayers of the people outside (Luke 1:8–10). Early in Acts, Peter and John ascend the Temple Mount to join other Jews "at the hour of prayer, at three o'clock in the afternoon" (Acts 3:1), the hour of the afternoon tamid. Later in Acts, in the coastal city of Caesarea, Cornelius prays to the God of Israel at the time of the afternoon tamid, and four days later he and his household receive the Holy Spirit at that same hour (Acts 10:2, 30).

We can see that Luke doesn't portray daily prayer as a *substitute* for the tamid offering in the temple, but instead as an essential *accompaniment*. Peter and John pray in the temple courts as the priests offer the tamid; Cornelius prays in his own house in Caesarea as the priests offer the tamid. All of them participate in the temple ritual through prayer.

This connection between worship in the temple and the prayers of the messianic community also involves the gift of the Holy Spirit. Just as fire fell from heaven to consecrate the altars of the wilderness tabernacle and Solomon's temple (Lev 9:24; 2 Chr 7:1), so tongues of fire rested on each of the disciples of Jesus gathered for the morning tamid prayer on Shavuot (Acts 2:3). This linkage points to the temple-like character of the messianic community. It's an expression of the human temple we discussed in the last chapter, God's people as the dwelling-place of his presence. After Shavuot and the great outpouring of the Spirit, Jesus' followers continued to gather in the temple of Jerusalem. Just as their prayers complemented rather than replaced the temple sacrifices, so their corporate presence didn't replace the temple, but elevated it, bringing into it a foretaste of the human temple of the age to come when God will dwell fully within his people.

Does Stephen Upstage the Temple?

This brief overview makes it clear that Luke has a high esteem for the temple. Many commentators, however, believe he undercuts that esteem in Acts 7 by allowing Stephen, a leader of the messianic community, to upstage the temple in his speech before the Jewish council. Here's how one commentator—who otherwise acknowledges Luke's high regard for the temple—characterizes this speech: "Stephen marks the beginning of a radical critique of the Temple on the part of the infant Christian movement."[2] But this sort of reading of Acts 7 doesn't really do justice either to the passage itself or to the message that runs throughout Luke and Acts. Does Stephen's speech, which Luke carefully recorded for all time, really entail "a radical critique" of what Luke consistently upholds elsewhere in his writings? Since this question is so critical to our whole understanding of Luke's theology, we'll look at Stephen's speech in some detail.

Stephen comes on stage amid mounting tensions within the messianic community over the distribution of resources among the needy. He's one of seven men chosen to coordinate this distribution, and he's listed first among them as, "a man full of faith and of the Holy Spirit." He doesn't limit himself to food distribution, but is doing "great wonders and signs among the people" (Acts 6:5, 8). His religious opponents can't stop him, so they stir up false witnesses against him, and have him arrested and brought before the Jewish council to give an account of himself. Before we hear Stephen's defense, though, we need to note the accusations that triggered it:

> Then they secretly instigated men who said, "We have heard him speak blasphemous words against Moses and God." ... And they set up false witnesses who said, "This man never ceases to speak words against this holy place and the law, for we have heard him say that this Jesus of Nazareth will destroy this place and will change the customs that Moses delivered to us." (Acts 6:11, 13–14)

2. Dunn, *Partings*, 67.

Part Two: The Besorah, the Temple, and the Covenant People

What is "false" about their testimony? Given the devotion to the temple shown by Jesus' followers in the previous chapters of Acts, we should start by assuming that Stephen's accusers are at least distorting his views about the temple. He's being framed. Therefore, as one commentator states, "it is quite amazing . . . that many scholars have concluded that though Luke tells us that the witnesses were false and the whole process rigged . . . nonetheless we should *believe these charges*."[3] Moreover, the false charges against Stephen are identical to the false charges later leveled against Paul (Acts 21:28), and Luke clearly shows that Paul is not guilty of such accusations. With these considerations in mind, and despite the view of various scholars, we wouldn't expect Stephen to say anything in his speech that will confirm the charges of his accusers.

The false witnesses charge Stephen with speaking against Moses, his Torah, and the temple. In defense, Stephen opens with a narrative drawn from the *Torah*, concentrating on the story of *Moses* (7:17–44). His aim is to present Jesus as the prophet like Moses (7:37; Deut 18:15–19). Moses suffers the opposition of his own people, and Stephen describes this opposition in words that hint at what Jesus (and his followers) will suffer among their own people: "This Moses, whom they rejected, saying, 'Who made you a ruler and a judge?'—this man God sent as both ruler and redeemer by the hand of the angel who appeared to him in the bush. . . . Our fathers refused to obey him, but thrust him aside" (Acts 7:35, 39a).

Stephen then shifts his focus from the Torah and Moses to the tent of witness, the sanctuary described in the Torah: "Our ancestors had the tent of witness in the wilderness, as God directed when he spoke to Moses, ordering him to make it according to the pattern he had seen" (7:44). Stephen displays the high regard for the sanctuary that we'd expect from a faithful Jew—it is made according to God's direction.

Throughout his speech, Stephen refutes the charge that he spoke "blasphemous words against Moses," or against the Law of Moses and its customs. He ends by turning the tables on his accusers, claiming that *they* are the ones who are disobeying Moses and the Torah by failing to honor the prophet whom Moses spoke of, concluding, "You are the ones that received the law as ordained by angels, and yet you have not kept it" (7:53).

But just before Stephen reaches this conclusion he says something that commentators often use to support the (false) accusation that he is speaking against the holy temple:

---

3. Witherington, *Acts*, 258; emphasis original.

> Yet the Most High does not dwell in houses made with human hands; as the prophet says
>
> "Heaven is my throne,
> > and the earth is my footstool.
> What kind of house will you build for me, says the Lord,
> > or what is the place of my rest?
> Did not my hand make all these things?" (7:48–50)

Stephen has already spoken in support of the tabernacle in the wilderness. And now he's not criticizing the "house," the first temple, built by Solomon (or the second, built by Zerubbabel), or the validity of worshiping God at this site. But he is criticizing *a distorted perception of the temple as the exclusive place where the divine presence dwells*—which is exactly what the Lord himself is saying through "the prophet" that Stephen cites above. This criticism applies as much to the original tent of witness commanded in the Torah as to the temples of Solomon and Zerubbabel that replaced it. Stephen pictures the infidelity of his fellow-Jews in his time as following the pattern set by the Israelites in the wilderness, who had the tent of witness yet consistently fell into idolatry (7:39–43). God is as accessible at the temple as he was at the tent, but the presence of God cannot be confined to either place, and neither place guarantees true worship.

The prophet Stephen mentions in Acts 7:48 is Isaiah, who refers to heaven and earth as made by God's hand (Isaiah 66), in contrast with the tent or the temple "made with human hands," as Stephen puts it. In this way, Stephen hints that the true temple in which God seeks to dwell is heaven and earth, the *entire cosmos* made by his own hand. The Jerusalem temple points to this reality, but when worshipers forget this and treat the temple as an end in itself, it ceases to fulfill its intended purpose and—like any sacred object treated as an end in itself—actually becomes an obstacle to true worship.

Nonetheless, Stephen has been accused of speaking "against this holy place," proclaiming that "Jesus of Nazareth will destroy *this place*" (Acts 6:13–14, emphasis added). In response, he cites God's promise to Abraham in Genesis 15: "'But I will judge the nation that they serve,' said God, 'and after that *they shall come out and worship me in this place*'" (Acts 7:7). Notice that the words we've italicized in this citation aren't from Genesis 15 but from Exodus 3:12, where they refer to Mount Sinai. The whole context of Stephen's speech, however, suggests that he's using these words to refer to the Temple Mount. His point: just as Israel worshiped God at Mount Sinai after its redemption from Egypt, so redeemed Israel later entered the land and worshiped on Mount Zion ("in *this* place").

There's further significance to the word "place" or *topos* in Greek. In the Septuagint, the widely-used classic Greek translation of the Tanakh, this word appears several times in the account of the offering-up of Isaac (Gen 22:3, 4, 9, 14). The "place" where Abraham had offered up his beloved son is Mount Moriah, and that is where Solomon's temple would be built centuries later (2 Chr 3:1). As one commentator states, "The promise in 7:7 anticipates a specific place of worship within the land, and that place will be the temple."[4]

Far from speaking against "this place," then, Stephen shows how central it is to God's purposes, and he implies that his accusers are out of touch with its true significance. Thus, Stephen's answer to the charge of speaking against the temple is identical to his answer concerning Moses and the Torah. In both cases, Stephen asserts that his accusers are the ones guilty of the very charges they unjustly level at him. Stephen's speech lines up with the overall message of Luke and Acts regarding the temple, the city of Jerusalem, the land of Israel, and the Jewish people. Even if the building "made by human hands" is destroyed, its "place" maintains a unique status in God's redemptive plan for Israel and the nations. The temple itself may be judged because of the sins of those in charge of it, but the Temple Mount will endure as the center of the city, the land, and the visible cosmos.

The Return of the LORD to Zion

We opened this chapter with Jesus' final entry into Jerusalem, and we can return there to gain more insight into the role of the temple in Luke's Besorah. While Jesus was still on his way to the holy city he had lamented over it, "O Jerusalem, Jerusalem, the city that kills the prophets and stones those who are sent to it! How often would I have gathered your children together as a hen gathers her brood under her wings, and you were not willing!" (Luke 13:34). As we saw in chapter 2, Jesus was speaking here on behalf of God himself. Otherwise the saying would seem out of place, because Jesus said this *before* he arrived at Jerusalem, before the city revealed to him that it was "not willing." But God had desired for centuries to gather Jerusalem's children under his wings and found them to be unwilling, and Jesus says these words in his name.

---

4. Tannehill, *Narrative Unity*, 92–93.

Later, Jesus speaks from the same prophetic vantage point as he is about to enter the city. He weeps over it because it does not recognize the time of its divine "visitation" (Luke 19:44). In this context, he is speaking of his entry into the city, and thus making that entry equivalent to the visitation of God himself. In Isaiah, the Lord's return to Zion brings glory and joy to Israel (Isa 40:3–5; 52:8–12), but in Luke, the Lord's appearance in Zion in the person of Jesus brings lamentation and a warning of judgment. Nevertheless, victory and joy will come later, when the "times of the Gentiles are fulfilled" (Luke 21:24) and the returning Messiah will "restore the kingdom to Israel" (Acts 1:6). This will be the true consummation of the story.

Jesus' lament over Jerusalem in Luke 13, then, helps us understand the destiny of the temple and Jerusalem itself. His lament concludes with these words: "Behold, your house is forsaken. And I tell you, you will not see me until you say, 'Blessed is he who comes in the name of the Lord!'" (Luke 13:35). The "house" that will be forsaken is the temple or perhaps the city as a whole—in this context, the two are virtually indistinguishable. Because of Israel's persistent rejection of God's prophetic messengers, Israel will no longer "see me"—that is, they will no longer experience the joy of encountering God in the "house" of the Jerusalem temple. Jesus is speaking here in the name of the God whom Jerusalem has time and again resisted. But his lamentation ends with a glimmer of hope: Jerusalem will once again "see God" (that is, will worship in a renewed temple, the house that is no longer forsaken) when it welcomes the Messiah "who comes in the name of the Lord!" These words are drawn from Psalm 118:26, where they are followed by the parallel line, "We bless you from the *house* of the Lord."

Jesus' reference to Psalm 118 here anticipates the words that will greet him later, when he finally enters Jerusalem riding on a donkey: "Blessed is the King who comes in the name of the Lord!" (Luke 19:38). The other Gospels describe those who cry out as "many people" or "crowds" who go before and follow after Jesus (Mark 11:9; Matt 21:8–9, 11). Luke is more specific: he calls the crowd "the whole multitude of *his disciples*" (Luke 19:37, emphasis added). They are neither Jerusalem residents, nor a crowd of pilgrims who happen to be on the scene, but people who were already following Jesus as their master. This distinction clarifies how Jesus' entry into the city relates to his lament and promise in Luke 13:34–35. The followers of Jesus shout the words of welcome from Psalm 118, but the city of Jerusalem itself remains silent, for it does not recognize the time of its visitation from God.

Ironically, then, Luke 19 depicts a "non-triumphal entry." But even this non-triumphal entry does enact the future return of the Lord to Zion. The prophetic symbolism is evident from Luke's twofold reference to the Mount of Olives (in Luke 19:29 and 37), which recalls Zechariah's words about the coming of the Lord: "On that day his feet shall stand on the Mount of Olives" (Zech 14:4a). This symbolism also drives Jesus' decision to ride into the city on a colt to fulfill the messianic promise of Zechariah 9:9:

> Rejoice greatly, O daughter of Zion!
>   Shout aloud, O daughter of Jerusalem!
> Behold, your king is coming to you;
>   righteous and having salvation is he,
> humble and mounted on a donkey,
>   on a colt, the foal of a donkey.

In Luke's account of Jesus' entry, however, Luke does *not* explicitly quote Zechariah 9:9. This is significant because it contrasts with both Matthew (21:5) and John (12:14–15). "Luke omits this material, perhaps because it suggests an eschatological focus: Jesus is entering Jerusalem to die, not to bring about the messianic reign just yet."[5] Messiah's entry into Jerusalem in the Gospel accounts does not signal the end of exile and God's promised return to Zion—at least not yet.

Rather, Jesus' entry symbolizes an event still to come, and the symbolism is clear if we remember the details given in Acts 1:11–12. There, Jesus *ascends* from the Mount of Olives, and the two men in white robes tell his bedazzled followers that he will *return* in the same way, implying the same location. So, in Luke, Jesus' dramatic entry from the Mount of Olives symbolizes the *future* coming of Israel's king, when the entire city of Jerusalem will welcome him in the same way that Jesus' followers did at his first entry. In that day, Jerusalem will "repent . . . and turn back" so that her sins "may be blotted out, that times of refreshing may come from the presence of the Lord" (Acts 3:19–20). In that day, the glory of God, whose departure from the temple and city was demonstrated by the Roman victory in 70 CE, shall return to the Temple Mount, just as Ezekiel promised (Ezek 43:1–7).

The return to Zion that Jesus prophetically enacts in Luke 19 points to a future day when the exile will be ended for good. In that day, Jerusalem will no longer be "trampled by the Gentiles," but will again be a Jewish city. In that day, Jesus, embodying the divine presence, will stand on the Mount of Olives, and will enter the city, which will welcome him with the

---

5. Levine and Witherington, *Luke*, 518.

words "Blessed is he who comes in the name of the Lord!" (Ps 118:26a). This future return will reach its climax on Mount Moriah/Zion, as the people of Jerusalem shout "We bless you from *the house of the Lord*" (Ps 118:26b; emphasis added).

Despite different interpretations of what the eschatological temple is like, "the house of the Lord" continues to be central to the prophetic future, and so does its place—Moriah—where Abraham had offered up Isaac, and Solomon had built the temple (Gen 22:2; 2 Chr 3:1). Luke's vision of the future bridges the great rift between the messianic community/church and the Jewish people, between Jesus and the whole Jewish story centered on Jerusalem and the Temple Mount. The temple of Jesus' day points beyond itself to the temple of the age to come—but without losing its significance as a particular *place*. In this way, the messianic hope borne by the Jewish people over the centuries converges with the hope that permeates the besorah of the crucified and risen Messiah.

The resurrection of Jesus constitutes both the *pledge* that the "return of the Lord to Zion" will be fulfilled and the *power* that will fulfill it. Moreover, the resurrection of Jesus intensifies the reality of Israel as the human temple. This becomes evident on the day of Shavuot, as the Messiah pours out the Holy Spirit on his Jewish followers—the remnant of Israel—in Jerusalem at the time of the morning tamid. Soon after, the resurrection extends the reality of the human-temple to the nations of the world, beginning with the gentile Cornelius in the gentile city of Caesarea, who receives the Holy Spirit at the time of the afternoon tamid. Still, the present age remains an ambiguous time, which involves *both* restoration *and* exile. Messiah's community in this age points prophetically to Israel's destined future, but represents only a partial and preliminary sketch of that future. In the besorah, as Luke tells it, the resurrection of Messiah bears the promise of a restoration yet to come for Jerusalem, a restoration that unlocks the fulfillment of God's purposes for all the nations. As we embrace Luke's message, the gospel once fractured is restored to become the prophetic besorah that brings hope for Israel and the world.

Conclusions

To wrap up our discussion of the temple (in chapter 4 as well as this chapter), we'll offer four conclusions. Our thesis throughout this book is that the besorah of Jesus the Messiah proclaims the restoration of Jerusalem and the Jewish people at its very core. Our first two conclusions remove obstacles from this thesis, and the second two conclusions strengthen our case for this same thesis.

1. *The first obstacle removed* is the frequent attempt among scholars to diminish the enduring character of Jerusalem (representing the Jewish people) by equating it with the transitory character of the temple. The destruction of the temple, in this line of thought, symbolizes the end, or at least the sidelining, of Jewish chosenness. But we've seen how the temple, though of paramount importance, operated on a different plane from the city of Jerusalem and the land and people of Israel. Each of these three elements maintained a stable identity and function through the varied and tumultuous epochs of Jewish history. This was never the case with the temple, which was inherently unstable and made up of diverse components. From its beginnings as the tabernacle in the wilderness, the temple combined the holiness of a particular place with the holiness of sacred furniture and architecture, resulting in a fragile and often disrupted institution. Moreover, the temple always functioned as a symbolic pointer to realities beyond itself. In those eras when the temple brought together its diverse components imperfectly, or when it ceased to function altogether, the realities to which it pointed never lost their relevance or their hold on the Jewish imagination.

   When the city of Jerusalem was taken by the Romans in 70 CE, it was the destruction of the temple that caused the greatest grief. It captured in one fiery image the catastrophe of the entire war. Thus, in the New Testament and in Jewish tradition as a whole, the destruction of the city is represented by the destruction of the temple. In his death, Jesus participates in the suffering that Jerusalem will endure four decades later, and bears in his body the blows that will fall on the temple that was her heart and soul. Nevertheless, the city, land, and the people remain in existence—wounded, but still alive, as Jesus foretold—even after the massive stones of the temple have been cast asunder. If the Babylonian destruction of the temple was any precedent, and the message of the prophet Ezekiel at that time is still to be believed, then the God of Israel continues to dwell among his people, and the city and land remain the proper objects of their hope.

2. *The second obstacle* is the idea that the New Testament focus on the heavenly temple, the human temple, and the eschatological temple derives from criticism of the earthly temple. We have shown, however, that this focus is inherent in the temple's essential symbolic role. The temple *always* served as a symbolic marker pointing to realities beyond itself, and the New Testament expressions of this symbolism don't differ in kind from those found in Hebrew scripture or Jewish tradition. In these texts, such symbolism is combined with respect for the earthly temple, and with reverence for the city, land, and people. There is no reason to assume that the New Testament is an exception to the rule, or that it invalidates the temple and its worship.

3. *Our first positive conclusion* concerns John's theology of the temple, which we covered in chapter 4. In John 1:51, Jesus pictures himself as Jacob's ladder: "You will see heaven opened and the angels of God ascending and descending upon the Son of Man." One midrash equates the ladder with Jacob himself, and John seems to be following this sort of reading to present Jesus as Jacob/Israel, who unites heaven and earth in himself. In the same scene, Jesus is also recognized as "the King of Israel" (1:49). As the divine presence dwelt among the people of Israel, even in the absence of the ark, the tent of meeting, or the Jerusalem temple—even in exile from the land of promise—so all the more the divine presence now rests upon the king of Israel, who represents his entire people.

   In John's Besorah, then, Jesus sums up the people of Israel in his individual person. The temple signifies God's dwelling in the midst of the people of Israel; therefore, Jesus in his individual person is the ultimate temple, as in John 2:19–21. In Jesus, God continues to dwell in the midst of Israel. Throughout this book, we've seen how the resurrected Jesus identifies with the Jewish people. If that is true, then his incarnation, death, and resurrection fulfill the gift of the divine presence among the Jewish people by intensifying its reality rather than removing it.

4. *Our second positive conclusion* concerns the temple-theology developed in Luke-Acts. This temple-theology advances our discussion by highlighting the enduring significance of the Temple Mount (that is, "the place") as a geographical site. Stephen's speech focuses on this place as a sacred element of the temple that is distinct from the temple building

and its furniture—and this element endures as long as the earth endures. In this way, Stephen's speech strengthens the case for the enduring significance of the city of Jerusalem even as it challenges misunderstandings of the temple and its purpose. Likewise, in Luke-Acts, as in John, Jesus embodies the divine presence; but for Luke, this reality will be fully realized only when Jesus himself returns to the Temple Mount via the Mount of Olives. This is the "return of the Lord to Zion" that both the Jewish people and the community of Jesus' followers await—the Lord's return to "the place" of the divine presence.

Our study of the temple has only strengthened our thesis regarding the city of Jerusalem, the land of Israel, and the besorah. Luke's presentation of the besorah links the death and resurrection of Jesus with the coming judgment and future restoration of Jerusalem. The besorah doesn't replace or set aside the Jewish people, but actually fulfills their most cherished hopes and expectations—even as it brings redemption to the rest of the human race. But how does this universal redemption apply specifically to the Jewish people? How can we uphold Israel's continuing covenantal identity and mission in this age in light of its communal failure to embrace its Messiah? In our next chapter, we will examine Luke and Acts for clues to answer this difficult question. If the besorah somehow leaves the Jewish people behind, it fails as a message of universal hope. But instead, as we'll see, the besorah remains a message of hope despite all our human failings.

Chapter Six

The Jewish People and the Restoration to Come

ONE OF THE PRACTICES that I've developed when I visit Jerusalem is to keep a good supply of five- and ten-shekel coins in my pocket whenever I go to pray at the *Kotel*—the Western Wall. As you make your way to the Wall, and even after you've arrived, you'll be approached by various people asking for donations, and it's good to be prepared. These people aren't simply beggars taking advantage of the big crowds at the Kotel; rather, they're providing an opportunity for *tzedakah* (often translated as "charity," but based on the Hebrew word for "righteousness" or "justice"). Jewish tradition teaches that it's especially worthwhile to practice tzedakah before or after prayer, as a way of offering a gift to God that is like offering sacrifice in the temple (see Acts 10:2, 4).

So it was probably nothing out of the ordinary for Peter and John to encounter a lame man asking for alms as they made their way to the temple to join in the tamid prayers one afternoon. The man was sitting with his back propped up against the stone wall at one of the entrances to the temple courts called the Beautiful Gate. Peter and John caught his eye, halted their walk, and said, "Look at us"—which the lame man was ready to do, thinking they were about to give him some coins. But Peter said, "I don't have any silver or gold, but I'll give you what I do have—in the name of Messiah Yeshua of Natzeret, rise up and walk!" Then Peter reached down, grabbed the man's hand, and pulled him up. The lame man began to walk, haltingly at first, and then to leap and shout praises to God as he realized what had happened to him.

The healed man entered the temple courts with Peter and John, and his shouting began to draw a crowd. Peter stepped forward to explain what was going on, just as he'd done a few days before on Shavuot, when the joyous shouts of Yeshua's Spirit-filled followers had also drawn a crowd. Now Peter reminded this crowd of how Yeshua had recently been handed over to the authorities and sentenced to death—and how some in the crowd had been among those demanding his execution. As he spoke these words, he thought he saw standing off to the side a small group of members of the council that had condemned Yeshua. "You killed the Author of life, whom God raised from the dead. To this we are witnesses," Peter declared. He went on to declare that it was this same Yeshua that had restored the lame man, who was still standing right there in front of them. His healing was a hint of the glorious age to come, the great Jubilee foretold by Isaiah, which will bring sight to the blind and liberty to all who are oppressed.

The crowd that Peter addressed included men who had turned on Yeshua just a couple of months before, but he called them "brothers" and said, "I know that you acted in ignorance, as did also your rulers."

> Repent therefore, and turn to God so that your sins may be wiped out, so that times of refreshing may come from the presence of the Lord, and that he may send the Messiah appointed for you, that is, Yeshua, whom heaven must receive until the time for restoring all the things about which God spoke by the mouth of his holy prophets long ago. (Acts 3:19–20 NRSV; 3:21 ESV)

Times of Refreshing

Peter tells this crowd of Jewish worshipers that Jesus is "the Messiah appointed for you." The redemptive work of Jesus brings blessing to all nations, but first and above all he is "the Messiah appointed *for you*"—the people of Jerusalem and the entire nation whom they represent. If they "repent and return," it will bring a divine intervention of cosmic proportions, a new era Peter describes as "times of refreshing" and restoration.

Peter's speech in Acts 3 connects with two crucial texts we have already discussed, Luke 21:24 and Acts 1:6-7. Peter's use of the words "times" and "until" here in Acts 3 recalls Jesus' words, "Jerusalem will be trampled underfoot by the Gentiles, *until* the *times* of the Gentiles are fulfilled" (Luke 21:24). This linkage implies that the times of refreshing and restoration concern the city of Jerusalem, and bring to an end the "times of the Gentiles," that is, the era of Israel's exile and Jerusalem's subjection to foreign powers.

Even more noteworthy is the connection between Peter's speech in Acts 3 and the dialogue in Acts 1:6–7:

> So when they had come together, they asked him, "Lord, will you at this time restore the kingdom to Israel?" He said to them, "It is not for you to know times or seasons that the Father has fixed by his own authority."

Here, as in Acts 3:19–21, two roughly synonymous nouns are paired, *chronoi* and *kairoi*—translated "time," "times," and "seasons." Even more significantly, Acts 1:6 employs the verb "restore," which appears in a related Greek form in Acts 3:21. This verb is a technical term used in other Jewish literature of the period to refer to the restoration of Israel to its own land. The contexts in Acts 1 and Acts 3 suggest that Luke is using the word with precisely that meaning. Thus, the second "sending" of the Messiah (Acts 3:20) will result in the restoration of the kingdom to Israel and the end of Israel's exile. Peter's speech, then, conveys two important facts:

- *First*, the return of Jesus will initiate the restoration of Israel's kingdom—with "Israel" here, as always in Luke-Acts, referring to the Jewish people as a community or nation in covenant with God.

- *Second*, the return of Jesus will occur only after, and as a consequence of, the faithful response by his own flesh and blood to his words and person.

Thus, the besorah of the resurrected Messiah concerns the Jewish people in a unique fashion—*they are an inextricable part of its core message*. Moreover, their corporate response to that message is required for it to be fulfilled, as Jesus tells Jerusalem, "You will not see me *until* you say, 'Blessed is he who comes in the name of the Lord'" (Luke 13:35b).

This unique relationship between the Jewish people and the besorah suggests that the besorah must be expressed in different ways to Jewish and gentile audiences, and this is exactly what we see in Acts—a two-fold, Jewish-gentile mission. This picture reflects the unique place of Jerusalem and the Jewish people within the besorah, their unique, continuing relationship with God, and their share in the restoration to come. The idea that somehow God is finished with Israel, which has often appeared in Christian teaching, hasn't a leg to stand on in the besorah as Luke presents it.[1]

---

1. Commentators sometimes seize on a phrase in Peter's speech as spelling the end of the special status of the Jewish people and the formation of a "new Israel" comprising

The Two-fold Mission in Acts

Peter's message in Acts 3 is just one of twenty-two speeches in Acts. Here's the breakdown:

- Sixteen are directed exclusively or primarily to Jewish audiences (eleven to Jews outside the messianic assembly and five to Jews within).

- Only five speeches are directed to gentile audiences; one of those to a group already loyal to the God of Israel (the household of Cornelius), and another to a Roman official responsible for the government of Judea (Acts 24:10–21).

- Of the three remaining speeches in a gentile setting, one is Paul's exhortation to his fellow shipmates urging them to be courageous in the midst of danger (Acts 27:21–26), and only two qualify as proclamations of the besorah to gentiles totally outside the Jewish sphere: Acts 14:15–17 and 17:22–31.

- This accounts for twenty-one of the twenty-two speeches. For the remaining speech, the Jewish and/or gentile composition of the audience is uncertain, as it is a set of leaders from Ephesus, one of Paul's diaspora congregations (Acts 20:18–35).

It's surprising that so few of the twenty-two speeches of Acts are directed toward gentiles, given the traditional assumption that Acts is all about the transition of the church from a Jewish to a gentile entity with a mission to gentiles and not to Jews. Even more surprising is the way Peter and Paul address Jewish audiences who have not yet accepted their message. They refer to their hearers as "men, brothers" (Acts 2:29; 13:26, 38; 23:1, 6; 28:17), or more simply as "brothers" (Acts 3:17; 23:5). Stephen adopts an even more respectful phrase—"brothers and fathers"—as does Paul later on (Acts 7:2; 22:1). These are family terms, the same terms that Peter and Paul use when they speak *within the messianic community* (Acts 1:16; 6:3; 15:7, 13; 21:20). Clearly, the Jewish community, not just its messianic subgroup, is family to Peter, Stephen, and Paul.

---

those who accept Jesus: "And it shall be that every soul who does not listen to that prophet [the prophet like Moses] shall be *destroyed from the people*" (Acts 3:23, emphasis added). *Jerusalem Crucified*, 147–56, provides a thorough analysis of this issue and concludes, "Rather than undermining our core thesis regarding the standing of the Jewish people, the prophet-like-Moses theme of Acts confirms that thesis."

In contrast, Peter and Paul never refer to members of a gentile audience as "brothers"—not even when the gentile in question is a pious God-fearer like Cornelius (Acts 10:28). When Paul speaks to the gentiles of Lystra (Acts 14:15), or his gentile shipmates en route to Rome (Acts 27:21, 25), he merely calls them "men." When he addresses the people of Athens, he employs the phrase "men, Athenians" (Acts 17:22). This impersonal terminology makes it clear that the relational bond is missing—even as it's clear that this bond remains with the Jewish people.

The speeches signal the honored spiritual status of their Jewish audiences in other ways as well. Using a variety of expressions, the speakers identify their hearers as heirs of the biblical tradition and sharers in a common covenant. Members of the Jewish audience are:

- "Men, Israelites" (Acts 2:22; 3:12; 13:16);
- part of "all the house of Israel" (Acts 2:36) or of "all the people of Israel" (Acts 4:10);
- "sons of the family of Abraham" (Acts 13:26);
- "sons of the prophets and of the covenant that God made with your fathers" (Acts 3:25);
- recipients of "the promise" (Acts 2:39).

As members of the same covenant family, Peter, Stephen, and Paul identify with their Jewish hearers and designate Abraham, Isaac, Jacob, and biblical Israel in general, as "*our* fathers" (Acts 7:2, 11, 12, 15, 19, 39, 44; 13:17, 32–33; 26:6; 28:17). Even more significantly, they speak of the Holy One as "the God of *our* fathers" (Acts 3:13; 5:30; 24:14) and "the God of this people Israel" (Acts 13:17).

Jews who fail to respond adequately to the besorah are in danger of divine judgment, but that doesn't change their covenantal status. Even disobedient Jews retain their identity as Israelites, descendants of Abraham's family, descendants of the prophets and of the covenant, and recipients of the promise. There's no evidence that Peter or Stephen or Paul withhold from their unfaithful kin the designation of "brothers," or are reluctant to include them when speaking of "the God of *our* fathers." In fact, the evidence suggests the opposite. According to Acts, the priestly council in Jerusalem, presided over by the high priest, consistently opposes the apostles and their message. The members of the council also bear primary responsibility for the crucifixion of Jesus. Nevertheless, the Holy One is

Part Two: The Besorah, the Temple, and the Covenant People

also the God of *their* ancestors (Acts 5:30); they are addressed as "brothers and fathers" (Acts 7:2); and the high priest (despite his culpable conduct) is acknowledged as "a leader of your people" (Acts 23:5).

Along with these terms of honor, the Jewish setting of most of the speeches of Acts suggests that the mission of the early church is uniquely oriented to the Jewish people. This mission expands to include gentiles, but speeches to gentile audiences actually play a minor role in Acts, and these audiences are never addressed with the terms of honor reserved for "the house of Israel." This distinction between the mission to the Jews and the mission to the gentiles is rooted in the content of the besorah itself.

The speeches of Acts proclaim Jesus as the Davidic Messiah by virtue of his resurrection from the dead (see Acts 2:24–36; 13:22–23, 32–37). They also imply that the resurrection of the Messiah ensures and will ultimately bring about the resurrection of the entire Jewish people along with its capital city. This glorious future constitutes the "hope of Israel" (Acts 26:6–8, 23; 28:20).[2] This constellation of texts demonstrates that the question of the eleven in Acts 1:6—"Lord, will you at this time restore the kingdom to Israel?"—reflects an accurate grasp of the message of the end times. But their question also demonstrates a misunderstanding of the times in which they were living. The kingdom, God's reign in Israel through the risen and glorified Son of David, has been inaugurated in the midst of Israel's exile under Roman occupation, but only later will it reach its fulfilment in a restored Jerusalem, capital of a regathered and resurrected Israel.

Most readers of Acts assume that the gospel is the same for both audiences: Individual Jews and gentiles are called to repent, believe in Jesus, be baptized, and enter the renewed Israel, which is the church. With this response they receive forgiveness of sins, the gift of the Holy Spirit, and the assurance of eternal life. Most readers assume that the message is the same, and the consequences of accepting or rejecting the message are the same. But when we pay close attention to the actual audiences of the speeches in Acts, to the way these audiences are addressed, and to the content of the words that are spoken, we see a different picture. The gospel, the besorah, is indeed for all—but its implications are different for Jewish and gentile audiences. Though often unobserved, this is a crucial point.

---

2. The resurrection of "the entire Jewish people" doesn't necessarily imply that every single Jew will share in it. Luke is thinking corporately, in contrast with the modern emphasis on the individual, much like Paul when he writes, "And so all Israel will be saved" (Rom 11:26).

Jewish Opposition and Paul's "Going to the Gentiles"

With this perspective in view, then, let's examine the key texts used by some scholars to argue that Luke-Acts nullifies the covenantal status of all Jews outside the community of Jesus' followers.

The Jewish Opposition

In various texts in Acts, Luke uses the phrase *hoi Ioudaioi* ("the Jews/Judeans") to designate Jewish opponents of the apostolic message. Many see this phrase as evidence that Luke views Jews outside the messianic community as losing their status as members of the people of God. But a closer look at Luke's use of the phrase reveals a different story.

The phrase *hoi Ioudaioi* first appears in the account of Paul's encounter with the risen Messiah on the road to Damascus (Acts 9:1–19). After that event, the phrase is found often, especially in contexts where groups of Jews are opposing the work of Paul.[3] This means that the phrase shows up with negative connotations almost exclusively in diaspora settings where Jews live as a minority community in the midst of gentiles.

However we interpret the significance of this phrase in Acts, we must avoid the anachronistic idea that Luke uses it to distinguish the category "Jew" from that of "Christian." Luke does speak of "*the* Jews" as a group hostile to the Jesus-movement, but he also sees the Jesus-movement as a *Jewish* reality, led by Jews and adhered to by many Jews. When Luke first introduces Aquila, for example, he identifies him not as a Jesus-follower but as "a *Jew* named Aquila" (Acts 18:2). He introduces Apollos in the same way (Acts 18:24). Paul identifies himself as "a *Jew*" (Acts 21:39; 22:3), and never as a "Christian."[4] Pagan critics of Paul and Silas in Philippi bring them before the Roman magistrates of the city, with the accusation, "These men are *Jews*, and they are disturbing our city. They advocate customs that are not lawful for us as Romans to accept or practice" (Acts 16:20–21). When Paul comes to Jerusalem, James tells him, "You see, brother, how many

---

3. Acts 9:23; 13:45, 50; 14:4; 17:5; 18:5–6, 12, 28; 20:3; 22:30; 23:12, 20; 24:9; 26:2; 28:19.

4. The term *Christianos* appears twice in Acts (11:26; 26:28) and only once more in the entire New Testament (1 Pet 4:16). In Acts 26:29, Paul implies that the term *could* be applied to him, but it never actually is.

thousands there are *among the Jews* of those who have believed." And they remain Jews, "zealous" for the Torah (Acts 21:20). When Jewish leaders attack Paul before the Roman authorities, they portray him as "one who stirs up riots *among all the Jews* throughout the world and is a ringleader of the sect of the Nazarenes" (Acts 24:5). Paul's accusers see him as a Jew who has a prominent position within a Jewish sect or party. Undoubtedly Luke recognizes the Jewish character of the Jesus-movement, and the Jewish identity of its leaders and its pioneering core membership.[5]

Therefore it's clear that the phrase *hoi Ioudaioi* (or "the Jews") in Acts doesn't encompass *all* Jews in a particular location, for those whom the Jews are opposing are also Jews. Instead, *hoi Ioudaioi* often means the Jewish community in a particular diaspora location acting—officially or unofficially—as a corporate entity.

Three Crucial Texts

This Jewish corporate entity responds to Paul's message in three texts that speak of Paul "turning to the gentiles."

1. In his initial missionary journey Paul delivers a lengthy speech in the synagogue of Antioch of Pisidia in Asia Minor (Acts 13:16–43). At first, the Jewish audience welcomes Paul's message, but the following week they turn hostile:

    > The next Sabbath almost the whole city gathered to hear the word of the Lord. But when the Jews [*hoi Ioudaioi*] saw the crowds, they were filled with jealousy and began to contradict what was spoken by Paul, reviling him. And Paul and Barnabas spoke out boldly, saying, "It was necessary that the word of God be spoken first to you. Since you thrust it aside and judge yourselves unworthy of eternal life, behold, we are turning to the Gentiles. For so the Lord has commanded us, saying,
    >
    > > "I have made you a light for the Gentiles,
    > > that you may bring salvation to the ends of the earth."
    > > (Acts 13:44–47)

2. In his second missionary journey, Paul receives a vision beckoning him to leave Asia Minor to begin a new work across the Aegean, which represents the advance of Paul's mission to the continent of Europe

---

5. This paragraph is drawn from Kinzer, *Postmissionary Messianic Judaism*, 116–17.

(Acts 16:9–10). Luke describes a scene in Corinth (on the edge of Europe) that resembles the earlier scene in Antioch of Pisidia, which is in the continent of Asia:

> Now when Silas and Timothy arrived from Macedonia, Paul became occupied with the message, urgently testifying to the Jewish people [*hoi Ioudaioi*] that Yeshua is the Messiah. But when they resisted and reviled him, he shook out his garments and said, "Your blood be upon your own heads—I am clean! From now on, I will go to the Gentiles." (Acts 18:5–6 TLV)

In the next two verses Paul goes to stay with a gentile "God-fearer" whose house is next to the synagogue, and the ruler of the synagogue soon "puts his faith in the Lord, along with his whole household." Clearly Paul's going to the gentiles doesn't leave out the Jews.

3. In the final chapter of Acts, Paul reaches Rome, the heart of Europe and the Empire. There he meets with the local leaders of the Jewish community, and speaks to them about the kingdom of God and Jesus (Acts 28:23). Their attitude toward his message is more welcoming than that of the Jews of Pisidian Antioch or Corinth: "And some were convinced by what he said, but others disbelieved. And disagreeing among themselves, they departed" (Acts 28:24–25a). Nevertheless, Paul responds in a fashion similar to the previous two episodes: "Therefore let it be known to you that this salvation of God has been sent to the Gentiles; they will listen" (Acts 28:28).

The Jewish leaders are divided in their response, with some accepting Paul's message and others rejecting it. Paul understands this divided response as equivalent in its effect to the Jewish communal rejection in Antioch of Pisidia and in Corinth: "The presence of disagreement among the Jews is enough to show that Paul has not achieved what he sought. *He was seeking a communal decision, a recognition by the Jewish community as a whole that Jesus is the fulfillment of the Jewish hope.* The presence of significant opposition shows that this is not going to happen."[6] In other words, the problem is not active rejection of the besorah, but the absence of a corporate acceptance of the message.

By ending his two volumes with this scene, Luke acknowledges that for the foreseeable future the Jewish community as a whole would

---

6. Tannehill, *Narrative Unity*, 347. Emphasis added.

not embrace the besorah, and in this way they would delay the return of Jesus. But this final scene doesn't imply that the community has lost its covenantal status, nor does it extinguish the hope that the community will someday welcome the message of the risen Messiah.

Paul's declaration that he is going to the gentiles is recounted three times in three geographical settings that represent three crucial stages of Paul's expanding sphere of leadership: Asia Minor, Greece, and Rome. As with the three accounts of Paul's vision on the road to Damascus (Acts 9:1–19; 22:6–16; 26:12–18), and the three accounts of Peter's encounter with Cornelius (Acts 10:1–48; 11:4–16; 15:7–9), this threefold repetition emphasizes the importance of these words of Paul, especially since the book concludes with the third of these episodes.

What is their significance, then?

Many interpreters see Acts concluding with a picture of the Jewish people rejecting the gospel, so that Paul finally turns away from them and toward the gentiles. Israel is left as a people without hope. The picture looks dramatically different, however, if we remember the two distinct missions of Acts. When Peter and Paul address Jewish audiences, they are speaking not just to a collection of Jewish individuals but to an organized *community*—their own community—that is the rightful recipient of the blessings brought by the Messiah. Jesus has been raised from the dead not only to save individual Jews, but also to accomplish "the redemption of Jerusalem." On the other hand, when Peter addresses Cornelius and his household, or when Paul speaks to gentiles in Lystra or Athens, they aim merely to win as many gentiles as possible to Jesus-faith. No *corporate* gentile response is sought or required.

As we've seen, *hoi Ioudaioi* in Acts refers to the communal body of Jews ordered under its leaders and acting in an official or semi-official capacity. One of the central themes of Acts is that many Jews respond with faith to the message of the resurrected Messiah. But another central theme is that the Jewish community *as a whole*, as embodied in its leadership and institutions, doesn't respond with faith, but instead opposes the new movement. This failure, however, doesn't mean that the Jewish community has lost its covenantal status. The hope remains that the community and its leaders will reverse their opposition toward Jesus in the end.

Israel's repentance and faith would have triggered Messiah's return and the establishment of his kingdom in Jerusalem; its failure to respond in this way not only delays the restored kingdom but also intensifies the sufferings of exile. This means that *the coming judgment actually confirms rather than annuls the enduring covenantal bond between God and the Jewish people.* Like the covenant curses of Leviticus and Deuteronomy, the fierce judgment of Jerusalem in 70 CE, anticipated in Luke-Acts, demonstrates the demands imposed on Israel as God's covenant partner. If Paul's turning to the gentiles meant that God was finished with Israel, then Israel would become like any other nation, and the punishment designated for violation of the covenant would no longer apply.

Luke retains hope for Israel's future, and regards Israel's present condition as enfolded within the covenantal purposes of God. Yes, leaders and groups within local Jewish communities actively oppose the spread of the besorah, but Luke doesn't portray the Jewish community as uniformly hostile to the message. The disciples of Jesus have friends and sympathizers in the wider Jewish world, such as the women who grieve for Jesus at his crucifixion, or the men who bury Stephen, and even among the Jewish leadership, such as Joseph of Arimathea, Gamaliel, the Pharisees of the Jerusalem Council to whom Paul appeals, and some of the official representatives of the Jewish community in Rome.

The opposition to the besorah of some within the Jewish community, and Paul's consequent threefold "going to the gentiles," do not nullify the promise of Israel's redemption. Israel finds itself still in exile—an exile that will be greatly intensified when Jerusalem is destroyed—but also still awaiting restoration.

Conclusion: the Promised Return of the Jewish People

When Peter stood in the temple courts, next to the lame man miraculously healed in the name of Jesus, he called on the Jewish crowd gathered around him to repent. He even offered this gift of repentance to men who had been involved in handing Jesus over to the Romans for crucifixion. Then he described the blessings that would result:

> Repent therefore, and turn to God so that your sins may be wiped out, so that times of refreshing may come from the presence of the Lord, and that he may send the Messiah appointed for you, that is, Jesus, whom heaven must receive until the time for restoring all the things about which God spoke by the mouth of his holy prophets long ago. (Acts 3:19–20 NRSV; 3:21 ESV)

Part Two: The Besorah, the Temple, and the Covenant People

As we've seen, Peter's message here shares vocabulary with the dialogue between the resurrected Jesus and his disciples in Acts 1:6–8. This overlap lets us know that the disciples' question—"Lord, is this the time when you will restore the kingdom to Israel?"—doesn't reflect a misunderstanding of Jesus' kingdom purpose. He *will* restore the kingdom to Israel, but "the time" will come only after Israel "repents" and "returns," only when all Jerusalem, and not just his followers, will say "Blessed is he who comes in the name of the Lord" (Luke 13:35b; 19:37–38).

Taken together, Acts 1:6–8 and 3:19–21 also shed light on Jesus' prophecy that Jerusalem will be "trampled on by the Gentiles, until the times of the Gentiles are fulfilled" (Luke 21:24). The two texts in Acts make it clear that the trampling of Jerusalem and the "times of the Gentiles" will be followed by Jerusalem's repentance and restoration. These three texts together—Luke 21:24 and Acts 1:6–8 and 3:19–21—demonstrate that Israel's repentance is both a *sufficient* and a *necessary* condition for the Messiah's return: *if—and only if*—Jerusalem welcomes Jesus, will God restore "all the things about which God spoke by the mouth of his holy prophets" (Acts 3:21). The restoration of all these things, which will benefit all humankind, is linked to the response of this tiny fragment of humankind, the Jewish people.

Against this background, it's hard to imagine Peter looking out at this crowd of fellow Jews and thinking they had lost, or could lose, their standing as members of the covenant people. And we shouldn't think so either. Many of those who heard Peter speak believed him (Acts 4:4), but it's true that most Jews have not believed in Jesus, received baptism, and entered the messianic community. Does this mean they have lost their right to be called members of the people of Israel? Are they no longer participants in the covenant? If that were the case, then who are the people whose repentance fulfills the *necessary* and *sufficient* condition for the return of the Messiah? And who are the people who will receive the kingdom that God will restore to Israel? Those who will ultimately fulfill these prophecies are the descendants of untold generations of Jews who have not believed in Jesus. Therefore, we must recognize that those same generations have successfully preserved and transmitted Israel's covenantal identity. After all, those who "repent" and "return" must themselves still *be* Israel in order for their repentance and returning to have prophetic significance.

Peter's words to his Jewish brothers in Acts 3 reveal his belief that the Jewish people *remain Israel*, God's covenant partner, despite their inadequate response to the besorah. Indeed, the theme of communal Jewish opposition becomes prominent in Acts *precisely because of Israel's enduring covenantal status*, not as the reason for its nullification. The Jewish people retain their unique position within the divine plan; the Messiah rises from the dead first for them, and his kingdom will have their beloved city as its capital. That kingdom will only come in its fullness when the Jewish people are able to honor Jesus the Messiah as their appointed sovereign, and greet him with the words, "Blessed is he who comes in the name of the Lord." Until that day comes, the Jewish people will be sustained and guided in their long journey through history by God's covenant faithfulness and through their loyalty to his Torah, as we'll see in our next two chapters.

Chapter Seven

The Jewish People and the Torah in the Besorah of Luke

SHIMON, THE ONE YESHUA called Peter, had followed the master through the hills and fields and fishing towns of Galilee. He loved to see the rabbi heal the sick people who came to him, drive out evil spirits that tormented some of them, and proclaim the kingdom of God. Most of all, he loved the times when he could just sit on the ground at Yeshua's feet and listen to his deep and mysterious words of Torah.

One day Shimon and a band of followers were returning to town from a retreat out in the hills with Yeshua. As they walked over the last rise on the way back, Shimon could see ahead a big crowd of people, doubtless waiting for a chance to see the Torah teacher and miracle-worker whom everyone was talking about in those days. Then Shimon saw one man, with a fancy robe and a dignified air, step out from the crowd as if he'd been waiting for just this moment. As Yeshua approached, the man spoke loudly enough for all to hear: "Rabbi, what shall I do to inherit eternal life?" It was a good enough question, but Shimon found himself wondering whether it was some kind of trap. He wasn't surprised when Yeshua, always the wise teacher, answered the question with another question: "What is written in the Torah? What do you read there?" Of course, life is to be found in the words of Torah, Shimon thought. That's what he heard every day at Yeshua's feet. He also noticed that Yeshua considered his questioner to be an expert in Torah—the master had assumed that the man could *read* its words for himself. Accordingly, the man answered Yeshua with words quoted from the Torah: "You shall love the Lord your God with all your heart, and with all your soul, and with all your strength, and with all your mind; and your neighbor as yourself."

Yeshua replied, "You have given the right answer; do this, and you will live" (Luke 10:17–28). Shimon thought that citing these two central commandments from the Torah should settle the question.

The Infancy Narrative in Luke

From the days when Jesus taught in Galilee until the modern era, when the Jewish religious consensus was shattered, the Torah gave the Jewish people a shared identity and a shared understanding of God and how to serve him. Daily, weekly, and yearly patterns of life were based on the Torah, as were the boundaries that distinguished the Jewish community from those outside. Just as important, the grand narrative of the Torah shaped the way Jews looked at the world and hoped for its final redemption.

Today, the age-old Jewish religious consensus is gone, but the word "Torah" is still a positive one to most Jewish people, conveying a sense of age-old wisdom, rich traditions, and deep spirituality. In contrast, in the Christian world the word "Torah" is often understood simplistically as "Law," with a negative connotation. To such Christians, Law means striving for "works-righteousness," for a right standing with God based on one's own efforts. This view draws on passages in Paul's writings, which are essential to Christian doctrine, but which need to be interpreted within the context of all of Paul's work. Most relevant to this book, they should also be read in balance with the distinctive view of the Torah revealed in Luke's writings.

Luke, from his earliest chapters, affirms the covenantal identity of the Jewish people and portrays a hope for the age to come that lines up with traditional Jewish expectations. This leads us to expect that Luke and Acts will also affirm the Jewish way of life rooted in the Torah. In this chapter we'll see how Luke shows Jesus affirming the Torah in his words and deeds, as he does with the religious expert who met him at the edge of the village. In the next chapter we'll return to Acts to see how Jesus' followers do the same. As in our study of the temple, we'll find that Luke's perspective on the Torah isn't neutral, but reinforces the vision of restoration for the land and people of Israel that lies at the heart of his Besorah.

This perspective on the Torah is evident from the very beginning of Luke. In his infancy narrative, the story of Jesus' conception, birth, and earliest years, it's hard to miss the emphasis on the city of Jerusalem, the temple, and the Jewish people. The main story occurs in or near *the city of Jerusalem*, and longing for the city's future "redemption" (2:38) animates

PART TWO: THE BESORAH, THE TEMPLE, AND THE COVENANT PEOPLE

the central characters. The story opens with a revelation to a priest in *the Jerusalem temple*, and returns there for prophetic announcements concerning the child-Messiah and for a description of his coming of age (1:5–23; 2:22–51). The salvation heralded by angelic messages and inspired songs concerns *"the people of Israel"* (1:16)—also referred to as "your people Israel" (2:32), "his servant Israel" (1:54), "the house of Jacob" (1:33), and the descendants of Abraham (1:55). The almighty Sovereign who will accomplish this salvation is "the Lord God *of Israel*" (1:68).

Within such a context rich in traditional Jewish imagery, we shouldn't be surprised to hear repeated mention of obedience to *the Torah* and its commandments (1:7; 2:22–24; 2:27; 2:39). Because of that context, we can be confident that these references to Torah-obedience are not incidental to the narrative but are deliberately included. Here the Torah functions as an essential mark of the Jewish people, ordering its life centered on the temple and shaping its hope towards a redeemed city and land.

A recent commentary summarizes the impact of Luke's introductory chapters:

> Luke's readers . . . would have heard a very positive description of Jewish piety, the openness of the Torah to the poor, the piety expressed by both men and women in the Temple, and Jesus' engagement with Jewish teachers. Luke presents Jesus as fully embedded, and at home, in the Judaism of his time.[1]

So, what is the purpose of all this traditional Jewish imagery in Luke's infancy narrative? Is it just a nostalgic attempt to establish continuity with the "Old Testament"? Is it just a way to buttress the church's claim on the inheritance of Israel's promises, despite the supposed demise of city, land, people, and Torah? If that were the case, we would expect to find in the remainder of the Besorah a gradual or sudden distancing from these hallmarks of Jewish identity and hope. We have already seen that this is not the case in regards to the city or the land, and we have argued the same concerning the Jewish people. What about the Torah?

In this chapter and the next, we will see how Luke's opening section serves as a carefully crafted introduction to his entire Besorah as well as Acts. These chapters aren't a nostalgic glance at the church's honored yet transcended Jewish origins, as readers sometimes suppose. Instead, they tell

---

1. Levine and Witherington, *Luke*, 73.

a story that embodies the enduring hopes and convictions of Jesus' early followers, which they shared with the wider Jewish community.

The Teaching and Practice of Jesus Himself

The Besorah of Luke shares much material with Mark and Matthew. Each Besorah is a reliable account of the life and teachings of Jesus of Nazareth, but each adds a different emphasis and perspective. Luke's distinct viewpoint becomes evident through details that are unique to his Besorah. In what follows, we will see how these features in Luke fully align with the perspective of his infancy narrative.

Supplementing, Not Canceling, the Torah

Jesus often refers to the Torah in Luke, but he rarely makes general statements about the Torah itself. The primary exception to this rule is found in Luke 16:16–18:

> [16] The Torah and the Prophets were proclaimed until John. Since then, the Good News of the kingdom of God is being proclaimed, and everyone tries forcing his way in. [17] But it is easier for heaven and earth to pass away than for a single serif of the Torah to fail. [18] Everyone who divorces his wife and marries another commits adultery. And he who marries one who is divorced from a husband commits adultery. (TLV)

Many scholars treat verse 16 as the key to Luke's whole scheme of history. In line with the widely used NRSV translation, they interpret the verse as meaning that the Torah is no longer "in effect." Of course, verse 17 then becomes highly problematic, because it clearly speaks of the Torah as a seamless garment, authoritative in all its details. But if we interpret verse 16 in light of verse 17 rather than the reverse, the two verses line up perfectly with each other. The original Greek text helps us here. It contains nothing to correspond to the NRSV's explanatory phrase "in effect," but simply says "the Torah [*nomos*] and the Prophets were until John." For Luke, the work and teaching of Jesus inaugurate a new era in the life of the people of God, in which "the Good News of the kingdom of God is being proclaimed." Jesus refers to the former era by the phrase "the Torah and the Prophets." Elsewhere in Luke, we read that "the Law of Moses and the Prophets and the Psalms" all point forward to the coming of Jesus the Messiah (24:27, 44–45).

As verse 17 indicates, however, the normative function of "the Torah and the Prophets" for Israel's way of life remains in effect. Therefore, as one Christian commentator notes: "The sense of Luke 16:16b has to be that Jesus' kingdom-preaching is a *supplement* to the law and the prophets of the Period of Israel. Now in the Period of Jesus, when he appears in the Lucan Gospel as the kingdom-preacher par excellence, he views the law and the prophets as normative, and his preaching of the kingdom is *supplemental* to it."[2]

The notion of "supplement" captures Luke's intent if we understand it properly. The work and teaching of Jesus *add* something decisive to the Torah, but don't *subtract* from it. This clarifies Luke's understanding of Jesus' prohibition of divorce, cited in the verse that follows (16:18). Here Jesus *adds* to the Torah by intensifying its stringency. He doesn't add a *new law*, but reveals the full meaning of the original law. And he *adds* the gift of the Holy Spirit, which will enable Israel to obey the true intent of the Torah in the way that Jesus himself does. From this perspective, *Jesus in his own person is the supplement*. Therefore, re-centering the Torah on him and his teaching does not merely lay an additional brick within the structure but re-orders the entire building. At the same time, the building itself and its constituent materials remain intact.

Torah, the Two Great Commandments, and Eternal Life

The continuing validity of the Torah stands out in the Parable of the Rich Man and Lazarus, which comes next in the narrative (Luke 16:19–31). A rich man suffers torment in "Hades" as punishment for his indifference to the needy, including the poor man Lazarus, who dies neglected at his gate. The Torah requires generosity to the poor, reflecting God's own generosity. The rich man should have known what awaited him when he withheld the crumbs from his table, even though he'd been blessed with such abundance that he could feast every day. He asks Abraham to send Lazarus—now exalted to Abraham's side—to warn his family of what awaits them if they act like him. This request sets up the conclusion of the parable:

---

2. Fitzmyer, *Luke the Theologian*, 182 (emphasis added).

But Abraham said, "They have Moses and the Prophets; let them hear them." And [the rich man] said, "No, father Abraham, but if someone goes to them from the dead, they will repent." He said to him, "If they do not hear Moses and the Prophets, neither will they be convinced if someone should rise from the dead." (Luke 16:29–31)

Abraham tells the rich man that Israel's scriptures, both Torah and the Prophets, show the way for his family to avoid future punishment, and even a resurrected messenger won't get through to his family if they're ignoring "Moses and the Prophets." Abraham's words echo the message of Luke 16:17: *the practical demands of the Torah remain foundational to Israel's way of life.* Far from negating or supplanting the Torah, the life to which the resurrected Messiah summons his disciples makes sense only in terms of that same Torah. If the family of the rich man desires eternal life, they need only follow what is written in the Torah.

Jesus gave a similar teaching in the story that opened this chapter. A lawyer, an expert in Torah, asks him, "What shall I do to inherit eternal life?" This is a practical, real-life question, not a theoretical one—the same sort of question that will be posed by a wealthy ruler in Luke 18, as we'll see. In response to both the ruler and the lawyer, Jesus indicates that the way to enter the life of the coming age is to *obey* the Torah, as summarized in two great commandments. The first commandment comes from the Shema, Israel's core declaration of trusting obedience, well-known to all Jews from that time to ours:[3] "You shall love the Lord your God with all your heart, and with all your soul, and with all your strength, and with all your mind; and your neighbor as yourself" (Luke 10:27).

The Torah expert, however, isn't satisfied. He shifts the discussion to a more theoretical level, and asks, "And who is my neighbor?" (Luke 10:29). In response, Jesus tells the story commonly known as the Parable of the Good Samaritan, which doesn't answer that question directly but instead returns to the practical issue of obedience. Jesus mentions the family or tribal status of the characters in his story who must decide whether they will obey Torah's commandment to love their neighbor—namely a priest, a Levite, and a Samaritan. But he doesn't reveal the status of the wounded traveler who needs their help. In a narrative twist typical of Jesus' parables,

---

3. The first two verses, Deut 6:4–5, are the best known, but the Shema comprises all of Deut 6:4–9, as well as Deut 11:13–21 and Num 15:37–41. Its unifying theme is loving and wholehearted service toward God.

it's the man whose status is ambiguous by Jewish standards—the Samaritan—who actually fulfills the commandment. And Jesus tells the lawyer, "Go and do likewise" (Luke 10:37). In other words, the real question is who *you* are, not who *they* are. Concentrate first on *living as a neighbor*, as a true Israelite, a true reflection of God's love toward those around you, rather than on analyzing the status of others to decide whether they qualify as neighbors. Then you will fulfill the commandment as God meant it to be fulfilled and attain eternal life.

The story of the rich ruler in Luke 18 also begins with a question about the path to eternal life. The story about the Samaritan provided the general answer: obey the Torah—as summarized in the two commandments to love God and neighbor—and then focused on the second of the two great commandments, "love your neighbor." Now Jesus offers the same general response to the ruler: "You know the commandments." He goes on to list the imperatives of the second table of the Ten Commandments, which deal with human relationships, the details of "love your neighbor." The ruler replies that he has observed all these since he was young (Luke 18:20–21).

> When Jesus heard this, he said to him, "One thing you still lack. Sell all that you have and distribute to the poor, and you will have treasure in heaven; and come, follow me." But when he heard these things, he became very sad, for he was extremely rich. (Luke 18:22–23)

Jesus doesn't challenge the ruler's claim to have obeyed the commandments of the second table of the Ten Commandments. Instead, he summons him to also obey the commandments of the first table, which deal with serving God. As Jesus says earlier, "You cannot serve God and money" (Luke 16:13). Thus, this second story focuses on the commandment to love God with all one's heart, soul, and strength—expressed in this case by selling all to follow Jesus—just as the first story focused on the commandment to love one's neighbor.

The first story concludes with the Parable of the Good Samaritan, and its moral: "Go and do likewise." Luke next tells of Jesus' visit to the house of Martha and Mary (Luke 10:38–42). Martha's diligence in practical service manifests her obedience to the commandment to love your neighbor, which Jesus had just emphasized in his instruction to the lawyer. Similarly, Mary's determination to remain in Jesus' presence and learn from his teaching manifests her love of God. When Jesus tells Martha that "*one thing* is necessary," we have a preview of what Jesus will say to the rich ruler. To follow

Jesus with all one has is to fulfill the commandment to love God with *all* one's heart, soul, and strength, as the Shema teaches. Thus, the two stories of Luke 10:25–42 should be viewed as a unit portraying the commandments of the Torah as the path that leads to eternal life. Jesus later emphasizes the same truth in his conversation with the rich young ruler.

Repentance

Luke also shows his high regard for the Torah by portraying Jesus as a preacher of repentance. Repentance plays a prominent role in Jewish thought in general, where it is termed *teshuvah*, meaning "return" or "turning." Teshuvah refers to a change of attitude *and* of behavior defined in relation to the commandments of the Torah. Luke reflects a similar emphasis on the commandments as the path to life, and repentance as returning to the path through obedience to the commandments.

The scholar E. P. Sanders has noted, "Repentance has a prominence in Luke that it does not have in Matthew and Mark."[4] This distinction among the Gospels is striking in Luke 5:30–32. Jesus is describing the shape of his mission, in response to being criticized for eating with sinners. According to Mark and Matthew, he says "I have not come to call the righteous but sinners" (Mark 2:17; Matt 9:13). Luke's version includes an additional phrase: "I have not come to call the righteous but sinners *to repentance*." Here Luke makes explicit what remains only implicit in the other Gospels: to follow Jesus, sinners must repent and reorient their lives to the commandments of God.

Further emphasizing this point, Luke devotes an entire chapter to the theme of repentance (Luke 15). The chapter begins with the same criticism of Jesus that we just saw in Luke 5:30: "And the Pharisees and the scribes grumbled, saying, 'This man receives sinners and eats with them'" (15:2). Jesus responds with three parables. The first parable focuses on a shepherd searching for a lost sheep, and the second depicts a woman hunting for a lost coin. Neither parable speaks directly about repentance, but they focus instead on the one who seeks what is lost, and especially on the heavenly celebration that greets the repentance of a sinner (verses 7 and 10). The final parable, the story of the prodigal son and his older brother, deals more directly with repentance. The younger son leaves his father's house, squanders his inheritance, and finally returns; the older

---

4. Sanders, *Historical Figure of Jesus*, 231.

son must decide whether to join in the celebration of his return. This parable also reflects Luke's balanced perspective on the Pharisees, which we mentioned back in chapter 2. In this parable, Jesus calls *all* to repentance and the heavenly banquet—Pharisees (as probably represented by the older brother) along with prodigals.

The complex interaction of divine and human initiative in repentance is also at play in the story of Zacchaeus (Luke 19:1–10). He's a tax collector, "small in stature," who's so eager to catch a glimpse of Jesus that he climbs into a sycamore tree to see him. Jesus rewards his zeal by choosing to stay at his house—and unleashes the same chorus of criticism we heard in Luke 5:30 and 15:2: "And when they saw it, they all grumbled, 'He has gone in to be the guest of a man who is a sinner.'" But Zacchaeus welcomes Jesus with joy—and evidence of real repentance: "And Zacchaeus stood and said to the Lord, 'Behold, Lord, the half of my goods I give to the poor. And if I have defrauded anyone of anything, I restore it fourfold.'" As E. P. Sanders notes, Zacchaeus fulfills the basic requirement of the Torah, but also goes beyond it:

> Zacchaeus offered a lot more than the law requires, which is that a person who defrauds another should repay him, add 20 percent as a fine, and then sacrifice a ram as a guilt offering (Lev 6.1–7). A person who did this, and who did not return to his former life, was no longer wicked.[5]

As in all forms of Judaism, Luke shows that repentance requires concrete action, action shaped by the commandments of the Torah. The Torah provides the normative template for repentance, and Luke assumes that a generous penitent will transcend the Torah's minimal demands and act in light of God's generosity as portrayed in the Torah.

The Parable of the Rich Man and Lazarus that we discussed above also underlines the connection between the Torah and repentance. The rich man asks Abraham to send Lazarus to his family to persuade them to repent and change their ways so they might escape the judgment that has befallen him. Abraham replies, "They have Moses and the Prophets; let them hear them" (Luke 16:29). Unsatisfied, the rich man argues, "If someone goes to them from the dead, they will repent" (Luke 16:30). He deems the Torah and the Prophets insufficient to motivate repentance, but Abraham disagrees. "If they do not hear Moses and the Prophets, neither

---

5. Sanders, *Historical Figure of Jesus*, 230.

will they be convinced if someone should rise from the dead" (Luke 16:31). *The way of repentance proclaimed by Jesus is not a substitute for the message of the Torah, but its fullest and most powerful embodiment.* Those unaffected by the sovereign claims of the Torah will likewise ignore the words of the resurrected Messiah.

Repentance plays an indispensable role in Luke's presentation of the besorah. The death and resurrection of Jesus prefigure the coming judgment upon Jerusalem and the final restoration that will surely come. For Jerusalem, however, there is an element that comes between death and resurrection/restoration, namely repentance. Or perhaps it would be more accurate to say that the resurrection/restoration of Jerusalem begins with repentance, as Jesus foretells: "And I tell you, you will not see me until you say, 'Blessed is he who comes in the name of the Lord!'" (Luke 13:35).

The Jewish "Customs" Given by the Torah

The commandments of the Torah are central to Jesus' teaching in Luke. They concern matters like the prohibitions against idolatry (the rich ruler) and defrauding others (Zacchaeus), and the injunctions to help the poor (the rich man and Lazarus) and care for the afflicted (the good Samaritan). These are all practical expressions of the two commandments of love that summarize the demands of the Torah, which is what the "expert" in our opening story was asking about (Luke 10:17–28). For the "sinners" who flock to Jesus and are despised by his critics, represented in parable form by the prodigal son, we may assume that repentance includes turning from "reckless living" (Luke 15:13; see 15:30) and obeying the Torah's commandments regarding marriage and sexual relations. For the pious critics, on the other hand, who appear in the parable as the prodigal's elder brother, repentance will mean surrendering their judgmental attitude and learning to celebrate the return of many prodigals.

These commandments have universal application, so we might ask how Luke presents the teaching and practice of Jesus regarding the commandments of the Torah that are particular to Israel's calling as a distinct people. To answer this question, we should begin with the Jewish institution that occupies a privileged position in the Torah and that all the Gospels recognize as a point of contention between Jesus and his critics, namely, the Sabbath. All the Gospels bear witness to Jesus' practice of healing on the Sabbath and to the controversy that this practice stirred up. How does Luke

Part Two: The Besorah, the Temple, and the Covenant People

present Jesus' understanding of the Sabbath? Does Jesus heal on the Sabbath in order to demonstrate that he has brought in a new era in which such "ritual" prescriptions have been transcended or marginalized?

To begin to answer these questions, we'll return to an early scene in Luke's account. After Jesus has been baptized in the Jordan River by John, and has fasted for forty days in the wilderness of Judea, he returns to Galilee to begin his public mission. All three of the Synoptic Gospels introduce this new phase of Jesus' life with a generalized description of his activity. Mark and Matthew focus on his "proclaiming" the kingdom of God (Mark 1:14–15; Matt 4:12, 13a, 17). But Luke introduces Jesus' Galilean ministry in a way that reflects his distinctive concerns:

> And Jesus returned in the power of the Spirit to Galilee, and a report about him went out through all the surrounding country. And he taught in their synagogues, and was glorified by all. (Luke 4:14–15)

Luke speaks of Jesus teaching (an act associated with Torah) rather than "proclaiming," and doing so in the synagogue. Elsewhere, Luke identifies Jesus' teaching in the synagogue as a Sabbath practice (Luke 4:31, 33; 6:6; 13:10), so it's safe to assume that he implies a Sabbath reference in this introduction to Jesus' mission in Galilee. Thus, alone among the Gospels, Luke begins by characterizing Jesus' central activity as *teaching*, identifying the characteristic location of that activity as the *synagogue*, and implicitly pointing to the *Sabbath* as the typical time in which that activity took place.[6]

Jesus and the Sabbath

With this background, let's return to the scene that we first visited in chapter 1, a scene that introduces Jesus' entire Galilean ministry: "And he came to Nazareth, where he had been brought up. And as was his custom, he went to the synagogue on the Sabbath day" (Luke 4:16). The phrase "as was his custom" is particularly noteworthy.[7] Luke stresses that Jesus made a habit of worshiping in the synagogue on the Sabbath. Luke uses the same Greek word translated as "custom" here to describe the communal "customs" of the Jewish people rooted in the Torah. And he doesn't use this term, as we

---

6. Chance, *Jerusalem, the Temple, and the New Age*, 59.

7. Luke uses the same phrase to characterize Paul's habitual synagogue attendance (Acts 17:1–2), presumably also on the Sabbath day (see Acts 13:14).

moderns might, as a way of minimizing the authority behind such practices, to contrast merely *human* customs with *divinely* given practices. Instead, Luke uses this term to describe the practices of the Torah that shape and define the Jewish way of life.

After establishing that Sabbath synagogue attendance is typical of Jesus' practice, Luke portrays him taking a central role in the worship of his home synagogue. "And he stood up to read. And the scroll of the prophet Isaiah was given to him" (Luke 4:16b–17). Jesus views the passage he will read from Isaiah 61 as announcing the mission he now inaugurates:

> The Spirit of the Lord is upon me,
>   because he has anointed me
>   to proclaim good news to the poor.
> He has sent me to proclaim liberty to the captives
>   and recovering of sight to the blind,
>   to set at liberty those who are oppressed,
> to proclaim the year of the Lord's favor. (Luke 4:18–19)

As we saw in chapter 1, Isaiah depicts the prophetic mission of the servant of the Lord with the imagery of the Jubilee year, in which slaves are freed, debts are remitted, and land is restored (Lev 25:10–54). The Jubilee occurs every forty-nine years, and functions as a sabbatical year of sabbatical years. Thus, the Jubilee year enacts the principle of the Sabbath day, in which Jews remember their slavery in Egypt and display to their families, servants, and domestic animals the same mercy God showed them when he released them from bondage (Deut 5:14–15). This is the liberating mercy that Jesus proclaims in his message of repentance and forgiveness (or "release" in Jubilee terminology,) and in the work of healing, which Luke sees primarily in terms of liberation from demonic forces. This work actualizes the meaning of the Jubilee year, which is also the meaning of the Sabbath day: to set free the captives and bring them into their inheritance of rest. What better way for Jesus to launch his Jubilee mission than to read Isaiah 61 in the synagogue on the Sabbath?

The next scene in Luke is another Sabbath visit to a synagogue, this time in Capernaum (Luke 4:31–37). In Mark (as well as Matthew), Jesus begins his Galilean mission by calling disciples, and then afterwards teaches and heals in the synagogue. But in Luke the calling of the first disciples is delayed until after these two synagogue scenes, in which Jesus first announces what he has come to do (to bring a sabbatical release to the captives), and then begins doing it (freeing a man from the oppressive power of an unclean demon). In this way, Luke further highlights the significance of the Sabbath and the traditional Jewish mode of honoring the day by gathering together for the reading of scripture. In his teaching and healing on the Sabbath, Jesus fulfills both the words of scripture and the sabbatical customs founded by those words.

Only later does controversy over Jesus' approach to the Sabbath emerge. Luke's perception of this controversy becomes clear in an episode found only in his gospel.

> Now he was teaching in one of the synagogues on the Sabbath. And behold, there was a woman who had had a disabling spirit for eighteen years. She was bent over and could not fully straighten herself. When Jesus saw her, he called her over and said to her, "Woman, you are freed [unloosed] from your disability." And he laid his hands on her, and immediately she was made straight, and she glorified God. But the ruler of the synagogue, indignant because Jesus had healed on the Sabbath, said to the people, "There are six days in which work ought to be done. Come on those days and be healed, and not on the Sabbath day." Then the Lord answered him, "You hypocrites! Does not each of you on the Sabbath untie [loose] his ox or his donkey from the manger and lead it away to water it? And ought not this woman, a daughter of Abraham whom Satan bound for eighteen years, be loosed from this bond on the Sabbath day?" (Luke 13:10–16)

Jesus doesn't defend his action by nullifying the laws of the Sabbath but by alluding to the Torah's injunctions to loose "your ox or your donkey" from burdens on the Sabbath, and to "remember that you were a slave in the land of Egypt, and the LORD your God brought you out from there" (Deut 5:14–15). Jesus tells this "daughter of Abraham," who had been "bound" by Satan, that she has now been loosed and set free. Jesus is bringing a messianic liberation that completes the redemptive purpose of the exodus, and thereby fulfills the intent of the Sabbath. Far from minimizing the Sabbath, Luke actually underlines its messianic significance as a fundamental part of Jewish life.

Jesus and the Temple

The Sabbath was the most important of Israel's "customs" commanded in the Torah. Of similar weight, and linked in various ways to the Sabbath, were the laws associated with the Jerusalem temple. Luke shows intense concern for these laws in his infancy narrative (Luke 1–2) and in Acts of the Apostles. But how does he portray Jesus' own approach to the temple and its customs? Before we close this chapter we'll take a quick look.

As Jesus is journeying to Jerusalem he enters a village near Samaria, and ten lepers come to him asking for help. He responds by commanding them to show themselves to the priests (Luke 17:11–14a). According to the laws of the Torah, a leper would only do this *after* being healed (Lev 14:1–32). Accordingly, in an earlier story of the healing of a leper, also found in Mark and Matthew, Jesus commands the man to go to a priest after his healing (Luke 5:12–16). In this later story, unique to Luke, Jesus demands more from his petitioners: they are to trust his word and set out on their journey to the priest in Jerusalem with the confidence that they'll be healed on the way. Their obedience to Jesus' command leads to their healing, but they must still do what is required by the Torah for someone healed of their disease.

The point of the story is the obedience of faith shown by the ten lepers, and (even more) the gratitude shown by the one Samaritan who returned to Jesus to give praise to God (Luke 17:15–19). But the drama of the story depends upon an assumption—shared by its author, earliest readers, and characters—that the priestly customs ordained by the Torah are sacred duties for all the children of Abraham (Jews and Samaritans alike). Furthermore, as we've already seen, when Jesus finally arrives in Jerusalem himself, his first move is to visit the temple and rid it of the corruption that violates its status as "a house of prayer." Then he continues "teaching daily in the temple" (Luke 19:45–47a).

Conclusion

The Gospel of Luke presents Jesus as a Torah-faithful Jew in both his teaching and his practice, a Jewish teacher who considers adherence to the commandments to be the way to eternal life, and who summons all who hear him to repentance in response to the Torah. Jesus focuses upon the two great commandments of loving God and neighbor, and supplements the Torah by demanding an even more radical conformity to its inner intent. At the same time, he also honors the distinctive Jewish institutions of the Sabbath and the temple. Thus, there is nothing in the Torah teaching and practice of Jesus that conflicts with the picture of Torah piety that Luke paints in his infancy narrative. Their coherence is evident.

Part Two: The Besorah, the Temple, and the Covenant People

In this way, Luke's Besorah upholds the chosenness of the Jewish people, which has always been expressed through obedience to the Torah. But what about the era inaugurated by the resurrection of Messiah and the outpouring of the Spirit? We've seen how the Torah and its practice remain central in the days of Jesus and in his own practice. Now we're ready to see how his followers, as pictured in the Book of Acts, relate to the Torah and the way of life that it mandates for Israel after Messiah's death and resurrection. It will become clear that the besorah honors the way of life founded on the Torah for Jesus' Jewish followers, as well as for the Jewish people as a whole in their journey through the centuries.

Chapter Eight

The Jewish People and the Torah in the Book of Acts

In the years after the great outpouring of the Spirit on Shavuot, Peter continued to serve as a spokesman and leader of the messianic community in Jerusalem. He also began to travel beyond the holy city, serving the groups of Yeshua's followers that were springing up throughout Judea and Samaria. One day when he was staying at the house of Simon the tanner in Jaffa, Peter went up to the rooftop to pray. It was about noon and his hosts were preparing some food below. As he wrapped up his prayers, Peter paused a moment to look out at the seashore not far off and breathe in the sea air, which relieved the smells of Simon's tanning operation. As he was gazing out at the horizon his mind drifted off and he fell into a trance.

The heavens opened up before him and he saw a large sheet being lowered to the ground by its four corners. Peter looked into it and saw all kinds of four-footed animals, reptiles, and birds—both clean and unclean. Then he heard a voice calling him by name and telling him to rise up, kill, and eat. The voice repeated this command two more times, but Peter refused to eat anything unclean. When he came out of the trance Peter wondered what the vision could possibly mean. Then he heard his name being called again. Three men down on the street were looking for him, and the Spirit directed him to "go with them without hesitation, for I have sent them." Peter went down and greeted the men, who told him they were messengers of a Roman officer named Cornelius, based up the coast in Caesarea, who supposedly had been directed by an angel to send for Peter. He invited them in and gave them lodging for the night—and then set out with them for Caesarea early the next morning. It was only on the long walk up the coast that Peter slowly began to understand the meaning of his vision.

Part Two: The Besorah, the Temple, and the Covenant People

The Teaching and Practice of Jesus' Disciples

When Luke describes the character of Cornelius and his household in Acts 10, as we'll see shortly, he uses words that echo his account of Jesus' birth and early years, discussed in the previous chapter. This linkage is just one example of how Luke's infancy narrative is foundational to the entire structure of his two volumes. And this foundation in turn rests firmly on the Torah.

Righteousness, Devotion, and the Torah

The infancy narrative is populated by a rich cast of Jews that Luke calls "righteous," beginning with Zechariah and Elizabeth: "Both of them were righteous before God" (Luke 1:6a). Indeed, Luke informs us that the Jewish world of the time included numerous people who were truly righteous, including Jesus' parents Joseph and Mary. Luke also offers a traditional Jewish definition of that righteousness: "living blamelessly according to all the commandments and regulations of the Lord" (Luke 1:6b). In Luke's infancy narrative, righteousness and observance of Torah are inseparable.[1]

Accordingly, here's how Luke introduces Simeon, the man who blesses Mary and her baby in the temple: "Now there was a man in Jerusalem whose name was Simeon, and this man was righteous and devout, waiting for the consolation of Israel, and the Holy Spirit was upon him" (Luke 2:25). Simeon is not only "righteous," he is also "devout," a term that indicates reverence or proper awe of God, and also implies the careful fulfillment of religious duties.[2] It describes a right posture toward God and a way of life that conforms to the standards of the Torah.

The "righteous" and "devout" Jews of the infancy narrative also hope in the Torah's promises to Israel. They are model Jews, "waiting for the consolation of Israel," and "waiting for the redemption of Jerusalem" (Luke 2:25, 38), who prefigure other "righteous" and "devout" people that will appear later. In Acts 2:5, for example, we read that during the feast of Shavuot or Pentecost, "there were dwelling in Jerusalem Jews, devout men from every

---

1. Readers of the New Testament will be aware of a broader discussion of righteousness and its relationship to the Law, especially in Paul's writings. Luke's perspective can be reconciled with the rest of the New Testament, but our focus here is on hearing and understanding his distinctive message.

2. Marshall, *Luke*, 118. The term in Greek is *eulabēs*, which appears also in Acts 2:5 and 8:2.

nation under heaven." Most likely, these Jews made their long journey to Jerusalem for Passover and remained in the city for Shavuot, revealing their "devout" character in their obedience to the Torah commandment to worship in the temple at these festivals.

Do these qualities of being "righteous" and "devout" continue within the community of Jesus' followers after Shavuot? The story of Paul's healing and baptism by Ananias provides an answer. Paul describes Ananias as "a devout man according to the Torah, well spoken of by all the Jewish people living there" (Acts 22:12 TLV). Ananias displays the same Torah-based devotion as the righteous Jews of Luke 1 and 2. In contrast with this array of righteous Jews, only one gentile is described as righteous—Cornelius. He's a Roman officer who adheres as fully as his circumstances allow to the teachings of the Torah: "he gave alms generously to the people [that is, the needy among the Jewish people] and prayed continually to God" (Acts 10:2). The phrase translated here as "continually" appears in the classic Greek translation of the Bible (the Septuagint) to render the Hebrew word *tamid*, which we discussed in chapter 5. It doesn't refer to a habit of praying every moment of every day, but to Cornelius's adoption of the Jewish custom of praying twice daily at the times of sacrifice in the temple (Acts 10:3-4).

Like Ananias, Cornelius is a man "well spoken of by the whole Jewish nation" (Acts 10:22). Notice how the opinion of the whole Jewish community, not just its messianic element, matters to Luke. Cornelius's love for the people of Israel and the God of Israel is a publicly acknowledged fact. As a righteous gentile who follows the provisions of the Torah that fit his status and circumstances, he becomes the perfect representative and first-fruit of those from the nations who are to be joined to the people of God. Peter will recount his story at the Jerusalem Council, as we'll discuss below (Acts 15:7-9). Cornelius's story helps shape the Council's decree that gentiles are to follow those commandments of the Torah given to outsiders who dwell in the midst of Israel. The Torah is honored and upheld throughout Acts, as it is throughout the Besorah of Luke.

The Prayer/Offering/Spirit Constellation

The account of Cornelius reflects another theme that first appears in Luke's infancy narrative, which we noted in our discussion of the tamid in chapter 5—a pattern of daily prayer linked to the offerings of the temple that is

Part Two: The Besorah, the Temple, and the Covenant People

also linked to the gift of the Holy Spirit. We'll call this pattern the prayer/offering/Spirit constellation. Just as a constellation is a configuration of stars that form a clear picture, so Luke-Acts includes a configuration of texts that picture an integrated pattern of prayer, temple offerings, and the gift of the Spirit.

The initial scene of Luke's Besorah unfolds in the Jerusalem temple, where the priest Zechariah enters the holy place to present the tamid offering of incense on the golden altar (Luke 1:8–9; see Exod 29:38–42; Num 28:1–8). Luke implies that Zechariah himself mingled prayer with the incense he burned, for, when the angel Gabriel appears to him, he says, "Do not be afraid, Zechariah, for your prayer has been heard" (Luke 1:13). And what is Zechariah praying about? Perhaps he prays for a son, since he and his wife are childless and of advanced age (Luke 1:7). But if that's really what Zechariah is praying about, it seems strange that he would doubt the angel's announcement that his wife will bear him a son, which would have been the exact answer to his prayer! More likely, Zechariah's prayer in the temple has the same content as the prayer of those Jews in the outer court, and of those Jews and righteous gentiles (like Cornelius) who turn towards Jerusalem and call upon God at the time of the twice-daily offering: they're all praying for the "redemption of Jerusalem" and the "consolation of Israel." This is the prayer that God is answering with the wondrous conception and birth of this child, who will be named John, and even more with the conception and birth of another child whose way John will prepare (Luke 1:17).

The son to be born to Zechariah and Elizabeth will be distinguished by a special gift: "even before his birth he will be filled with the Holy Spirit" (Luke 1:15). Mention of the Holy Spirit here may seem like an incidental detail, but what follows in Luke and Acts should make us think otherwise. As an unborn child, John is moved by the Spirit when his mother is visited by Mary and immediately "filled with the Holy Spirit" (Luke 1:41, 44). Years later, when John describes the mission of the one whose way he is preparing, he says that the coming one "will baptize you with the Holy Spirit and fire" (Luke 3:16). Thus, the incense *offering* of Zechariah and his *prayer*, joined with the prayers of devout Jews in Jerusalem and around the world, are answered in the birth of a child filled with the *Holy Spirit*, and in the birth of another child who will bestow the Holy Spirit on faithful Israel.

In the opening scenes of his Besorah, Luke links the daily temple offerings, ordained by the Torah, to the daily practice of prayer undertaken by devout Jews, proselytes, and righteous gentiles. He also pictures both the temple service and the prayers as ordered toward the "redemption of Jerusalem," and hints that the long-awaited redemption begins with the impartation of the Holy Spirit.

Clearly, then, this prayer/offering/Spirit constellation has a major role in Luke's Besorah, but what about Acts? Acts 2 emphasizes one element of the three-part constellation—the gift of the Holy Spirit (Acts 2:4, 17–18, 33, 38)—but the other two elements (prayer and temple offerings) are implicit.

- **Prayer:** Acts 1 concluded with the followers of Jesus together in an upstairs room, where they "were devoting themselves to prayer" (Acts 1:14). Acts 2 then opens, "When the day of Pentecost arrived, they were all together in one place. And suddenly there came from heaven a sound like a mighty rushing wind, and it filled the entire house where they were sitting" (Acts 2:1–2). The "one place" of Acts 2:1 and the "house" of Acts 2:2 seem to be equivalent to the "room upstairs" of Acts 1:13, just mentioned as the place of prayer. The prayer of Jesus' band of followers provides the setting for what comes next.[3]

- **Temple Offerings:** The Holy Spirit is poured out on the disciples around "the third hour of the day," or approximately 9:00 am (Acts 2:15). This timing relates to the temple worship schedule. The morning tamid commenced at daybreak, and would normally conclude no later than the fourth hour, around 10:00 am.[4] Since the morning incense-offering came before both the priestly benediction and the sacrifice of the burnt-offering, it would take place at about the third hour.[5] This means that the messianic community received the Holy Spirit at approximately the time when the priests in the temple offered incense, and thus also at the same time of day that Zechariah had entered the holy place and received the promise of redemption from the angel Gabriel.

The prayer/offering/Spirit constellation implicit in Acts 2 reflects the biblical accounts of the dedication of the tabernacle in the wilderness and the temple in Jerusalem. Both of these rites reach their climax when fire falls from heaven and consumes the offering on the altar (Lev 9:24; 2 Chr 7:1). On Shavuot "divided tongues as of fire appeared to the disciples and rested

---

3. The scene soon shifts to a more public setting and the transition is unclear, but the backdrop of prayer remains.

4. This is according to the Mishnah, M. Eduyot 6:1, and Talmud, b. Berachot 26b–27a.

5. Edersheim, *The Temple*, 107–8.

on each one of them. And they were all filled with the Holy Spirit and began to speak in other tongues as the Spirit gave them utterance" (Acts 2:3–4). The "tongues as of fire" represent the Spirit, who fills the disciples. The praying community itself becomes the offering, not consumed by the fire from heaven but instead transformed and empowered by it.

This same constellation of prayer, offering, and Holy Spirit is clearly visible in Acts 10–11. As we've seen, Cornelius is a man who habitually prays to the God of Israel at the time of the tamid offering. He's praying at the hour of the afternoon tamid when an angel appears to him and tells him that his prayers and alms "have ascended as a memorial before God" (Acts 10:4). This terminology suggests that the prayer of Cornelius (like that of Zechariah) has been mingled with the incense of the Jerusalem temple, which "ascended" at the same hour, and has been received with favor. For Zechariah (in Luke 1) and for the apostolic community (in Acts 2), the acceptance of *prayer* and *sacrifice* results in a direct response of God by the *Spirit*. But Cornelius will need a different kind of response, since he is a gentile, not part of the people of Israel. The angel therefore commands him to send for Peter, who is part of Israel, and will be the human agent through whom the saving message will be proclaimed and the Spirit bestowed. Since the gift of the Spirit in this case is humanly mediated, a delay separates it from the prayer and offering, but the final result is the same as in Luke 1 and Acts 2. The *prayer* of a righteous person, accompanying Israel's *offering*, leads to the bestowal of the *Spirit*. This paradigm, which first appears in Luke's infancy narrative, plays out in the whole history of the followers of Jesus. The Holy Spirit is revealed in the midst of Israel's Torah-ordained way of worship.

The Family of Jesus and the Jerusalem Assembly

Luke portrays Zechariah and Elizabeth, as well as Joseph and Mary (along with Simeon and Anna), as righteous and devout according to the Torah. In particular, he presents Joseph and Mary as obeying specific Torah commandments related to ritual purity, circumcision, and the redemption of a firstborn son (Luke 2:21–24). Mary had already taken center stage as a model of Torah obedience because of her faithful response to the message of the angel Gabriel. After being told that she would be the mother of the Messiah, Mary answered, "Behold, I am the servant of the Lord; let it be to me according to your word" (Luke 1:38). Unlike Zechariah, who, though "righteous before

God" (Luke 1:6), doubted Gabriel's message, Mary takes the posture of a "servant" and places herself humbly at God's disposal.

When Mary visits her kinswoman Elizabeth, the older woman proclaims, "And blessed is she who believed that there would be a fulfillment of what was spoken to her from the Lord" (Luke 1:45). Mary is "blessed" because she responded to God's word with faith. Later in the narrative, angels appear to shepherds outside Bethlehem, who then find Mary and Joseph, with the newborn Jesus, and tell them what they had heard from the angels concerning the child. Luke informs us that "Mary treasured up all these things, pondering them in her heart" (Luke 2:19). Mary had taken seriously the word of Gabriel and offered herself as a servant in response; now she received and guarded in her heart these words concerning another angelic appearance that confirmed what she had heard earlier. In this way, Mary demonstrates the whole-hearted devotion to God's word that marks Torah-faithful Israel.

With this picture of Jesus' family, and Mary in particular, we shouldn't be surprised by the make-up of the messianic community in Jerusalem before Pentecost: "All these [the eleven apostles] with one accord were devoting themselves to prayer, together with the women and Mary the mother of Jesus, and his brothers" (Acts 1:14). Mary's presence in the upper room seems as appropriate as her presence (along with Joseph) with the shepherds of Bethlehem and the prophets of the temple.

Furthermore, Luke's portrayal of Jesus' family in his early chapters sets the stage for the appearance of a family member whose crucial role in Acts might otherwise be inexplicable—namely Jesus' brother, James. When Peter is forced to flee from Jerusalem, he treats James as the leader of the community (Acts 12:17). Later, as leader of this Torah-zealous Jerusalem community, James receives Paul and counsels him to publicly demonstrate his own loyalty to Torah (Acts 21:17–26). James is continuing the family tradition that Luke portrays so vividly in his infancy narrative, a tradition that could be captured well by the phrase, "they are all zealous for the Torah" (Acts 21:20).

In the Besorah of Luke, Mary, Joseph, Zechariah, and Elizabeth, as well as Simeon and Anna, are all "righteous" and "devout" according to the Torah. In Acts, so also are the twelve apostles, as well as Mary and James, and the entire Jerusalem assembly. As the pious Jews in Luke show special reverence for the temple and its Torah-mandated rites, so does the

Jerusalem assembly in Acts, both under the leadership of the twelve (Acts 2:46; 3:1; 5:12, 19–21, 42; 6:7) and under James (21:23–24, 26).

Paul and the Torah in Acts

The imagery of Torah-faithful Israel, so prominent in the infancy narrative, remains central to the whole story that Luke tells, well into the later chapters of Acts. But the featured protagonist of Acts isn't James, leader of the messianic Jewish community in Jerusalem—it's Paul, light to the nations. Therefore, it is significant that Luke portrays Paul following the pattern established in the infancy narrative as closely as James does. Three particular Torah practices pictured in the infancy narrative recur in Paul's story, and each one plays an even more significant role in Paul's story than in the infancy narrative. In the story of Paul, each practice is pivotal to the plot, and all three come together at one of its climactic moments.

1. **The pilgrimage to Jerusalem**

    The opening chapters of Luke recount Joseph and Mary's custom of traveling each year to Jerusalem for Passover (Luke 2:41). This pilgrimage-to-Jerusalem story becomes the model for three accounts that follow: (1) Jesus' pilgrimage to Jerusalem, which dominates most of Luke's Besorah (starting at Luke 9:51); (2) the outpouring of the Spirit on the pilgrim-feast of Pentecost (Acts 2:1–5); and (3) Paul's final pilgrimage to Jerusalem, hoping to arrive, "if possible, on the day of Pentecost" (Acts 20:16). When Paul arrives in Jerusalem, he immediately meets with James, and this meeting raises the issue that will dominate the final eight chapters of the book—namely, Paul's approach to Judaism and the Jewish people (Acts 21:17–26). Paul's pilgrimage to Jerusalem provides the framework for a major section of the entire Book of Acts.

2. **The Nazirite vow**

    When the angel Gabriel promises a son to Zechariah and Elizabeth he says their son "must not drink wine or strong drink," a central component of the Nazirite vow (Luke 1:15; Num 6:3). This vow, whether temporary or lifelong, imposed obligations upon an individual similar to those that bound the high priest, and imparted to the person a status of sanctity that was appropriate to John as one filled with the Holy Spirit from before birth.

John's lifelong status as a Nazirite prepares the reader for a temporary vow that Paul undertakes just before traveling to Jerusalem (Acts 18:18–23). As in the infancy narrative, Luke doesn't use the term "Nazirite," but provides enough detail to show that this Torah practice is in view. In Luke 1, the relevant fact is the prohibition of wine and strong drink; in Acts 18, the key details are the "vow" itself and the cutting of Paul's hair (v. 18; see Num 6:1, 5, 18).

The significance of this vow becomes clear when Paul arrives in Jerusalem for Pentecost, and James tells him about a problem: The messianic Jews of Jerusalem, who are "all zealous for the Torah," have heard that Paul has been teaching "all the Jews who are among the Gentiles to forsake Moses" (Acts 21:20–21). James knows this rumor to be false, and we do too, since we've just read about Paul's Nazirite vow and his exertions to reach Jerusalem for Pentecost. But how can Paul prove his innocence? James suggests that he join four men in the community "who are under a vow . . . and purify yourself along with them and pay their expenses, so that they may shave their heads. Thus all will know that there is nothing in what they have been told about you, but that you yourself also live in observance of the law" (Acts 21:23–24).

Now we see the importance of Luke's earlier mention of Paul's vow. He'd taken it upon himself in a context that implied no motive other than devotion to God, so now we can believe that he'll sincerely participate in the vows of these four fellow Jewish disciples, making it clear that he also is a Jew "zealous for the Torah."

The first two Torah practices—the pilgrimage and the Nazirite vow—converge when Paul reaches Jerusalem at Pentecost and reports to James. The third practice, circumcision, becomes significant on the same occasion.

3. Circumcision

The first chapter of Luke's infancy narrative reaches its climax at the circumcision of John (Luke 1:59–79). In the second chapter, Luke recounts briefly the circumcision of the Messiah: "And at the end of eight days, when he was circumcised, he was called Jesus, the name given by the angel before he was conceived in the womb" (Luke

2:21). No heavenly visions, no ecstatic songs of praise, no ominous prophecies, no mention even of guests at the joyful event—the boy is circumcised (as the Torah required) and named (as the angel commanded), and that is enough.

Circumcision receives attention again in Acts, but now it becomes a major point of contention. Paul and Barnabas have completed their first missionary journey and returned to their home base, the city of Antioch. "But some men came down from Judea and were teaching the brothers, 'Unless you are *circumcised according to the custom of Moses*, you cannot be saved'" (Acts 15:1, emphasis added). Circumcision symbolizes the whole issue of the Torah and its application to gentiles, for circumcision was the doorway for gentiles into membership in the Jewish people, which entailed a commitment to the whole body of Mosaic Law. The debate in Antioch becomes so intense that the messianic community sends Paul and Barnabas and some others to Jerusalem, to bring this question to the elders.

As we'll see in a moment, the Jerusalem Council will rule that circumcision is not required for gentile followers of Jesus. But for readers of Acts another question arises: What about the *Jewish* disciples of Jesus? Are they still obliged to circumcise their sons, and to keep the Torah? This is exactly the question raised within the Torah-zealous messianic Jewish community of Jerusalem concerning Paul. If he were really teaching "all the Jews who are among the Gentiles to forsake Moses" as rumors had it, then he'd be invalidating circumcision for Jewish disciples as well as gentiles. That's why it is of enormous significance that immediately after the account of the Jerusalem Council the next chapter of Acts begins with Paul's circumcision of Timothy, son of a Jewish woman and a gentile man (Acts 16:1–3). Clearly in Paul's practice, circumcision still applies to messianic Jews.

The three key Torah practices of Paul—his pilgrimage to Jerusalem for Pentecost, his Nazirite vow, and his circumcision of Timothy—all prepare us for the Torah-positive act that he undertakes under James's instruction in Acts 21. This act demonstrates that Paul has always been and now remains a faithful Jew, observing the Torah and living in loyalty to his people (cf. Acts 25:8; 26:5; 28:17).[6]

---

6. The epistles of Paul align with this picture of him as a faithful Jew who remains Torah-observant throughout his life. For contemporary scholars who support this view, see Nanos and Zetterholm, eds., *Paul within Judaism*; Rudolph, *A Jew to the Jews*; Thiessen, *Paul and the Gentile Problem*.

These three Torah practices repeat three elements from Luke's infancy narrative: the annual pilgrimage to Jerusalem of Jesus' family, the Nazirite status of John the Baptist, and the circumcisions of John and Jesus. When these same three elements recur in Paul's narrative we can see how the rich Torah imagery of Luke's first two chapters now applies to the messianic era inaugurated by Jesus. The emphasis on Torah observance in the infancy narrative establishes a paradigm for the teaching and practice of Jesus and his disciples in the coming years. Moreover, this material isn't marginal to the author's concerns, but plays a prominent role in his whole narrative. Luke's appreciation for the distinctive character of the Jewish way of life attests to the enduring centrality of the Jewish people in his theological vision.

The Jerusalem Council

Nevertheless, many commentators believe that Luke-Acts views the Torah as no longer applicable in the new era inaugurated by Jesus. They often cite the ruling of the Jerusalem Council as evidence, a definitive "report of how the Gentile Church is declared free from the Law."[7] But more recently, other commentators have argued that the Council's ruling implies the exact opposite, so let's consider the ruling in more detail.

When Paul and Barnabas and the delegation from Antioch arrive in Jerusalem and report on their work among the gentiles, they're greeted warmly, "But some believers who belonged to the party of the Pharisees rose up and said, 'It is necessary to *circumcise them and to order them to keep the law of Moses*'" (Acts:15:5, emphasis added). After much debate the Council decides that gentile followers of Jesus need only abstain from "what has been sacrificed to idols, and from blood, and from what has been strangled, and from sexual immorality" (15:29; see also v. 20). One of the key factors in reaching this decision was a speech by Peter that is often interpreted as anti-Torah:

> God, who knows the heart, showed that he accepted them [Cornelius and his Gentile household] by giving the Holy Spirit to them, just as he did to us [Jews who received the Spirit on Pentecost]. He did not discriminate between us and them, for he *purified their hearts* by faith. Now then, why do you try to test God by putting on the necks of Gentiles a yoke that neither we nor our ancestors have been able to bear? No! We believe it is through the grace of

---

7. Conzelmann, *Theology of St. Luke*, 212.

our Lord Jesus that we are saved, just as they are. (Acts 15:8–11 NIV, emphasis added)

These gentiles received the same purification of heart as the Jewish disciples of Jesus did at Shavuot. And, as this terminology implies, this purification, or cleansing, of heart is identical to what God promised Israel through the prophet Ezekiel:

> I will sprinkle clean water on you, and you shall be clean from all your uncleannesses, and from all your idols I will cleanse you. And I will give you a new heart, and a new spirit I will put within you. And I will remove the heart of stone from your flesh and give you a heart of flesh. And I will put my Spirit within you, and cause you to walk in my statutes and be careful to obey my rules. (Ezek 36:25–27)

Peter's allusion to Ezekiel hints at what he means by "the yoke that neither we nor our ancestors have been able to bear" (v. 10b). He's not criticizing the Torah for being too burdensome, nor asserting that every individual Jew has failed to keep its commandments. Remember, Luke himself describes Zechariah and Elizabeth as "righteous before God, walking blamelessly in all the commandments and statutes of the Lord" (Luke 1:6). Likewise, the claim that the yoke refers to the Torah as an "unbearable burden" seems incompatible with the attitude of those "thousands" of messianic Jews who were "zealous for the Torah" (Acts 21:20). They appear to have embraced this supposedly unbearable burden with enthusiasm.

Peter may be echoing Ezekiel 36 to refer to Israel's *corporate* failure to keep the Torah adequately, both in the present and the past ("neither we nor our ancestors have been able to bear" its requirements). This *corporate failure* led to the exile that Ezekiel warns of. In response, God has acted through the Messiah to pour out the Holy Spirit—not to free the people of Israel from the burden of the Torah, but to empower them "to walk in my statutes and be careful to obey my rules" (Ezek 36:27). Now, by giving the same Spirit to the gentile believers in Jesus, God has shown that there is a place for them *as gentiles* within the community of God's people. These gentiles are to keep the "statutes" and "rules" of the Torah that are appropriate to them. Thus, Peter's words are not a critique of the Torah but instead a critique of Israel's corporate response, past and present, to the Torah.

After Peter denies that gentile believers in Jesus should be required to be circumcised and to keep all the provisions of the Torah incumbent upon Jews, he explains why: "We believe it is through the grace of our Lord Jesus that we are saved, just as they are" (Acts 15:11). The "yoke" that Israel failed to bear was the responsibility of fulfilling the Torah *as a condition for receiving salvation*. This is the "yoke" that some Torah-zealous Jewish disciples of Jesus seek to impose on new gentile disciples when they insist, "Unless you are circumcised according to the custom of Moses, *you cannot be saved*" (Acts 15:1). Peter sees a different logic at work in his encounter with Cornelius as interpreted through Ezekiel 36. The gift of the Spirit bestows the saving power of God and the blessing promised to Israel by purifying the heart and inspiring obedience to the commandments—for *both* Jews and gentiles (though in a differentiated manner). This grace of salvation is manifested in the gift of the Holy Spirit as a result of the work of Jesus and a response of faith in him.

Commentators traditionally treated the decision of the Jerusalem Council as a declaration of independence from the Torah for the (gentile) church. They often saw the call to avoid the four behaviors listed by the Council as no more than a pastoral recommendation aimed at promoting harmony between Jews and gentiles. Jewish members of the church would find the excluded behaviors to be repulsive, so the gentile believers were being asked to bear in love with some of the excessive scruples of their Jewish brothers and sisters.

More recently, however, scholars have been developing an alternate understanding of the Council's decree. In this view, the four prohibitions derive from commandments found in Leviticus 17–18 that apply to gentiles dwelling among the Israelites. James, speaking for the Council, concludes the ruling by stating, "For in every city, for generations past, Moses has had those who proclaim him, for he has been read aloud every Sabbath in the synagogues" (Acts 15:21). He means that, "Everyone who truly hears Moses knows that the decree expresses what Moses demands from Gentiles in order that they may live among Israelites."[8] Therefore, the significance of the Jerusalem Council in relation to the Torah is the exact opposite of what has usually been thought: "It is false to speak of the Gentiles as free from the law. The church, on the contrary, delivers the law to the Gentiles as Gentiles. Thus Luke succeeds in showing complete adherence to the law as well as the salvation of Gentiles as Gentiles."[9] Far from constituting a declaration of independence from the Torah, the Jerusalem Council actually demonstrates the Torah's enduring power in the age of the Messiah, applying it appropriately to both Jewish believers and gentile believers.

---

8. Jervell, *Luke and the People of God*, 144.
9. Jervell, *Luke and the People of God*, 144. Many current scholars support this view.

If the Jerusalem Council affirms the authority of the Torah for the lives of *gentile* followers of Jesus, how much more does it do so for the lives of *Jewish* followers! Or to flip that around, if Jewish Jesus-followers were no longer expected to keep the commandments of Torah, the question of Torah obedience for gentiles wouldn't even have been considered.[10] But Jewish members of the Jesus community are to maintain their observance of Torah, and the Jerusalem decree defines a form of Torah obedience for gentile members as well.

Peter's Vision Revisited

Before we conclude, let's return briefly to Peter's vision. Like the Jerusalem Council, it's frequently cited to support the idea that the resurrection of Jesus brings Torah observance to an end—or at least radically changes it—even for Jewish followers of Jesus. Peter sees a multitude of animals, clean and unclean according to the Torah, and hears a voice saying, "Rise, Peter; kill and eat" (Acts 10:13). It's a shocking command to a Jew accustomed to obeying the Torah, and we might well wonder what it means. F. F. Bruce offers a traditional interpretation that this vision was meant to remind Peter of Jesus' words "that it is not what goes into a man's stomach that defiles him, but what comes out of his heart" (Mark 7:14ff.).[11] Bruce goes on to claim that this saying in Mark "was in effect an abrogation of ceremonial food laws and much else of the same character, but it was not until much later, as a result of his experience on the roof at Joppa, that Peter appreciated this."[12] But Peter actually doesn't seem to "appreciate this" even then. Instead, he remains puzzled until he reaches a different conclusion: "God has shown me that I should not call any *person* common or unclean" (Acts 10:28b, emphasis added).

Peter boldly refuses three times to disobey the "ceremonial food laws" of the Torah, but when the Spirit tells him to go with the messengers from Cornelius "without hesitation," he quickly obeys (vv. 17, 20). When Peter arrives, he tells Cornelius and his household, "You yourselves know how unlawful it is for a Jew to associate with or to visit anyone of another nation, but God has shown me that I should not call any person common or unclean. So when I was sent for, I came without objection" (Acts 10:28–29a).

---

10. Wyschogrod, *Abraham's Promise*, 209.

11. For the view that Mark 7 does *not* abrogate the food laws of Torah, see Boyarin, *The Jewish Gospels*, 102–28; Kinzer, *Postmissionary Messianic Judaism*, 50–58; and Rudolph, "Jesus and the Food Laws."

12. Bruce, *Acts*, 206.

We should note that visiting the home of a gentile is not "unlawful" according to the Torah (as eating unclean food would be), but it did violate the standards of many Jews of the time.

Peter's vision, then, challenges the way his community has been "making a distinction" between Jews, who are "clean" and "holy," and gentiles, who are "unclean" and "common" (Acts 10:15, 28; 11:12; 15:8–9). But Cornelius and like-minded gentiles have repented of defiling practices like idolatry, sexual immorality, and murder, and should no longer be viewed as "unclean." Furthermore, when Cornelius and his household receive the Holy Spirit it shows that they have now been sanctified and rendered part of the holy people, and are no longer "common" either. This fact provides background for the Jerusalem Council of Acts 15. Nevertheless, the categories of clean/unclean and holy/common remain in effect. The status of gentiles who enter the messianic community is altered from "unclean" to "clean" and from "common" to "holy," as symbolized in Peter's vision by the change in status of unclean animals. There is no evidence in the narrative, however, that this symbolic change implied an abolition of the dietary laws of the Torah.

All this adds up to a compelling refutation of the claim that Peter's vision in Acts 10 entails the abolition of the dietary laws of the Torah. When viewed in the wider context of Luke and Acts—in which the Torah plays such a prominent role and the distinctive customs of the Jewish people are repeatedly affirmed—this standard traditional interpretation lacks the slightest trace of plausibility.

Conclusion

Just as Luke affirms the enduring significance of the temple in a way that upholds the lasting significance of Jerusalem (as we saw in chapters 4 and 5), so he affirms the enduring place of the Torah in a way that underlines its ongoing connection with Jewish national life (as we've discussed here in chapters 7 and 8). As Jacob Jervell writes, "Luke is concerned about the law *because it is Israel's law*. . . . The law is to him not essentially the moral law, but *the mark of distinction between Jews and non-Jews. The law is the sign of Israel as the people of God.*"[13] Just as the Temple Mount remains a holy place when the temple building has disappeared, so also the distinctive Jewish national customs of the Torah—circumcision, Sabbath, holidays, and dietary laws—continue to define the identity of the Jewish people even when the sacrificial service is defunct.

13. Jervell, *Luke and the People of God*, 137. Emphasis added.

Throughout Luke-Acts, then, the Torah remains in effect in the age inaugurated by the death and resurrection of Jesus. The Torah retains its significance as a sign of Israel's calling as a people. Therefore, Luke draws our attention to the faithful Torah practice of Jesus and his followers. And since they treat the Torah as authoritative it must also remain authoritative for the Jewish people as a whole. The Jerusalem Council reveals that the Torah applies, although in distinct ways, to gentile believers in Jesus as well. Therefore, the death and resurrection of Jesus and the gift of the Spirit have not ushered the messianic community into a new Torah-free zone. Much less have they invalidated the Torah for all Jews. Levine and Witherington note, "Luke presents Jesus as fully embedded, and at home, in the Judaism of his time,"[14] and one can say the same thing about Jesus' Jewish followers, particularly in Jerusalem.

How does this portrayal of Torah observance fit into the larger context of the besorah? Practice of the Torah binds the Jews together as a people, ensuring that there will be a Jerusalem in the final days that can cry out, "Blessed is the one who comes in the name of the Lord." Luke's universal vision for all nations remains rooted in Israel's particular national hopes based on the Torah and the Prophets. The particular calling of the Jewish people is never lost, even within the ever-expanding horizon of the universal community of Jesus' followers.

Our analysis of Luke and Acts has revealed much about the besorah and its message concerning the resurrected Messiah and his relationship to the Jewish people and the land of promise. The Jewish people, of course, have corporately failed to recognize this relationship. But we also must note that the historical Jesus-community, the church, failed to absorb Luke's message regarding the Jewish people. Instead, it embraced a gospel that must be seen as fractured and incomplete because of this failure. In our final two chapters we will trace signs of healing of both this fracture and the ancient estrangement between the church and the Jewish people. Our focus will not be on the theological course-correction taking place within Christian thought today, but instead on two paradigm-shifting events: first, the Jewish return to Zion; and second, the restoration of a Jesus-believing remnant within the wider Jewish community. Both events are signs in modern history that the fractured besorah and the fractured community of God's people are being healed.

---

14. Levine and Witherington, *The Gospel of Luke*, 73.

Part Three

The Besorah, Present and Future

Chapter Nine

The Return to Zion in Light of the Besorah

Joseph trudged along a dusty path through the rocky hills and valleys of Dothan, searching for his ten older brothers who were tending the family's flock. Joseph was seventeen and his brothers were all grown men, some already with children of their own, but their father, Jacob, had sent Joseph to check on them: "Go now, see if it is well with your brothers and with the flock, and bring me word." Tracking down the brothers turned out to be a long and hard task, but Joseph wore the richly ornamented tunic, the sign of favor his father had given him, the whole way.

Finally, he spotted his brothers and their encampment, and they saw him. When a couple of his brothers rushed out toward him, he expected a hug of greeting. Instead, they grabbed him with rough hands, stripped off his tunic, shoved him to the edge of a pit near the camp, and threw him in. Joseph cried out to his brothers, begging them to pull him out of the pit, but they left him there until they finally spotted a passing band of traders bound for Egypt and sold Joseph to them.

Joseph endured long years of bondage and imprisonment in Egypt, first as a household slave and then locked up in a dungeon. Finally, through another prisoner, he got the chance to interpret a mysterious set of dreams that was troubling Pharaoh. His interpretation and evident wisdom so impressed the king that he elevated Joseph out of bondage to his right hand, to help prepare Egypt for the seven-year famine that the dreams foretold.

Joseph became second only to Pharaoh, in charge of the whole agricultural system of Egypt. When the years of hunger arrived, he was in charge of the food distribution, skillfully saving the lives of the Egyptians as well as surrounding peoples. Finally, Joseph's brothers showed up in his court, seeking food, but didn't recognize him. Rather than simply selling them the food they needed, Joseph tested his brothers until he detected enough remorse among them that he was willing to reveal himself.

> Then Joseph could not control himself before all those who stood by him. He cried, "Make everyone go out from me." So no one stayed with him when Joseph made himself known to his brothers. And he wept aloud, so that the Egyptians heard it, and the household of Pharaoh heard it. And Joseph said to his brothers, "I am Joseph! Is my father still alive?" But his brothers could not answer him, for they were dismayed at his presence.
>
> So Joseph said to his brothers, "Come near to me, please." And they came near. And he said, "I am your brother, Joseph, whom you sold into Egypt. And now do not be distressed or angry with yourselves because you sold me here, for God sent me before you to preserve life." (Gen 45:1–5)

The story of Joseph and his brothers is a prime example of a recurring pattern in biblical stories. Over and over, God works to bring redemption despite and even through the evil deeds of human beings. It's fitting therefore that Stephen gives the story of Joseph a prominent place in his speech before the Jewish council (Acts 7:9–16). As in Joseph's story, God will work redemptively through the evil actions of the Jewish leaders of Stephen's day, to bring salvation not only to the nations but also to the Jewish people itself. Luke's writings can't include that happy ending as an accomplished event, but they do point beyond themselves to a coming day when a new Joseph will finally be recognized by his brothers and bring salvation.

Luke assumes that human beings make their own decisions, and are held accountable for those decisions. Even when God brings good out of evil, as with the crucifixion of Jesus, the martyrdom of Stephen, and the destruction of the temple, Luke acknowledges the evil at play in those events and the suffering it causes (Luke 23:27; Acts 8:2; Luke 13:34; 19:41–44). Human beings aren't marionettes, and history is not a puppet show with a controlling deity hovering over the stage. Human beings act freely, and often badly. Luke accepts this fact, but he also affirms God's power to bring good out of evil, and to effect his good purposes despite—and even through—the tragic twists and turns of history. The story of Joseph makes it clear that the God of Israel is the Lord of history, even when his presence is clouded. His plan for history is evident in Luke and Acts, and we must ask how it shapes the later history of Jesus' followers and the Jewish people. How does the big story of Jesus the Messiah and his early followers shed light on the later, often troubled, story of those related to him by flesh and/or by Spirit?

Fractured Community, Fractured Besorah

The early community of Jesus' followers received and transmitted the essentials of what became the Christian faith: the Jewish scriptures; the teachings and life story of the crucified and risen Messiah; the good news he extended to all nations through his apostles; a way of life founded on the pillars of New Testament scripture, community, the Lord's Supper, and prayer (Acts 2:42); and the hope that Jesus would return to establish the kingdom of God. The early Jesus-community guarded this rich treasure and kept it safe for generations through the fierce storms of history, and we should be grateful for her faithful stewardship.

But the community lost sight of other crucial elements of the besorah. It soon dismissed the significance of the earthly Jerusalem and the land of Israel. It denied or downplayed the enduring covenantal status of the Jewish people and its priestly calling on behalf of all nations. It nullified the Torah as Israel's defining national constitution. In keeping with this hostility to Jews and Judaism outside her walls, the community also suppressed any Jewish expression within her walls. It thereby lost its own character as a community uniting Jews and gentiles.[1] Its vision of salvation became so spiritualized and individualized that it lost the New Testament hope for a transformed earth peopled by resurrected nations.[2]

These failures helped fracture the besorah portrayed in Luke and Acts. The Jewish people as a whole contributed to this fracturing when they refused or ignored the heart of the besorah, namely, the message concerning the crucified and risen Messiah. As a result, the coming of God's kingdom was delayed, and Israel's exile grew more intense. But as the dust settled following the failure of a second Jewish revolt against Rome (135 CE), and heirs of the Pharisees gained in power and influence within the Jewish community, an amazing thing began to happen. Over the next few centuries, the very elements of the besorah that the emerging church had abandoned were preserved as central aspects of the Jewish worldview. The new rabbinic Judaism that arose after the second Jewish revolt preserved

---

1. On the early history of these developments, see Kinzer, *Postmissionary Messianic Judaism*, 181–212.

2. See Wright, *Surprised By Hope*; Farrow, *Ascension Theology*.

the Torah as Israel's national constitution. It preserved a vision of the earth as the place of redemption and renewal; the prophetic significance of the land of Israel, Jerusalem, and the Temple Mount; and the unchanging bond between the God of Israel, the Messiah of Israel, and the descendants of Abraham, Isaac, and Jacob.

We are not the first to claim that the people of God were fractured when the Jesus-community and the Jewish people became estranged. But traditionally Christians have blamed this fracture entirely on the Jewish rejection of the gospel. In light of our previous chapters, that view seems simplistic. In reality, the besorah itself became fractured, as each side rejected that part of the besorah that the other side preserved. The two sides need each other, then, and the besorah needs both in order to come to completion.

Once we recognize the besorah as a proclamation about Jesus the Messiah *and* about the Jewish people, we can discern the marks of God's plan in the history of the two communities. In his resurrection as the firstfruits of Israel's coming rebirth, Jesus establishes an unbreakable bond with the Jewish people as a whole. We are not speaking here about individual salvation, the issue of life in the age to come. We are speaking of the Messiah's ongoing relationship with the Jewish people as a whole, which is an inherent part of the besorah.

In his death on the cross, Jesus anticipates and bears in himself the punishment that will fall on Jerusalem forty years later. In this way, he transforms that event, rendering it not only a punishment for the rebellion of past generations but also a purifying fire that can bring renewal. The Roman destruction of Jerusalem sets the stage for renewal by ending the reign of the priestly aristocrats who were most responsible for the execution of Jesus and the persecution of his early disciples. It prepares the way for the influence of the Pharisees, which will shape Jewish life and tradition in the coming centuries. The risen Messiah remains unrecognized within this tradition, like Joseph the son of Jacob, who acts for the welfare of his family while keeping his true identity hidden. But Jewish tradition derives its power from the hope of a messianic future—a hope kept alive by the veiled Messiah whose resurrection guarantees that he will one day "restore the kingdom to Israel" (Acts 1:6).

According to this reading of Luke and of the subsequent events of history, we receive the besorah in its fullness only when we see its truth transmitted through *both* Christian and Jewish traditions. The bad news is that the besorah, like the people of God itself, suffered fracture. The good news is that the besorah is still accessible in its fullness and integrity—but only through a restored partnership between the two fragments of that fractured community.

As in the story of Joseph that Stephen told at his trial, and as in many incidents in the narrative of Luke and Acts, God works with the flawed material presented to him by human failure in order to bring good out of evil. His people and his message are in fragments, but those fragments have endured, and the pieces can still be reassembled. Surprisingly, the Jewish religious tradition is essential not only to sustain the identity of the Jewish people but also to restore the besorah of Jesus the Messiah. The preservation of the Jewish people and the Jewish tradition are thus a gift of God for the Christian community and for the entire world. And, despite the many hardships Jews have suffered at the hands of Christians, the enduring witness of the church will also in the end prove to be a precious gift to the Jewish people.

We've focused so far on God's work in preserving the besorah in the distant past. But what about recent history? What we are to make of the extraordinary events of modern Jewish history? Two of these events are associated with features of the besorah as we've presented it, and both are keys in bringing the besorah to completion. The first is the Jewish return to Zion, which was not enacted primarily in the realm of religion, but on the political, diplomatic, and military stage of the secular world. We'll consider it in the rest of this chapter. The other historical development is quieter and more confined to the religious world, but no less momentous—the rise of Messianic Judaism, which is the focus of our concluding chapter.

A Biblical View of Zionism

For simplicity, we'll discuss the Jewish return to Zion under the term "Zionism," the movement dedicated to establishing a "national home for the Jewish people" in the land promised to the biblical patriarchs and matriarchs.[3] With

---

3. This language is drawn from the Balfour Declaration adopted by the British government in 1917. In this text, addressed by the British Foreign Secretary, Arthur James Balfour, to Lord Rothschild, the following is conveyed: "I have much pleasure in conveying to you, on behalf of His Majesty's Government, the following declaration of sympathy with Jewish Zionist aspirations.... His Majesty's Government view with favour the establishment in Palestine of a national home for the Jewish people...." The vagueness of the phrase "national home" was one of its advantages in 1917—it could refer to a state,

the establishment of the Jewish state in 1948, Zionism refers to a movement that views this "national home" as an essential part of Jewish identity and destiny, and aims to support and strengthen Jewish life in the land.[4]

Contrary to the claims of some critics, Zionism is not the product of nineteenth-century European nationalism. Its roots go back to the Bible itself, and are evident in the prayers of the Jewish people from earliest times. Prayer for Israel's return to the land of its ancestors occupies a central position in the collection of petitions recited by observant Jews three times daily; the formal grace recited after every meal; the mystical prayer that welcomes the Sabbath each Friday evening; the blessings after the weekly reading from the Prophets; and the Jewish wedding service. The saddest day in the Jewish year is the Ninth of Av, when Jews remember the destruction of Jerusalem by the Babylonians (in 586 BCE) and the Romans (in 70 CE). The Passover Seder and the Day of Atonement both conclude with the same ecstatic words of hope: "Next year in Jerusalem!" Throughout the centuries after the fall of Jerusalem, this hope was sustained not only by prayer but also by the continual presence of a Jewish community in the land of Israel.[5]

Given this history, it's not surprising that traditional Jewish religious practice and the study of traditional Jewish religious texts have thrived in contemporary Israel. While most of the founders were "secular Jews," today a majority of Israeli Jews no longer identify with that label. Israeli Jews speak and write the language of the Jewish literary classics, order their public and private lives according to the rhythm of the Jewish religious holidays, and live in cities with streets named after Jewish religious icons like Hillel and Maimonides. Even those who identify as "secular" often take an interest in Talmud, Midrash, Kabbalah, or Hasidism. Israel is unquestionably modern, but its ties to traditional Jewish life are manifold. Zionism is a modern movement, but it is also an expression of values, longings, and utopian dreams cherished by Jews for millennia.

How then are we to understand this movement in light of the besorah? As we've seen, the besorah envisions the restoration of Jewish life in the land of Israel as an essential fruit of the resurrection of Israel's messianic king, Yeshua. Against the backdrop of this besorah the

---

but it could also refer to another form of national existence.

4. "To be a Zionist is to be personally committed or loyal to the existence of the State of Israel as a Jewish polity" (Novak, *Zionism and Judaism*, 1).

5. For an extended treatment of the history of Jewish presence in the land of Israel, see Kinzer, *Jerusalem Crucified*, 241–49.

re-establishment of Jewish national life in the land, with Jerusalem as its capital, has prophetic significance. Could this be a decisive outworking of the divine plan in history? Might it be just as much a part of God's purposes as the flourishing of Jewish life after the fall of Jerusalem, or even as the spread of the besorah itself?

It's clear from our reading of Luke and Acts that Jewish life is to be restored in the land of Israel, but this vision doesn't necessarily require that restoration to happen in this age, before the Messiah's return. Instead, one might still defend the view that was common in Jewish thinking before the modern era: only *after* the Messiah comes in power will Israel return to the land and renew there its national life. This view led many traditional Jews to minimize or even oppose the Zionist movement in its early years. But now that Jewish national life in the land has revived *before* the Messiah's coming, we must ask whether this historical development fits the besorah, even if the besorah doesn't strictly demand it. And clearly it does fit.

Some texts from Luke and Acts presume a form of Jewish national life in the land before Jesus' return—especially those crucial texts that *anticipate* (Luke 13:35), *describe* (Luke 19:28–46), or *look back* (Acts 1:6–12) to Jesus' entry into Jerusalem on Palm Sunday. In the first of these texts, Jesus grieves over the holy city and concludes with words drawn from Psalm 118: "you will not see me until you say, 'Blessed is he who comes in the name of the Lord!'" As we noted earlier, in this passage Jesus looks ahead to his entry into Jerusalem before his crucifixion (Luke 19:28–46) as a prophetic sign. The enthusiastic acclamation by his own disciples at that time prophetically represents the welcome the entire Jewish population of the holy city will offer when he returns. Since Jerusalem's repentance is a condition for the messianic restoration (Acts 3:19–21), we should see the city's readiness to welcome Messiah as a sign of repentance and a catalyst for his return.

The prophetic character of Palm Sunday is also confirmed in Acts 1:6–12, where the disciples are told that Jesus "will come in the same way as you saw him go into heaven." As we previously noted, this implies that Jesus will *descend* to the Mount of Olives, the same place from which he *ascended* in this scene from Acts. Earlier, a few days before his final Passover, Jesus had begun his triumphal entry on the Mount of Olives (Luke 19:29), as an indication that the triumphal entry to come would commence from the same location (in accordance with Zechariah 14:4–5). All this suggests that in some sense Jerusalem must be a Jewish city *before* Jesus returns to it, just as it was when he presented himself to it before his crucifixion.

Part Three: The Besorah, Present and Future

For disciples of Jesus today, who live after the establishment of a Jewish state, the question of Zionism's relationship to biblical prophecy is unavoidable. But it's striking that this question first became a matter of lively discussion among Christians centuries before Zionism emerged as an explicit program among Jews. Theologian Gerald McDermott recounts how Anglo-American Protestants of the seventeenth century first began to discuss an expectation of Jewish return to the land.[6] Commenting on Increase Mather's *The Mystery of Israel's Salvation* (1669), McDermott states, "One of Mather's innovations was to charge that the Jews would regain their ancient land *before* they would convert. It would be only 'after the Israelites shall be returned to their own Land again' that the Holy Spirit would be poured out on them."[7] This view eventually became widespread in Anglo-American Protestant circles, and that movement was especially favorable to the Zionist project once it was launched in the nineteenth century. Our reading of Luke and Acts suggests that this theological perspective was not a fluke, but a response to the illuminating work of the Holy Spirit.

We can note then four weighty pieces of evidence relevant to a biblical assessment of Zionism and the Jewish state:

1. the restoration of Jewish life in the land of Israel is a fundamental component of the besorah;

2. an expectation that this restoration would occur before Messiah's return lines up with key texts in Luke and Acts;

3. some Christians began to understand the New Testament as teaching such a Jewish national restoration centuries before the emergence of the Zionist movement; and

4. the Zionist movement itself, whether explicitly religious or not, arose from the matrix of Jewish religious tradition that was sustained in history by God's design.

These four pieces of evidence lead us to conclude that the establishment of a Jewish national home in the land of Israel—that is, the success of the Zionist enterprise—was itself ordained by God's design, and constitutes a historical fact of enormous theological significance.

A grim fifth factor confirms this assessment. The establishment of the Jewish state occurred just three years after the conclusion of World

6. McDermott, "A History of Christian Zionism," 59–61.
7. McDermott, "A History of Christian Zionism," 61.

War II. In the twelve years of Nazi rule, the Jewish people suffered the most devastating catastrophe in its long history of persecution and martyrdom. One out of every three Jews in the world was murdered. As a result of this modern horror, many Christians began to revise their views concerning the Jewish people, and to discard the notion that Jewish suffering could be attributed solely to Jewish sin. Some Christians proposed that the Shoah (Holocaust)—and the centuries of persecution that made it possible—revealed a profound connection between the Jewish people and Jesus the Messiah. In a mysterious fashion, the persecuted Jewish people were participants in the suffering of Jesus.[8]

We have repeatedly argued that the besorah of the life, death, and resurrection of Jesus the Messiah includes the life, death (or exile), and resurrection/restoration of Jerusalem and the Jewish people. The besorah reflects an unbreakable bond between Jesus and his own Jewish people. If the Shoah reveals the bond between the Jewish people and the death of Jesus, then the establishment of the Jewish State three years later likewise reveals the bond between the Jewish people and the resurrection of Israel's Messiah on the third day.

Just as "modern antisemitism was the catalyst for the rise of Jewish nationalism rather than its cause," so the Shoah was the catalyst for the establishment of the Jewish State rather than its cause.[9] But it was an effective catalyst, and the connection between the Shoah and the birth of the State of Israel is no historical accident. The partial communal death of the Shoah helped prepare for a partial communal rebirth in 1948. Together, these two events made the 1900s "the most dramatic century in the dramatic history of the Jewish people."[10] If we believe the Jewish people remain chosen by God, then the two-act drama of that century cannot be spiritually insignificant.

---

8. For examples of such theological perspectives, see Kinzer, *Postmissionary Messianic Judaism*, 226–30, which refers to the comments of Edith Stein, Pope John XXIII, Clemens Thoma, Thomas F. Torrance, and Joel Marcus.

9. Ottolenghi, "A National Home," 59. See also the words of Martin Buber in 1946: "Modern political Zionism . . . was only prompted and intensified, but not caused by modern anti-Semitism" (Buber, *A Land of Two Peoples*, 181).

10. Shavit, *My Promised Land*, 412.

Part Three: The Besorah, Present and Future

A Theological Objection to Zionism

Christian critics of Zionism raise an objection that deserves comment. As one critic puts it, Christian Zionists "fail to point out the indisputable biblical motif that land promise is strictly tied to covenant fidelity."[11] Israel has a "right" to the land only so long as it remains faithful to its God. Moreover, such critics would claim, once expelled from the land for its unfaithfulness, Israel's return is promised only on condition of its repentance (Deut 4:26–31; 30:1–5). Did the Zionist movement arise as an expression of such renewed covenant fidelity? Was this movement not dominated by secular Jews who rejected the authority of the Torah and who often lacked even minimal faith in God?

Such critics of Christian Zionism have a point. Deuteronomy does make faithfulness to the covenant a condition for Israel's national restoration. It is a mistake to view Zionism as a strictly secular movement and the State of Israel as a strictly secular state, but it's true that neither one can be seen as primarily religious in nature. Furthermore, like all political movements and states, this movement and this state may reasonably be charged with acts of injustice that violate the ethical demands of God's covenant.[12] So then, do these two facts undermine the claim that the Zionist movement and the Jewish state are in some way a fulfilment of the words of Israel's prophets?

To answer that question, we need to recognize two distinct strands of prophetic teaching about Israel's return from exile. As noted, Deuteronomy requires Israel's repentance as a condition for its national restoration.[13] But another strand of prophetic teaching approaches the topic quite differently. In Ezekiel 36, for example, God restores Israel "for the sake of my holy name," and "not for your sake, O house of Israel" (vv. 21–23; 32). God acts not because Israel has fulfilled a condition of the covenant, but because God's name is tied to Israel and Israel's desolate state brings dishonor to God's name. Ezekiel describes an act of restoration that *begins* with a return to the land (v. 24), and then follows up with a transformation that enables Israel to obey God's ordinances and live in a renewed covenant relationship with him (vv. 25–28). For Ezekiel, Israel's repentance is a *result* of God's

---

11. Burge, *Jesus and the Land*, 123.

12. "Christian Zionists who champion the prophetic fulfillments of modern Israel must likewise be ready to apply the prophetic ethical demands of these same writers" (Burge, *Jesus and the Land*, 124).

13. This viewpoint is also found in prophetic texts such as Jeremiah 31:18–20.

restorative work rather than its *condition* (v. 31). Moreover, Israel's repentance *follows* rather than precedes its return to the land. A similar scenario appears in Isaiah 40–66, where God's forgiveness and redemption serve as the motive for Israel's repentance, rather than its result.

If Luke expects a return of Israel to its land before it welcomes Jesus with the words "Blessed is he who comes in the name of the Lord," then his writings may combine these two strands of the prophetic tradition. First God acts (in accordance with the teaching of Ezekiel and Isaiah) to partially restore Israel to its own land. Only afterward does God give Israel a new heart, opening the way for the full restoration of Israel, and all creation with it (Acts 3:19–21). This sequence of restoration brings together not only the full array of Lukan texts, but also diverse strands in Torah and the Prophets. From this perspective, nothing prevents us from seeing Zionism as an integral yet imperfect expression of God's plan at work in human history.

A Biblical Response to Zionism

How does this besorah-based understanding of the Jewish return to Zion shed light on realities in the Middle East today? In this section we're not advocating any particular political program or policy. Our aim is to clarify the practical implications of our positive assessment of Zionism in light of the besorah. To provide this clarification we address five questions that might be raised by those seeking to understand what biblical support for Zionism looks like in the real world today.

Question #1: Does a positive biblical view of Zionism mean that the Jewish state of today is the beginning of the redeemed order of the world?

We believe that the rebirth of Jewish national life in the land of Israel is a divine work with prophetic implications. But this doesn't mean that the *State* of Israel should be regarded in exactly the same way. The State of Israel is a political arrangement for the ordering of Jewish national life in this age; it serves the nation or people, but is not identical to it. The Jewish state is an instrument, not an end in itself, and could take a variety of different forms and still fulfill its purpose. In the world-to-come, the reign of the Messiah will heal the *nations* (Rev 21:24, 26; 22:2), but will end *states* as we now know them, including the State of Israel, by establishing a *kingdom* in its place (Acts 1:6).

Part Three: The Besorah, Present and Future

Question #2: Does a positive view of Zionism mean that the State of Israel must retain sovereignty over all the land it now controls?

We should not exaggerate the continuity between this broken world and the redeemed world to come. If the State of Israel were the first stage of redemption, destined to change gradually into the messianic kingdom (the issue in Question #1), then one might justly argue against it making any territorial concessions. But the State of Israel is best understood as a preliminary sign of the messianic kingdom to come. The life of the Jewish people in the land of Israel constitutes a sign pointing beyond the exile to the coming kingdom of God—yet the exile continues, even for Jews in the land. We will only see the true end of exile when God steps into human history to establish his kingdom. In the meantime, the State of Israel is free to make territorial concessions if it determines that they would advance the welfare of its people and promote the good of its region.

Question #3: Does a positive view of Zionism mean that the State of Israel must retain total sovereignty over a politically united city of Jerusalem?

Our answers to questions #1 and #2 underline the provisional character of the Jewish state in this age, and this character applies to Jerusalem as well. Any political arrangement concerning Jerusalem must account for the city's unique role as the center not only of the Jewish state but also of the Jewish people throughout the world. Administration of the city must always enable Jewish life to thrive there, and assure freedom of access to Jewish holy sites. But once those conditions are met, the Jewish state could negotiate any number of possible political arrangements that would be compatible with the besorah. Disciples of Jesus should not try to limit the state's right to develop solutions to complex political and diplomatic problems. It is unlikely that the State of Israel would agree to any political arrangement that compromises its sovereignty over Jerusalem, and we're not arguing for or against that position. We merely seek to define the boundaries of permissible political options in light of the besorah of the crucified and resurrected Messiah.

Question #4: Does a positive view of Zionism mean that the State of Israel should claim ownership of the Temple Mount and seek to rebuild the temple?

All Jews treat the Temple Mount as the holiest place on earth. For most of the past nineteen centuries Jews have been unable to worship on the mount itself. Instead, they have expressed their devotion to it by praying at the Western Wall, part of the mount's supporting structure, although at times governing authorities prevented even that. After the Jewish state took control of the Old City of Jerusalem in 1967, rabbinic rulings prohibited Jews from going up to the Temple Mount itself to avoid profaning the holy place.

Whether or not a Jewish temple adorns the site, the place itself retains its unique character. This quality is reflected in Luke's portrayal of the mount. Therefore, disciples of Jesus should affirm the enduring connection between the Jewish people and the Temple Mount, and defend Jewish rights of worship at the Western Wall.[14]

Jews have traditionally believed that the temple would be rebuilt by the Messiah, and therefore Jewish longing for the temple was enfolded in a greater longing for the messianic era. This approach lines up with the New Testament orientation to the temple and the messianic era. But after Israel took control of the Old City of Jerusalem, a few Israelis began to think that the temple should be rebuilt *now*, before the coming of the Messiah.[15] This program has gained momentum in recent years and, while still marginal, has a growing number of Israeli adherents. Of course, this program also would likely entail destroying some or all of the Muslim religious sites that currently reside on the Temple Mount. That act would dishonor structures held sacred by a billion Muslims around the world, isolate the Jewish state even from its allies, and likely ignite a violent conflict with the Palestinians and other Muslim neighbors. Since building the temple before the coming of the Messiah is required by neither Jewish tradition nor the besorah, this is not a course of action that disciples of Jesus need support or applaud.

Question #5: Does a positive view of Zionism mean that disciples of Jesus should always support the policies and actions of the government of the State of Israel?

In contrast with the previous four questions, the answer to this one should be obvious: if disciples of Jesus need not approve of every policy and

---

14. This may appear to be a non-controversial statement. That this is not the case is demonstrated by an April 15, 2016 UNESCO resolution that spoke of the "Al-Haram Al Sharif" (the "noble sanctuary") solely as a "Muslim holy site of worship," and referred to the Western Wall as "Al-Buraq Plaza" (with "Western Wall Plaza" mentioned parenthetically, in quotation marks). The resolution ignored the biblical connection between the Jewish people and the Temple Mount. See https://www.haaretz.com/israel-news/full-text-of-unesco-s-resolution-on-jerusalem-1.5450617 (accessed 6/28/20).

15. See Shavit, *Promised Land*, 215–17.

action undertaken by the governing authorities of their own religious communities, of course they need not do so in regards to the Jewish state. And if traditional Jews who consider themselves Zionists don't believe they're obligated to always support policies of the State of Israel—and none to our knowledge do—then why should followers of Jesus be required to do so?

Instead of unquestioning support for everything the Israeli government does, our attitude should be one of solidarity with the people who elected the particular government in power and whose continued assent provides it with legitimacy. A disciple of the Jewish Messiah cannot retreat to a neutral posture in thinking about Middle-East politics, standing at an equal distance from all parties and giving the benefit of the doubt to none. Instead, we stand in solidarity with the people of Israel, even if we must at times disagree with specific Israeli policies.

It's worth reviewing the reasons for such solidarity:

1. All disciples of Jesus—gentile as well as Jewish—are bound to the Jewish people as brothers and sisters.

2. Disciples of Jesus should view the overall Zionist enterprise as a miracle of God's Spirit in history, tied intimately to the besorah. Just as we cannot consider the ovens of Auschwitz apart from the cross of the Messiah, so we cannot consider the life of this nation apart from his resurrection.

3. Disciples of Jesus should be vividly aware that the diabolical forces that culminated in the Shoah have not been banished by its manifest horrors. The spirit of anti-Semitism is identical to the spirit of anti-Christ, and it is alive and well today in both guises. Not all anti-Zionism serves as a cloak for anti-Semitism, but some of it surely does.

We stand in solidarity with Israel even when we must disagree with specific Israeli policies. We begin from a position of faith in the work of God in history. Like any government entangled in a web of inter-national, inter-cultural, inter-ethnic, and inter-religious hostility and violence, the government of Israel has committed and will continue to commit misdeeds of varying degrees of gravity. But doesn't this reality echo the biblical narrative itself, in which God weaves his own redemptive tapestry out of our frayed and tangled cords? We can acknowledge the misdeeds of the Jewish state and pray and labor for their correction, even as we also admit our limited capacity to discern the precise outlines of God's design in current affairs. At the same time, we can place our hope in the God who works redemptively in history, as he did in turning the sin of Joseph's brothers into salvation for both the sons of Jacob and the nations of the world.

Conclusion

Within the broad framework of Zionism, there is ample room for debate and disagreement concerning the practical details. We are not raising our five questions to establish a political position, but to provide some theological parameters within which advocates of the right, left, and center can all work out their positions. But as we consider these parameters we shouldn't lose sight of the most amazing thing—that we are able to ask these questions at all. There's a restored Jewish presence—large and thriving—in the ancient homeland, and it's not hard to recognize that this is part of the prophetic scheme of history. God is in this restoration, and the stage is set for Jerusalem to recognize and embrace its long-hidden Messiah, just as Joseph's brothers recognized and embraced him after long years of estrangement. The result of both moments of recognition is blessing for Israel and the entire world.

The turning-point in the story of Joseph and his brothers arrives when he reveals himself to them, saying, "I am Joseph! . . . Come near to me, please," and the brothers come near (Gen 45:3–4). In like manner, Messiah Yeshua will present himself again to his brothers—to Jerusalem—after his return to the Mount of Olives, and his brothers will fully recognize him with the words, "Blessed is he who comes in the name of the Lord." Joseph was estranged from his family for more than two decades; Yeshua for nearly two millennia. But finally in our days Jerusalem's words of welcome are possible with a restored Jewish population in the city. Let's not take the momentous possibilities of our own times for granted, but instead be alert to the day in which we live, which holds unexpected promise for Israel and the nations.

We are now ready to consider an additional amazing sign of God's activity in our days—a sign that is intimately connected to the prophetic besorah and a hint that its fulfilment is at hand—the restoration of a remnant for Messiah Yeshua within the Jewish people.

Chapter Ten

Messianic Judaism and Restoration of the Besorah

IN OUR EARLY SOJOURN at Templo Cristiano, Jane and I, and our Jewish hippie friends Andrew and Connie, learned that the Book of Acts is for today. At that time we understood this truth to mean that the power and gifts of the Holy Spirit were still present and available to all followers of Jesus. We spoke about the "baptism in the Holy Spirit" as an initiation into the power and gifts of the Spirit, but we hadn't yet experienced it. During this period, we also learned more about repentance, not just as a one-time part of accepting Jesus, but also as an ongoing work of the Spirit in our lives. Jane and I realized (a bit belatedly) that we needed to get married and we did. We dedicated ourselves and our two little boys to the Lord and the two of us were baptized, immersed in a big stock tank by Brother Limas (introduced in the Preface). That same evening, a few months after our initial encounter with Jesus, we were finally baptized in the Holy Spirit. We received power from on high, not just to believe in Jesus, but to actually follow him.

Later we came to realize that the axiom of Acts-for-today would also apply to its picture of a thriving Jewish remnant, living in the heart of the Jewish world, "zealous for Torah," and faithful to Jesus (Acts 21:20). Many of us Jewish counter-culture types who had become followers of Jesus spent a few years figuring out exactly how being Jewish and believing in Jesus— which most Jews and Christians alike thought were incompatible—actually fit together. The picture in Acts was our guiding light. We weren't sure how to think of ourselves, or even what to call ourselves. We started out as Hebrew Christians, and then Jewish Christians, meaning that we were Christians with the modifier "Jewish" attached to our label. But before long we began to hear the phrases "Messianic Jew" and "Messianic Judaism" more often, and finally began to apply them to ourselves. This meant that we were

Jews with the modifier "Messianic" attached. Jesus—whom we soon started to call "Yeshua"—was Messiah and Lord, and the central reality of our lives, and we embraced him as Jews. We weren't Christians who somehow remembered that we were, or once had been, Jewish; we were Jews who had received the revelation that Yeshua was our Messiah, Israel's Messiah. And we sought to live our lives accordingly.

It has taken years to fill out what "living our lives accordingly" means in detail—and we're still filling it out. This book about the besorah as good news for Jerusalem and the Jewish people is a big part of that process. When my old friend Andrew and I responded to the gospel on that night on the Mesa long ago, we knew it was all about the crucifixion and resurrection of Jesus. This message transformed our lives, but we didn't yet see how it applied to us specifically as Jews, or to our Jewish people. Much less did we realize what Mark Kinzer and I are now presenting in this book—that in his crucifixion and resurrection Jesus is not only enacting my own individual death to sin and resurrection into new life, but also Israel's death of exile and its resurrection in the age to come. The resurrection of Messiah doesn't displace the hope of Israel promised in all of our prophets, but is the means by which that hope will be accomplished.

So, we called ourselves Messianic Jews, members of a remnant-community for Messiah in the midst of our people Israel. We remained loyal to our Jewish people and to our life and tradition, even as we remained loyal to Yeshua as our Messiah. Just as surely as the Jewish return to Zion is evidence of God's work in current history, as we saw in our last chapter, so is the existence of this Messianic Jewish remnant. These two modern historical phenomena are of equal relevance to the besorah, and both are essential to its fulfilment. To understand the relationship and strategic importance of these two movements, let's take a brief look at the history of Messianic Judaism in relation to the history of Zionism.

Messianic Jewish Exile

Jerusalem in Luke and Acts is the city of God and the city of Messiah, with the Temple Mount at its heart. It is the holiest point in the land of promise, the most precious part that represents the whole. And for Luke, Jerusalem is also the city of Torah-faithful Jews devoted both to Jesus the Messiah and to the people of Israel. Simeon, Anna, Joseph of Arimathea, James the brother of Jesus, the thousands of Jews who are zealous for the Torah—these are the citizens of Jerusalem whose lives represent the city's prophetic destiny.

In the decades after the close of Acts, however, the Jewish people centered in Jerusalem endured two wars with Rome—and two defeats—that would shape Israel's national existence for almost two millennia. As a result of these wars, although communities of Jews continued to live in the land of promise, they were banned from Jerusalem for centuries. These two wars also played a decisive role in weakening and eventually destroying the early messianic Jewish community. As it turned out, the "times of the gentiles" (Luke 21:24) would involve the elimination of a visible Jewish communal presence not only in Jerusalem but also within the Jesus-community. Sadly, most believers in Jesus of the second century and beyond had lost the vision of Jerusalem as a holy city, and actually celebrated the destruction of the city. And they also rejoiced in the demise of the messianic Jewish community, which they viewed as in error or even heresy.

The sufferings of Jewish exile were most cruel for messianic Jews. Like the rest of the Jewish people, they had lost their beloved city and temple, and had endured national humiliation. But it soon became evident that they had also lost their place in both the Jewish community and the Jesus-community. If they wished to maintain their Jewish identity they were required to renounce their faith in Jesus. If they wanted to maintain their connection with the Jesus-community they were compelled to surrender their Jewish identity and be absorbed into the gentile church. The church's loss of a vision of Jerusalem meant that Jewish disciples of Jesus would be required to suppress their connection to the holy city and, as a consequence, be exiled from themselves.

But although the Jewish people lost Jerusalem and their national home in the land of Israel, they never gave up hope for a future restoration. When the Messiah would finally come, he would lead his people back to their promised inheritance. Just as the besorah hints, the connection between Messiah Yeshua and his own people is profound and unbreakable, even if it will only be revealed in fullness at the end of the age. In the meantime, Jews could only pray and wait for the coming of Messiah and the promised redemption.

At the same time, the gentile church retained its own glimmer of hope for the Jewish people. At the end of the age the Jews would be "converted to Christ," and then Jesus would return. This meant that the church never totally forgot about Israel's unique covenantal status among the nations of the earth. The land of Israel, however, had no part in this picture. Furthermore, the church believed that the covenantal status of Jewish people could only be fulfilled when they believed in Jesus (and, paradoxically, gave up their Judaism and their distinct national identity). So the Jewish people were an essential part of the divine plan for the final redemption of the world, but in the meantime Jews lived under a curse, and the most that Christians could do was pray for them and wait for the return of Christ—which ironically reflected the prayer and waiting for Messiah among the Jewish people.

The First-Fruits of Messianic Jewish Restoration

As we saw in our last chapter, however, as early as the seventeenth and eighteenth centuries some Christians began to envision a collective return of Jews to their ancestral land *before* the return of the Messiah.[1] Similarly, by the early eighteenth century some Christians began to envision communities of Jewish disciples of Jesus who would adopt the essential components of a traditional Jewish way of life—a prototype of today's Messianic Judaism.[2] They saw the Jerusalem community of Acts as a model worthy of emulation by latter-day Jewish disciples of Jesus. These Christians were a century ahead of their time, as this vision would not gain traction among Jewish disciples of Jesus until the late nineteenth century.

The beginning of the nineteenth century also brought a decisive change of attitude toward exile in the mainstream Jewish community, when followers of the preeminent Gaon (or Sage) of Vilna emigrated to the land of Israel seeking to build religious and communal institutions there. In the same period, Jewish believers in Jesus in England took a step without precedent since the fourth century. They publicly affirmed the enduring character of their Jewish identity and its spiritual significance, and began to form bonds with each other as well as institutions to strengthen those bonds. In 1813 forty-one Jewish disciples of Jesus established a London association called *Beney Abraham* (the Children of Abraham). In 1866 the Hebrew Christian Alliance was born, again in England.[3] The participants in

---

1. Some Jews had entertained the same notion in the medieval period, but this view lived on at best as a marginal belief in Jewish circles until the nineteenth century.

2. Rudolph, "Messianic Judaism," 25–26.

3. This organization continues to exist, now under the name "The Messianic Jewish Alliance." There are autonomous national branches of the Alliance (like the British Alliance, described above), as well as an international branch, which was founded in 1925.

these organizations were loyal members of various churches, and were not attempting to create distinct Jewish-Christian congregations. Nevertheless, they had broken with a centuries-long practice of total Jewish assimilation within the gentile church.

Not long afterwards, in the 1880s and 90s, Zionism as a movement assumed its mature form. In 1881 Czar Alexander II of Russia was assassinated, and many blamed the Jews. Pogroms and anti-Jewish legislation followed, as did massive emigration to the biblical homeland. In the history of Israel, this period is traditionally known as "the First Aliyah," when some 25,000 Jews made their way from Eastern Europe to the Jewish homeland, then part of the Ottoman (Turkish) Empire. In January of 1882, a central committee was established in Romania to coordinate the transport of groups of Jews to the land, and to help them become part of new Jewish agricultural settlements there. The first such settlement, Rishon Lezion, today Israel's fourth-largest city, was founded in the same year. In 1895 Theodore Herzl wrote *The Jewish State* (published in 1896), and in 1897 he led the First Zionist Congress in Basel, Switzerland. In these decades, Zionism emerged as a well-defined movement seeking to establish a distinct Jewish presence in the land of Israel.

One of the many Eastern European Jews caught up in the Zionist discussions of the 1880s was Joseph Rabinowitz (1837–99). In 1882 he traveled to the land to investigate whether collective immigration might be a solution to the ills plaguing the Jewish people in Europe. While gazing on the holy city from the Mount of Olives (which Jesus had descended on his way into Jerusalem for his last Passover), Rabinowitz was suddenly convinced that "*Yeshua Achinu*" (Jesus our Brother) was the Messiah, and that he alone was the solution for Israel.[4] He returned to his home city of Kishinev, in what is now Moldova, and began to gather a group of Jewish disciples of Jesus, whom he called "Israelites of the New Covenant." This group would follow the biblically ordained practices of the Torah, such as circumcision, the Sabbath, and the Jewish holidays, and—while seeking friendly relationships with the Christian churches—would guard their autonomy as a *Jewish* community. But Rabinowitz was unable to win governmental authorization to baptize individuals and to establish a congregation, and his Kishinev group was unable to survive his death in 1899. Nevertheless, during his lifetime he enjoyed extraordinary success in

---

4. Kai Kjaer-Hansen, *Joseph Rabinowitz*, 11–22.

gaining an international hearing for his program.[5] Rabinowitz has rightly been called "the Herzl of Jewish Christianity."[6] As a result of his efforts, the vision of a distinct Jewish community within the worldwide community of Jesus, which was formerly inconceivable, became a matter of active debate among Jewish disciples of Jesus, and also among gentile disciples of Jesus who labored in Christian missions to the Jews.

As the ideas of Rabinowitz spread among sympathetic Jewish disciples of Jesus, and some began to employ the term "Messianic Jew" to describe themselves, the longstanding members of the Hebrew Christian Alliance reacted fiercely. In 1917 they officially denounced Messianic Judaism as a heresy.[7] This draconian measure succeeded in delaying the growth of Messianic Judaism for five decades, but it could not destroy the idea that Rabinowitz and others had championed.

The seismic events of the 1940s united the Jewish world in support of Zionism and the fledgling Jewish settlement fighting for its life in a hostile Middle-East. The Hebrew Christian world experienced a similar shaking two decades later in the wake of the Six-Day War. That conflict had begun amidst realistic fears that Israel would be annihilated, and concluded with Jews returning in triumph to pray at the Western Wall. In those days, Jewish disciples of Jesus shared the sense of wonder that prevailed within the Jewish world as a whole, and many now began to reconsider the Messianic Jewish "heresy" that had been suppressed a half-century earlier. They began to realize that Jewish disciples of Jesus might need their own communal identity to ensure their survival as Jews and to maintain solidarity with the rest of their fellow Jews, especially those in the land of Israel. The restoration of Jerusalem as the capital of the Jewish people after nearly two millennia of exile was also a paradigm shifter in the Christian world. Was it not an appropriate time for the worldwide body of Jesus' followers to renounce its self-imposed exile and recover its own Jewish remnant—its Jerusalem within?

In this Spirit-infused atmosphere, the Messianic Jewish movement of the 1970s was born. As its fruit, congregations and groups of Jewish followers of Jesus now exist who identify as Jews rather than as Christians,

---

5. Rabinowitz traveled to Germany, Hungary, England, Scotland, and the United States, attracting attention wherever he went (Kjaer-Hansen, *Joseph Rabinowitz*, 75–90, 171–78).

6. Kjaer-Hansen, *Joseph Rabinowitz*. See his subtitle, *The Herzl of Jewish Christianity*.

7. On this conflict, see Rudolph, "Messianic Judaism," 26–29.

and who seek to live according to the Torah.[8] Some of them even embrace rabbinic tradition as an essential aid in shaping that way of life.[9] Since the heady days in which it first took root, the Messianic Jewish movement has developed diverse expressions—some of impressive theological and spiritual depth, others embarrassingly shallow. In producing mixed fruit, Messianic Judaism once again resembles Zionism. But mistakes and failures don't mean that God is absent. Indeed, as Luke-Acts often illustrates, human frailty provides the normal material upon which the Spirit works in redemptive artistry. The intertwined history of the Jewish return to Zion and the rise of Messianic Judaism suggests that the same divine Spirit is at work in both—especially since both are reflected in the same besorah. Just as we can recognize and respond to the Spirit's work in both movements, so we may yet witness the recovery of the besorah—the integrated message of good news for Jerusalem and the world through Messiah Yeshua—which was fractured soon after its initial proclamation.

Healing the Fracture

Like the Jewish return to the land of Israel, the reborn movement for Jesus among the Jewish people is a foretaste of the restoration that the besorah points to. This movement is also a key to healing the fractured gospel, as it brings together the two estranged elements—the Jewish people and the Jewish Messiah—within itself.

In our early days at Templo Cristiano, we learned that the Book of Acts is for today. For us that meant that the infilling and gifts of the Spirit were still available and, more than that, *essential* for us as we sought to follow Jesus. Later we realized that the picture in Acts of a thriving, indigenous Jewish movement for Jesus that embraced Jewish life and tradition was also for today. And there was a third lesson from those early days: "Jesus is coming again!" Jesus would return to complete his work of redemption and rule all the nations of humankind in justice and compassion from his throne in a restored Jerusalem.

---

8. Messianic Jews refuse to identify as "Christians" because that term invariably connotes a form of religious life *distinct from* and *incompatible with* Judaism. They do not treat the term with contempt, but see it as an honorable designation appropriate for members of the gentile church.

9. See, for example, the Messianic Jewish Rabbinical Council, of which we are members: http://ourrabbis.org/main/.

These were the days of Hal Lindsay's blockbuster, *The Late, Great Planet Earth*,[10] and we were sure that the second coming wasn't far off. We heard lots of different teachings about the end times, about when and how Jesus would return, and what might need to happen first. It could get confusing, but what is clear today from our study of Luke and Acts is that two elements are essential to set the stage for Messiah's return and the coming of his kingdom, two elements that only in our times are being set in place: 1) a Jerusalem qualified to welcome Messiah on behalf of all Israel—Jerusalem for the first time in millennia not only the center of Jewish prayer and vision, but literally the center of the Jewish world; and 2) a remnant of Jews following Yeshua from within and among their Jewish people.

We've covered these two elements and now we'll add a third prophetic element of the times in which we're living: healing of the age-old rift between Jews and Christians. We have seen how Luke emphasizes the need for a Jewish return to God—repentance—to prepare the way for Messiah's return. But the worldwide Jesus-community is also called to repentance, to a return to God, which is mysteriously tied to the return of Messiah. Just as the Jewish people must turn away from neglect and denial of Jesus as Messiah, so must the community of Jesus turn away from its neglect and denial of Israel as a priestly nation still in covenant with God. Just as the rise of Messianic Judaism is a prophetic sign of the coming Jewish welcome of Messiah Yeshua, so its acceptance and influence within the Jesus-community is a prophetic sign of the gentile church coming into alignment with Israel as a people. In both cases, repentance brings healing, healing of God's fragmented people and healing of the fractured gospel.[11]

Since we're writing from a Jewish perspective, we're not speaking of repentance as only a change of heart or attitude. And it's also not merely a matter of remorse and confession of sin, although these provide a starting-point. Rather, repentance means turning away from wrong behavior and turning towards right behavior. One sign of this repentance on the

---

10. Published in 1970. Amazon.com explains the significance of this book: "Hal Lindsey's blockbuster served as a wake-up call on events soon to come and events already unfolding—all leading up to the greatest event of all: the return of Jesus Christ."

11. A fourth element in setting the stage for Messiah's return is beyond the scope of this book. It is the globalization of the Jesus-community, so that China and Africa, in place of Europe and North America, are now centers of Christian life and influence. This massive shift reflects Yeshua's words, "And this gospel of the kingdom will be proclaimed throughout the whole world as a testimony to all nations, and then the end will come" (Matt 24:14).

Christian side is widespread support for Israel as the restored Jewish homeland, especially within the evangelical community. As we noted in our last chapter, this support doesn't mean blanket acceptance of every Israeli policy and action, but it does mean solidarity, standing with and not against the Jewish people.

Another sign of healing is growing recognition in the Christian world that Jewish followers of Jesus can and should remain Jewish, that they should not be pressed to assimilate into the Christian community, but should be honored in—and encouraged to maintain—their distinctive way of life. A generation ago, Orthodox Jewish theologian Michael Wyschogrod called the church to this exact response: "Had the Church believed that it was God's will that the seed of Abraham not disappear from the world, she would have insisted on Jews retaining their separateness, even in the Church."[12] Later he made this exhortation even clearer: "Jews who embrace Christ must be persuaded by the church to retain their identity as the seed of Abraham. . . . They must also remain loyal to the Torah and its commandments, with their faith in Jesus as the Christ as the only characteristic differentiating them from other Jews."[13] As Messianic Jews, we'd use different terminology, but we can totally affirm this statement. We can also affirm those in the Christian world who are echoing Wyschogrod's call. Prominent evangelical Bible scholar Craig Keener, for example, writes: "The Messianic Jewish movement challenges the arbitrary dichotomy between Jewish identity and faith in Jesus, reminding us, as the apostolic church did, that these are not mutually exclusive options."[14] We would add that not only are Jewish identity and faith in Jesus "not mutually exclusive options," but their union within the Messianic Jewish community is *essential* to the healing of the fractured gospel.

This restored gospel, the besorah, will look much more like good news to Jewish people than the narrower gospel of individual salvation. That gospel has often been interpreted as demanding a choice between being Jewish and accepting Jesus—with the implication that all the Jewish generations that came before us were lost. In contrast, our Messianic Jewish colleague Stuart Dauermann interprets the good news in a way similar to our portrayal of

---

12. Wyschogrod, "Israel, the Church, and Election," 183.

13. Wyschogrod, "Paul, Jews, and Gentiles," 198.

14. Keener, "Interdependence and Mutual Blessing in the Church," 194. In light of the history we've recounted, the dichotomy between Jewish identity and faith in Jesus isn't really arbitrary, but Keener's point remains.

the besorah. He traces this message in key texts from the Hebrew prophets. In particular, Dauermann highlights Ezekiel 37:21–28 (which he calls "the Ezekiel Agenda") as a seven-part summary of the destiny of Israel.

> Ezekiel lists the facets of the good news in this order:
> - The ingathering of the Jewish people to our homeland, Israel (thus, Aliyah)
> - The restoration of the unity of the people of Israel
> - Repentance-renewal for the people as a whole
> - Messiah reigning in the center of this gathered people
> - Torah living as the communal life of this people
> - National experience of the divine presence
> - And because of all this, and in the sight of the nations, vindication of the Jewish people as the people of God, and the God of Israel as faithful to his promises.[15]

Dauermann notes that "Ezekiel places Messiah in the center of these items" (number four of seven), but he emphasizes that the gospel as a message for the Jewish people includes all seven of these aspects of Israel's hope. "Anything less and anything other is at best someone else's truncated gospel."[16] In place of a "truncated gospel," we have the besorah—the account of the Messiah crucified in union with his people Israel and resurrected to fulfill all that the prophets, including Ezekiel, promised to Israel. The besorah will reach completion as the Jewish people are restored to their land, restored to their God through repentance and forgiveness, and living in faithfulness to God and his ways under the rule of Messiah, with the Spirit of God in their midst. This restored Israel becomes a source of God's blessing to all the nations.

> They shall dwell in the land that I gave to my servant Jacob, where your fathers lived. They and their children and their children's children shall dwell there forever, and David my servant shall be their prince forever. I will make a covenant of peace with them. It shall be an everlasting covenant with them. And I will set them in their land and multiply them, and will set my sanctuary in their midst forevermore. My dwelling place shall be with them, and I will be their God, and they shall be my people. Then the nations

---

15. Dauermann, *Converging Destinies*, 164.
16. Dauermann, *Converging Destinies*, 164.

will know that I am the Lord who sanctifies Israel, when my sanctuary is in their midst forevermore. (Ezek 37:25–28)

Conclusion

The gospel of the life, death, and resurrection of Jesus of Nazareth has transformed countless lives over the centuries, and is in the process of transforming all of human history. We have argued in this book, however, that the gospel itself has been fractured, and is proclaimed in partial fashion, through neglect of one of its main components. The texts of Luke-Acts reveal that the death and resurrection of Jesus are linked inextricably to the destruction and promised restoration of Jerusalem, the city that personifies the Jewish people as a whole. To highlight this expanded understanding of the gospel and its recovery, we have used the term besorah throughout this book.

The besorah is a prophetic message of salvation both for Israel and for all nations, a message that reflects the words of the Hebrew prophets as well as the New Testament accounts of the death and resurrection of Messiah. This prophetic besorah, which we introduced in chapter 1, overcomes the age-old notion that Israel—that is, the Jewish people, whose story is so deeply rooted in the biblical texts they share with the Christian community—has been replaced by the church. The besorah as presented in Luke-Acts, in contrast, ties the death and resurrection of Messiah inextricably with the exile and restoration of Jerusalem, as we demonstrated in chapters 2 and 3.

From there we returned to our critique of replacement theology by examining one of its pillars, its interpretation of the temple. Since the temple was destroyed by Rome in the first century, and allegedly marginalized or redefined in the New Testament, its destruction was seen as a sign that God is also finished with Israel as a people, or at least that God sets Israel aside for its failure to recognize Jesus as Messiah and will only return to it in the prophetic future. To counter this doctrine, we showed in chapters 4 and 5 how the temple and the tabernacle that preceded it played a complex and shifting role within the divine drama from their beginnings. The role of the temple in the New Testament is complex, but consistent with its role in Moses and the Prophets. In all these texts, the destruction of the temple was foretold, along with its eventual restoration—just as the exile and restoration of the people were foretold. What Luke-Acts adds to the New Testament picture is its consistently positive view of the temple, and its linkage of the temple's story to the death and resurrection of Messiah.

As we saw in chapter 6, the besorah of the death and resurrection of the Messiah is directed principally to the Jewish people, and reinforces their irrevocable covenant identity. That identity is also reinforced by the enduring significance of the Torah, as we discussed in chapters 7 and 8. The community within which Jesus is born and comes of age is positive toward the Torah, as he and his band of followers continue to be. After the resurrection, the followers of Jesus, centered in Jerusalem, continue in this Torah-honoring way of life, a way of life that has sustained the Jewish people throughout long centuries of exile, despite their corporate failure to recognize Jesus as Messiah. As with the temple, the besorah doesn't present the Torah in contrast with God's ultimate purposes for Israel and the nations, but as essential to them.

The Spirit has encoded hints of this besorah within the flow of history in the last two millennia, and especially the last two centuries, as we've seen in these final chapters. Two events of recent history, the Jewish return to Zion and the rebirth of an indigenous Jewish Jesus-movement, are signs that the fractured gospel is being healed. As a further sign, the church—the community called into being to embody and proclaim the besorah—is beginning to rediscover in this "good news" for Israel her own identity as Israel's extension and partner.

In regaining her vital connection to the people Israel, the church also learns the reality of her own fractured character and history. The wound is deeper than first imagined. The rift between Israel and the church of the nations makes the divisions between Catholic and Protestant, East and West, look superficial and merely symptomatic of that more radical underlying condition. But this harsh lesson also holds out hope for recovery for the worldwide Jesus-community. Renewed appreciation for the rich and multifaceted message that brought her into being can bring with it a renewal of her own identity and mission. It can free the church from the religious competition and cultural domination that have marred her history since they arose in the original rift with Israel. Understanding the besorah as a prophetic message for Israel and all humankind also frees the church from the individualized spirituality that mars her identity today, at least in her expression in the global West.

The worldwide Jesus-community is the body of Messiah, the Messiah of Israel. As such she lives and serves her Lord faithfully only as

PART THREE: THE BESORAH, PRESENT AND FUTURE

she is properly related to Israel, the people for whom, first, Messiah died, and for whom, first, he was raised from death. This realignment of the Jesus-community with Israel enlivens hope for the promised healing of all nations in the age to come.

Hope also springs from a geographical place, a site that is indissolubly bound up with Jesus the Messiah and the Israel for whom he died and now lives. The Jewish people have endured as one people through centuries of exile by never losing sight of Jerusalem, the "place that the LORD your God will choose out of all your tribes" (Deut 12:5). Before 70 CE the holy city represented also for the disciples of Jesus, Jewish and gentile alike, an institutional center and object of messianic hope. After 70, the gentile disciples of Jesus looked to other cities for identity and orientation—Rome, Alexandria, Constantinople, Moscow, Canterbury—but never again recovered a single site that could unite them all in love and eschatological longing.

But we live in a new day, and Jerusalem restored is a signpost of the age in which we live. It points toward the culmination of this age, when the resurrected Messiah will appear again on the Mount of Olives and make his promised entry through the city gates. From the ramparts, voices of welcome will arise—voices already sounding among a remnant of Yeshua's Jewish followers. As Jerusalem receives her king, she will finally become "the joy of the whole earth" (Ps 48:3 [2]). Her holy mountain will become what it has always been destined to be, a "house of prayer for all peoples" (Isa 56:7; Mark 11:17), "and all the nations shall flow to it" (Isa 2:2).

In this way, the hope of the Jewish people is also the hope of the worldwide Jesus-community, and this shared hope has the potential to unify the whole people of God—Jewish and gentile, Protestant and Catholic, Eastern and Western. Just as the besorah calls all who hear it to a share in the death and resurrection of Jesus, so it calls all who hear it to a share in the exile and restoration of Jerusalem. Just as Jews find their spiritual home in Jerusalem, so also shall those whose descent from Abraham and Sarah is by faith and not by genealogy:

> Among those who know me I mention Rahab and Babylon;
>   behold, Philistia and Tyre, with Cush—
> "This one was born there," they say.
> And of Zion it shall be said,
>   "This one and that one were born in her." (Ps 87:4–5)

When the church of the nations rediscovers this truth she will join with the Jewish people in taking the words of the Psalmist as her own sacred promise:

> If I forget you, O Jerusalem,
>   let my right hand forget its skill!
> Let my tongue stick to the roof of my mouth,
>   if I do not remember you,
> if I do not set Jerusalem
>   above my highest joy! (Ps 137:5–6)

In the prophetic besorah, Jerusalem the site of the holy temple, of the sacrificial death and glorious resurrection of Messiah, of Israel's promised return from exile, becomes the signal of hope for all the nations.

Epilogue

DECADES HAVE PASSED SINCE I began my journey with Yeshua and within the emerging Messianic Jewish community. Much has changed in my life and in the world around all of us. For me, God's presence in Messiah Yeshua remains the constant, but my understanding of Messiah and what it means to follow him as a Jew has continued to grow from the earliest days until now.

My first stage of growth, to put it simply, was to realize that I was still Jewish after I came to believe in the one the Christians recognized as Lord and Christ, and that being Jewish as I followed Yeshua was okay. From there I went on to realize that it wasn't just okay, but essential to God's plan for me and my place in the world. To put this another way, the whole direction of my growth as a Jewish follower of Yeshua has been toward seeing Jewish calling as central to the work of Messiah—not just consistent or compatible with it, nor just a legitimate add-on, but at the heart of Yeshua's whole story, both in the here-and-now and in the age to come.

Another part of my spiritual growth, which might seem unrelated at first, has been to realize the depths of the brokenness and dysfunction in the world, including the religious world. The idea of a broken or fractured gospel came to light for me only recently as I read *Jerusalem Crucified, Jerusalem Restored*, but it helped me understand my own journey from its earliest days. The original besorah, a message of good news for the Jewish people, had long since become a gospel that somehow seemed like bad news for the Jewish people. When I heard it back in our log house in New Mexico, it seemed at first to mean an end to my Jewish identity and connection. It seemed to present an impossible Sophie's-choice between my people and my Messiah. The fractured gospel threatened to fracture part of me, even as it brought me into the light of salvation. But if this gospel is really fractured, it can be healed, and this means healing the split in my own identity, even if the healing won't be complete until Messiah returns.

The Messianic Jewish movement of the early twenty-first century also seems fractured and in need of healing. After decades of serving the Messianic Jewish vision, I'm often frustrated that even many of its advocates don't seem to grasp the radical nature and potential impact of this vision. Over the years, Messianic Judaism has often presented itself as an updated (or sometimes outdated) Jewish style of contemporary Bible-church Christianity. It has often focused on outward symbols—Lion of Judah graphics and Star of David-shaped tambourines—and not on its prophetic heartbeat. My concerns have only intensified throughout the profoundly disordered year of 2020. But even now, Yeshua the Messiah remains constant and so does his healed and healing gospel, that message of hope we call the besorah.

For me, this hope is intensely personal, and I imagine it is for many of you who are reading this as well. We are among the millions who can say that Yeshua, Jesus, makes all the difference in our lives. I believe that the restored besorah intensifies and expands that difference, for reasons that you may find as compelling as I do.

First, the besorah frees us from the hyper-individualized gospel of the modern West, which is prey to the narcissism and consumerism promoted by our dominant culture. The besorah includes individual salvation, of course, but is far broader, and it draws us into a vision and life-purpose far beyond finding personal peace and happiness—a purpose that is paradoxically more likely to yield peace and happiness than are the various paths to personal satisfaction on the market today. As I was writing this paragraph, I took a break to check my email, and I saw this subject-line on a piece sent by a Bible app: "Become the person God created you to be." That appeal isn't necessarily narcissistic, but it hints at the current tendency to reduce the gospel to me and my spiritual journey. The besorah's impact, however, is always far grander than personal fulfillment and it frees us from being absorbed with ourselves.

Further, the besorah reverses the alienation between the Jewish Messiah and the Jewish people. Just as discord within an earthly family creates an atmosphere of tension and strain among all its members, so Jews and Christians today seem to live without the profound peace—the shalom—of which the scriptures continually speak. Many people today are sick of the discord and divisiveness that are rampant in the world—and many people find it hard to consider Jesus when his followers seem to be the most divisive of all. This tendency (which is often made to seem even worse in media portrayals) is rooted in the original unholy divisions between Israel and the church, and between Jesus and his own people. The besorah, in contrast, reveals Jesus as the Prince of Peace, who took upon himself the alienation and exile of Israel and reversed it through his resurrection. We can share this besorah as a message of peace, a message we can be proud of even in the twenty-first century

Finally, the restored besorah is prophetic. It's a message of hope that stands up to all the setbacks and shortcomings of this present age. I grew up in the generation of kids who went through air-raid drills in elementary school. A siren would go off at some random moment and we'd slide out of our seats as we had been instructed to do, crouch on all fours under our desks, and cover the back of our necks with our hands, just in case the Russians had decided to drop an H-bomb on our town. I came of age in the shadow of the "Population Bomb," which threatened to bring famine and chaos to planet earth. And I've watched the mounting pollution and exploitation of our environment, along with wild fluctuations in the global climate. The besorah portrays the renewal of all things as inherent to the sacrificial death and resurrection of Jesus the Messiah. It doesn't promise us a ticket out of this broken world, but a share in the restored world to come. Our lives gain meaning and impact, and more benefit to others, as they are infused with such hope.

For all these reasons, I believe *Besorah: The Resurrection of Jerusalem and the Healing of a Fractured Gospel* will make a difference in the world.

I've been a follower of Yeshua for a long time now, but I don't intend this book as a swan song, and I'm sure Mark Kinzer doesn't either. Instead, my hope for this book is that it becomes itself an instrument of healing of the fractured gospel and the fractured people of God, and of our own fractured lives as well. May the healer-king, Yeshua the Messiah, and his message, the besorah of resurrection for Israel and all the nations, take root and thrive in our hearts!

Bibliography

Armstrong, Karen. *Jerusalem: One City, Three Faiths*. New York: Ballantine, 1996.
Boyarin, Daniel. *The Jewish Gospels: The Story of the Jewish Christ*. New York: New Press, 2012.
Brawley, Robert L. *Luke-Acts and the Jews: Conflict, Apology, and Conciliation*. Atlanta: Scholars, 1987.
Bruce, F. F. *Commentary on the Book of the Acts*. Grand Rapids: Eerdmans, 1988.
Buber, Martin. *A Land of Two Peoples*. Chicago: University of Chicago Press, 2005.
Burge, Gary M. *Jesus and the Land: The New Testament Challenge to "Holy Land" Theology*. Grand Rapids: Baker Academic, 2010.
Chance, J. Bradley. *Jerusalem, the Temple, and the New Age in Luke-Acts*. Macon, GA: Mercer University Press, 1988.
Chilton, Bruce, and Jacob Neusner. *Judaism in the New Testament: Practice and Beliefs*. London: Routledge, 1995.
Conzelmann, Hans. *The Theology of St. Luke*. Translated by Geoffrey Buswell. Philadelphia: Fortress, 1982.
Dauermann, Stuart. *Converging Destinies: Jews, Christians, and the Mission of God*. Eugene, OR: Cascade, 2017.
Dunn, James D. G. *The Partings of the Ways*. Philadelphia: Trinity, 1991.
Edersheim, Alfred. *The Temple: Its Ministry and Services*. 1874. Reprint, Peabody, MA: Hendrickson, 1994.
Farrow, Douglas. *Ascension Theology*. London: T. & T. Clark, 2011.
Fitzmeyer, Joseph A. *Luke the Theologian: Aspects of His Teaching*. Mahwah, NJ: Paulist, 1989.
Jervell, Jacob. *Luke and the People of God: A New Look at Luke-Acts*. Minneapolis: Augsburg, 1972.
Juel, Donald. *Luke-Acts. The Promise of History*. Atlanta: John Knox, 1983.
Keener, Craig. "Interdependence and Mutual Blessing in the Church." In *Introduction to Messianic Judaism: Its Ecclesial Context and Biblical Foundations*, edited by David Rudolph and Joel Willitts, 187–95. Grand Rapids: Zondervan, 2013.
Kinzer, Mark S. *Jerusalem Crucified, Jerusalem Risen: The Resurrected Messiah, the Jewish People, and the Land of Promise*. Eugene, OR: Cascade, 2018.
———. *Postmissionary Messianic Judaism*. Grand Rapids: Brazos, 2005.
———. *Searching Her Own Mystery: Nostra Aetate, the Jewish People, and the Identity of the Church*. Eugene, OR: Cascade, 2015.

BIBLIOGRAPHY

Kjaer-Hansen, Kai. *Joseph Rabinowitz and the Messianic Movement: The Herzl of Jewish Christianity.* Grand Rapids: Eerdmans, 1995.
The Koren Siddur, with introduction, translation, and commentary by Rabbi Sir Jonathan Sacks. Jerusalem: Koren, 2009.
Levenson, Jon D. *Sinai and Zion: An Entry into the Jewish Bible.* New York: Harper & Row, 1985.
Levine, A. J., and Ben Witherington III. *The Gospel of Luke.* New Cambridge Bible Commentary. Cambridge: Cambridge University Press, 2019.
Lindsey, Hal. *The Late, Great Planet Earth.* Grand Rapids: Zondervan, 1970.
Marshall, I. Howard. *The Gospel of Luke.* New International Greek Testament Commentary. Exeter, UK: Paternoster, 1978.
McDermott, Gerald R. "A History of Christian Zionism." In *The New Christian Zionism: Fresh Perspectives on Israel and the Land,* edited by Gerald R. McDermott, 45–75. Downers Grove, IL: IVP Academic, 2016.
Moffitt, David M. *Atonement and the Logic of Resurrection in the Epistle to the Hebrews.* Leiden: Brill, 2013.
Nanos, Mark D., and Magnus Zetterholm, eds. *Paul within Judaism: Restoring the First-Century Context to the Apostle.* Minneapolis: Fortress, 2015.
Novak, David. *Zionism and Judaism: A New Theory.* Cambridge: Cambridge University Press, 2015.
Oliver, Isaac W. *Torah Praxis after 70 CE: Reading Matthew and Luke-Acts as Jewish Texts.* Tubingen: Mohr Siebeck, 2013.
Ottolenghi, Emanuele. "A National Home." In *Modern Judaism,* edited by Nicholas de Lange and Miri Freud-Kandel, 54–65. Oxford: Oxford University Press, 2005.
Rudolph, David J. "Jesus and the Food Laws: A Reassessment of Mark 7:19b." *Evangelical Quarterly* 74.4 (2002) 291–311.
———. *A Jew to the Jews: Jewish Contours of Pauline Flexibility in 1 Corinthians 9:19–23.* 2nd ed. Eugene, OR: Pickwick, 2016.
———. "Messianic Judaism in Antiquity and in the Modern Era." In *Introduction to Messianic Judaism: Its Ecclesial Context and Biblical Foundations,* edited by David Rudolph and Joel Willitts, 21–36. Grand Rapids: Zondervan, 2013.
Sanders, E. P. *The Historical Figure of Jesus.* New York: Penguin, 1993.
Shavit, Ari. *My Promised Land: The Triumph and Tragedy of Israel.* New York: Spiegel & Grau, 2013.
Tannehill, Robert C. *Luke.* Abingdon New Testament Commentaries. Nashville: Abingdon, 1996.
———. *The Narrative Unity of Luke-Acts: A Literary Interpretation, Volume 2.* Minneapolis: Fortress, 1990.
Thiessen, Matthew. *Paul and the Gentile Problem.* Oxford: Oxford University Press, 2016.
Tiede, David L. "Glory to Thy People Israel: Luke-Acts and the Jews." In *Luke-Acts and the Jewish People,* edited by Joseph B. Tyson, 21–34. Minneapolis: Augsburg, 1988.
Witherington III, Ben. *The Acts of the Apostles: A Socio-Rhetorical Commentary.* Grand Rapids: Eerdmans, 1998.

BIBLIOGRAPHY

Wright, N. T. *Jesus and the Victory of God.* Minneapolis: Fortress, 1996.
———. *Surprised By Hope: Rethinking Heaven, the Resurrection, and the Mission of the Church.* New York: HarperCollins, 2008.
Wyschogrod, Michael. "Israel, the Church, and Election." In *Abraham's Promise: Judaism and Jewish-Christian Relations,* edited by R. Kendall Soulen, 170–87. Grand Rapids: Eerdmans, 2004.
———. "Paul, Jews, and Gentiles." In *Abraham's Promise: Judaism and Jewish-Christian Relations,* edited by R. Kendall Soulen, 188–201. Grand Rapids: Eerdmans, 2004.

Scripture Index

Hebrew Bible (Old Testament)

Genesis

1:1—2:3	61
12	23
15	79
22	59
22:2	59, 83
22:3, 4, 9, 14	80
22:4	80
22:9	80
22:14	59, 80
45:1–5	134

Exodus

3:12	79
4:22	64
23:14, 17	38
23:14–17	25
23:17	38, 48
25	61
25:8	62, 69
25:9	61
25:9, 40	61
25:40	61
29:38–42	76, 118
35–40	61
40:18–21	58

Leviticus

	21
6:1–7	108
9:24	76, 119
14:1–32	113
17–18	127
25 LXX	20
25:10	20
25:10–54	111

Numbers

6:1, 5, 18	123
6:1–21	24
6:3	122
6:5	123
6:18	123
11:29	13n1
15:37–41	105n3
28:1–8	76, 118

Deuteronomy

	142
4:26–31	142
5:14–15	111
6:4–5	105n3
6:4–9	105n3
11:13–21	105n3
12:5	59, 160
16:1–17	25
18:15–19	78
30:1–5	142

Scripture Index

Joshua

18:1	58

Judges

20:26–28	58n2

1 Samuel

3:3	58
4:1—7:2	58
10:6	13n1
19:20–24	13n1
21:1–9	58
22:6–23	58

2 Samuel

4:10	15
7:1–13	58
18:19–27	15

1 Kings

	61
8:46–53	59

Isaiah

	5, 17, 18, 21, 28, 81
2:2	160
6	76
6:1	60
40	14, 15, 17, 18
40:1	19
40:3–5	81
40:4–5, 9 ESV	15
40:9 ESV	15
40–66	xxii, 5, 13, 143
51:12	19
51:12—52:12	19
52	19
52:1–12	19
52:7–8	18
52:8	63
52:8–12	81
52:9	19
52:12	19, 63
52:13	19
52:13—53:12	19
53	19
53:4	19
53:10–11a	20
54	19
54:1	19
55:3	40
56:6–8	66
56:7	160
61	5, 13, 17, 18, 20, 111
66	79
66:18–23	66

Jeremiah

3:14	16
31:18–20	142n13

Ezekiel

8:3–4, 6	63
8:6	63
8–11	63
9:3	63
10:1–22	63
10:18–19	16
11:16	16
11:23	16, 48
36	126, 127
36:21–23, 32	142
36:22	xxiv
36:23–27	xxiv
36:24	142
36:25–27	126
36:25–28	142
36:26–27	xxiv
36:27	126
36:31	143
36:32	142
37:21–28	157
37:25–28	157–58
40	62
43:1–7	82

Scripture Index

43:2	48
43:2, 3b-5	16
43:2–7	63
43:3b-5	16
47:1–5	62
47:9	62
47:12	62

Joel

2:28	13n1
3:18	62

Zechariah

	62
8:18–19	50
9:9	82
14	48, 49
14:2–5	47
14:4–5	139
14:4a	82
14:6–8	62
14:9, 16	49
14:16	49

Malachi

3:1	14n2
3:7	16

Psalms

2	40
16	38, 40
16:10	38
48:3	160
69:10	70
87:4–5	160
110	39
114:2	63
118	81, 139
118:26	81
118:26a	83
118:26b	83
137:5–6	161

Daniel

	59
6:10	59

1 Chronicles

16:37–40	58
21:15—22:1	58
21:29	58

2 Chronicles

1:3–6	58
3:1	58, 80, 83
7:1	76, 119

Rabbinic Works

Mishnah,
M. Eduyot 6:1   119n4
Talmud,
b. Berachot 26b-27a   119n4

New Testament

Matthew

	4, 28, 32, 42, 103, 107, 111, 113
4:12, 13a, 17	110
4:13a	110
4:17	110
9:13	107
21:5	82
21:8–9, 11	81
21:9	28
21:10—22:46	28
21:11	81
23:37	28
23:37–39	28
23:39	xxiv, 28
24	32
24:14	155n11

Scripture Index

Mark

4, 5, 14, 17, 18, 20, 32, 42, 103, 107, 111, 113

1:2–4	14
1:4	17
1:14–15	110
1:14–15 NRSV	17
1:15 CJB	xxii
2:17	107
7	128n11
7:14ff	128
11:9	81
11:17	160
13	32
13:14	32
13:19	32

Luke

1	30, 120, 123
1–2	113, 117
1:3	4
1:5–23	102
1:6	121, 126
1:6a	116
1:6b	116
1:7	102, 118
1:8–9	118
1:8–10	76
1:8–22	75
1:13	118
1:15	118, 122
1:16	102
1:17	118
1:33	102
1:38	120
1:41, 44	118
1:44	118
1:45	121
1:54	102
1:55	102
1:59–79	123
1:67	31
1:68	30, 102
1:68–79	30
1:69	37
1:70	30
1:71	30
1:72	30
1:73	30
1:77	30
1:79	30
2:19	121
2:21	123–24
2:21–24	120
2:22–24	102
2:22–51	102
2:25	116
2:25, 38	116
2:27	102
2:32	102
2:38	30, 101, 116
2:39	102
2:41	48, 122
2:43	37
2:48b–49	37
2:49	37
3:4–6	15
3–9	42
3:16	34, 118
4:14–15	110
4:16	110
4:16–30	13
4:16b–17	111
4:16ff	5
4:18	13
4:18–19	20, 111
4:31, 33	110
4:31–37	111
4:33	110
4:43	13
5:12–16	113
5:30	107, 108
5:30–32	107
5:33–35	50
5:35	50
6:6	110
9:51	42, 122
9:51—18:14	42
10:17–28	101, 109
10:25–42	107
10:27	105

Scripture Index

Reference	Page
10:29	105
10:37	106
10:38–42	106
12:49–50	34
13	34, 81
13, 19	34
13:10	110
13:10–16	112
13:22	27, 42
13:31–33	27
13:31–35	27, 28, 34
13:34	28, 80, 134
13:34–35	28, 81
13:35	28, 29, 31, 33, 48, 81, 109, 139
13:35b	89, 98
15	107
15:2	107, 108
15:7, 10	107
15:10	107
15:13	109
15:30	109
16:13	106
16:16 NRSV	103
16:16–18 TLV	103
16:16b	104
16:17	103, 105
16:18	104
16:19–31	104
16:29	108
16:29–31	105
16:30	108
16:31	109
17	104
17:11	42
17:11–14a	113
17:15–19	113
18	105, 106
18:20–21	106
18:22–23	106
18:31–33	75
19	30, 34, 82
19:1–10	108
19:28–46	74, 139
19:29	139
19:29, 37	82
19:37	29, 81, 82
19:37–38	48, 98
19:38	81
19:38–39	29
19:41–44	29, 30, 31, 34, 82, 134
19:42	30
19:43–44	30
19:44	30, 81
19:45–47a	113
21	32
21:6	31
21:20	32
21:20–24	31, 34
21:23	34
21:24	46, 81, 88, 98, 148, 150
22:1, 7–8, 11, 13, 15	48
22:7–8	48
22:11	48
22:13	48
22:15	48
23	34
23:27	134
23:27–31	31, 33
23:31	34
24:27, 44–45	104
24:41	31
24:44–45	104
24:49	43
24:52–53	75
24:53	43

John

Reference	Page
	4, 6, 70, 86
1:14	70, 71
1:49	85
1:51	85
2:14–15	55, 70
2:16	70
2:17	70
2:19	71
2:19–21	85
2:21	71
4	56
4:10–22	55
4:21, 23	56, 71

John *(continued)*

4:23	56, 71
5:1	70
5:1, 14	55
5:14	55
7:14, 28	70
7:28	70
8:20, 59	70
8:59	70
10:23	70
12:14–15	82

Acts

1	47, 89, 119
1:1	4
1:3–4	43
1:6	46, 81, 89, 92, 136, 143
1:6–7	88, 89
1:6–8	43, 98
1:6–12	75, 139
1:7	46
1:8	44, 45
1:9b–12	47
1:11–12	82
1:13	119
1:14	119, 121
1:16	90
2	48, 119, 120
2:1	119
2:1–2	119
2:1–5	122
2:2	119
2:3	76
2:3–4	120
2:4, 17–18, 33, 38	119
2:5	116, 116n2
2:15	119
2:17–18	119
2:22	91
2:24–36	92
2:27	38
2:29	90
2:29–32 NRSV	39
2:33	119
2:33–36 NRSF	39
2:36	91
2:38	119
2:39	91
2:42	135
2:46	xviii, 44, 75, 122
3	7, 88, 89, 90, 98
3:1	75, 76, 122
3:1–10	44
3:12	91
3:13	91
3:13, 26	37
3:17	90
3:19–20	82
3:19–20 NRSV	88, 97
3:19–21	89, 98, 139, 143
3:20	89
3:21	89, 98
3:21 ESV	88, 97
3:23	90n1
3:25	91
3:26	37
4:1–2	44
4:4	98
4:25	37
4:27, 30	37
4:30	37
5:12, 19–21, 42	122
5:12, 20–21, 42	44
5:12, 42	75
5:19–21	122
5:20–21	44
5:30	91, 92
5:33–39	33
5:42	xviii, 44, 75, 122
6:3	90
6:5, 8	77
6:7	122
6:11, 13–14	77
6:11–14	75
6:13–14	77, 79
7	6, 77
7:2	90, 92
7:2, 11, 12, 15, 19, 39, 44	91
7:7	79, 80
7:9–16	134

7:11	91	13	44, 75
7:12	91	13:14	110n7
7:15	91	13:16	91
7:17–44	78	13:16–43	94
7:19	91	13:17	91
7:35, 39a	78	13:17, 32–33	91
7:37	78	13:22–23	40
7:39	91	13:22–23, 32–37	92
7:39–43	79	13:26, 38	90
7:39a	78	13–28	4
7:44	91	13:32–33	91
7:48	79	13:32–37	92
7:48–50	79	13:33–35	40
7:53	78	13:34	40
8	75	13:38	90
8:1, 4–25	44	13:44–47	94
8:2	33, 116n2, 134	13:45, 50	93n3
8:4–25	44	13:50	93n3
9:1–2, 10, 19	44	14:4	93n3
9:1–19	93, 96	14:15	91
9:10	44	14:15–17	90
9:19	44	15	7, 129
9:23	93n3	15:1	124, 127
9:26–29	44	15:2	45
10	7, 44, 116, 129	15:5	125
10:1–48	96	15:7	14
10:2	117	15:7, 13	90
10:2, 4	87	15:7–9	96, 117
10:2, 30	76	15:8–9	129
10:3–4	117	15:8–11 NIV	125–26
10:4	120	15:10b	126
10–11	120	15:11	126
10:13	128	15:13	90
10:15	129	15:20	125
10:17, 20	128	15:21	127
10:20	128	15:29	125
10:22	117	16:1–3	124
10:28	91	16:9–10	95
10:28–29a	128	16:10–17	4
10:28b	128	16:20–21	93
10:30	76	17:1–2	110n7
11:2	44	17:5	93n3
11:4–16	96	17:22	91
11:12	129	17:22–31	90
11:26	93n4	18	123
11:27–30	44	18:2	93
12:17	121	18:5–6, 12, 28	93n3

Acts *(continued)*

18:5–6 TLV	95
18:12	93n3
18:18	123
18:18–23	123
18:22	45
18:24	93
18:28	93n3
20:3	93n3
20:5–15	4
20:16	49, 75, 122
20:18–35	90
20:24	14
21	124
21:1–18	4
21:4, 10–14	75
21:10–14	75
21:17—23:11	45
21:17–26	121, 122
21:17–28	75
21:20	90, 94, 121, 126, 148
21:20 TLV	xviii
21:20–21	123
21:23–24	123
21:23–24, 26	122
21:26	122
21:28	75, 78
21:39	93
22:1	90
22:3	93
22:6–16	96
22:12 TLV	117
22:17	76
22:30	93n3
23	40
23:1, 6	90
23:5	90, 92
23:6	4, 40, 90
23:6–10	33
23:12, 20	93n3
23:20	93n3
24:5	94
24:9	93n3
24:10–21	90
24:11–13	75
24:14	91
24:14–21	4
24:15, 21	41
24:21	41
25:8	4, 75, 124
26:2	93n3
26:5	124
26:5–7	4
26:5–8, 22–23	41
26:6	91
26:6–8, 23	92
26:12–18	96
26:22–23	41
26:23	92
26:28	93n4
26:29	93n4
27:1—28:16	4
27:21, 25	91
27:21–26	90
27:25	91
28	7, 46
28:17	4, 45, 90, 91, 124
28:19	93n3
28:20	41, 92
28:23	95
28:24–25a	95
28:28	95
28:30–31	46
28:31	49

Romans

1:1–4	1
1:16	1
9:4	64
11:26	92n2
11:29	2
12:1	64
15:15–16	64

Scripture Index

1 Corinthians

	65
6:19–20	64
9	65
9:13	64
10:16	65
10:16–21 NRSV	65
10:18	65
10:21	65
15	3
15:1, 3–5	1
15:3–5	1

2 Corinthians

6:14—7:1	64

Ephesians

	65
1–3	66n7
2:11–22	66, 66n7
2:14	66
2:17–18	66
2:21–22	66

Philippians

2:17	64
4:18	64

Hebrews

	6, 44n1, 67, 68, 69, 70
6:19–20	66
7:14	68
7:16	68
9:6–10	56
9:11–12a, 24 NRSV	67
9:12	67
9:24 NRSV	67
10:19	66
10:37	68

1 Peter

4:16	93n4

Revelation

	6, 68, 69, 70
5:5	69
5:6–14	69
21:3	69, 71
21:16	69
21:22	56, 69
21:24, 26	143
21:26	143

Early Christian Writings

Hegesippus, *Ecclesiastical History* 2.23	24n3

www.ingramcontent.com/pod-product-compliance
Lightning Source LLC
Chambersburg PA
CBHW031428150426
43191CB00006B/444